The Bodyguard

TRAVEL COMPANION COOKBOOK
A VEGAN FOOD GUIDE FOR MEXICO AND CENTRAL AMERICA

The Bodyguard: Travel Companion Cookbook
A Vegan Food Guide for Mexico and Central America

Layout and design by Dave Paco
Cover art by Sonny Kay
Illustrations by Kevin Hennessy

ISBN 978-0-9824008-3-8 (pbk)
1. Vegetarian Cooking.   2. Vegan Cooking.   3. Travel.   4. Guidebooks.   I. Title

Published by Paco Garden Enterprises
March, 2017
San Diego, California
U.S.A.
92116

Table of Contents

DISCLAIMER

This book is a collection of food and nutrition-based ideas, many of which have been handed down to me by small communities and friends throughout southern Mexico and Central America. I am not a doctor and have no formal medical or nutritional training. I'm just an Average Joe who thinks that this kind of information is both useful and important. The ideas expressed in this book should not be taken as medical fact, but rather popular belief. These are dietary options that have worked well for me and for others. However, in addition to reading this book, I highly recommend that you continue to research and learn more about the astounding world of plant-based food and medicine.

Thanks and Dedication

-To friends & family without whom this book could never exist-

Mom and Dad, Penny Cahill & Catfish Keith, Patty and Jim Brenner, Daniel Landes, Sonny Kay, Jason Heller, Kevin Hennessy, Josiah Hesse, J.Frede, Shane Ewegan, Brian Polk, T.Vy Jeannie Nguyen, Silva Vásquez Juarez, Erika Melchor García, María and the Ramos family, Andrés Urrutia David, and the many others I met along the journey who have shared insights, information, kitchens, and recipes with me.

Thank you to Marisol Garcia (little bean) for the continuous support, help, love, and criticism.

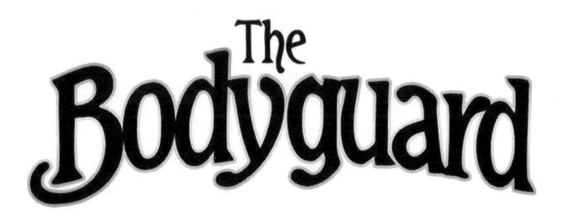

Introduction

Everything was spinning. The sticky, sultry afternoon threatened to cook me alive, buried within the bowels of a congested Costa Rican market. I couldn't think. My brain boiled over into a slushy cerebral soup. I was hungry... and anxious. My clothes clung to me, heavy and uncomfortable. I felt the dull persistent pangs raging against my weakened stomach walls. The dead weight of my brow drove my head mindlessly as it swung side to side from my limp neck. I had been nibbling on some fruit here and there, but that wouldn't quench the deepened hunger. I needed food. A real meal. A real meatless meal. Every turn I took through this labyrinth of goods led only to fish or flesh. I was a traveling vegetarian who had wandered into a non-veggie zone.

....

It's easy to associate international travel with the physical act of being born. Time passes while you ride in the belly of a bus or plane – sleeping, thinking, or snacking. Changes happen outside, though you may or may not be aware of them. Scenery passes; mountains melt into beaches, beaches end at the sea. Fields, jungles and cities swarm all around you, but within the womb of your chariot everything stays the same.

Sooner or later, though, a door opens and POP! You're pushed out into a strange new world. The sights, sounds, and smells envelope you. Maybe you've traveled halfway around the earth to a place where no one looks like you, where all the chattering voices meld into incomprehensible static. You look around and don't know where to go or what to do. But one thing is certain: You're hungry! Maybe you begin to imagine savory chana masala or a warm falafel sandwich – some far-off craving – and you think that if you could just get your hands on this or that you could make do.

For some of us, however, the solution isn't so simple. There's nothing worse than being hungry and surrounded by absolutely nothing that you want to, or even *can*, eat. Stepping out into an obscure city can be strenuous for those of us who follow a strict diet, vegetarian or otherwise. Sometimes a hot dog or chicken leg just won't cut it. A little hunger can turn into a big headache if you can't speak the language and don't find what you're looking for. Vegetarians and vegans often find themselves in this very predicament when traveling.

Whatever your reasons for following or exploring a plant-based diet, one thing's for sure: The body needs a wide variety of vitamins and nutrients to function properly. Although a vegetarian diet can be extremely healthy, becoming a vegetarian and omitting animal-based products from your plate doesn't automatically mean you will be consuming the necessary variety and quantity of these essential items. Chances are, without a little studying, you probably won't be.

One great weapon against falling prey to an unhappy stomach is taking control of what you put into it. This book will help you take such control. When your stomach calls out for Green Thai Curry and you know just where, when, and how to prepare it... you're one step closer to winning the battle. Of course, if you don't feel you possess the knowledge or experience to prepare enjoyable, wholesome food from scratch, especially in a completely foreign environment, taking on the responsibility to care for both your health and your taste buds can become daunting or stressful. It can be like learning to walk all over again.

This book is going to help you take those first steps toward preparing delicious, nutritious, plant-based foods. Any major change in diet demands an increase in knowledge as well: We have to *relearn* how to eat. And to do so we must reconnect ourselves with our foodstuffs and how we prepare them. In a sense we have to be "reborn." And there's no better way to do that than to break out of the routine and hit the reset button somewhere away from home. But this act of being born into an unknown culture or lifestyle helps us realize more about ourselves as well as our neighbors. When we're forced out of our comfort zone, we're forced to grow. We're forced to process situations we may never have encountered otherwise. By continually engaging new territory we place ourselves in a current of constant growth and adaptation. These new and uncomfortable situations lead to greater strength and understanding. Like an insect or reptile sheds its skin to grow, we shake off old ideas to make room for fresh, refined, better-developed ones.

....

I quit eating meat around the same time that I started traveling. However, that doesn't mean I became healthier from one day to the next. I was fifteen years old, still within that tender and resilient age when the body seems invincible and could probably be fed dirt and doughnuts all day long without complication. Throughout most of my adolescence, my diet leaned pretty heavily on massive amounts of cola and seven-layer burritos from fast food joints. "Healthy" vegetarian food, at least to me, was either unknown or unpalatable. Even when I turned to a full-on vegan diet the following year, it was more likely that I would be caught eating a cheese-less pizza than a lush Mediterranean salad. Some time would pass before I would begin to equate being vegetarian with the eating of vegetables.

It's not that I detested vegetables. I was actually quite fond of them, but short of making a salad (unlikely for a teenager), I didn't know what else to do with them. I knew how to heat stuff up but had no idea how to cook. Around the holidays I would receive gifts like dried beans or peas that would sit on the shelf for months as I stared at them, not knowing where to start. I wanted to eat better but lacked the education. I relied exclusively on whatever pre-packaged vegetarian products I could get from the store. During those years the options were few for young vegetarians who couldn't cook. Tofu was a four-letter word, and if you mentioned that you were vegan people would recoil in shock as if you had a disease. Eating out was a nightmare.

Traveling from state to state within the U.S. was often difficult. There were drastic differences between the coasts and the middle of the country. Vegetarian restaurants were common in California or New York, but unheard of in places like Kentucky. Throughout most of the country grocery stores would either have a brand or two of veggie burgers and some dry, boxed falafel mix or nothing at all.

My challenges at home were nothing compared to the intense alienation I experienced when I began to travel internationally. All of a sudden my go-to foods were gone, replaced by strange new packages marked by unintelligible foreign script, like lines of Japanese characters printed on flashy hot pink foil. I was still dependent on packaged products and couldn't make sense out of any of them. Restaurants were expensive and street food -- made up of ingredients impossible to decipher without speaking the local language -- was difficult to identify as meat-free.

I was now in my mid-twenties and starting to notice changes in the way my body operated. I had already eliminated most of the junk food and caffeine from my diet, and was beginning to feel what it was like to live under the influence of real foods, albeit packaged or canned ones. I noticed that my energy would surge and crash. Huge ups and downs. Lethargy. Weakness. I found that eating certain foods at certain times had a positive effect on my moods and general well-being. I began to pay closer attention to what I was putting into my mouth.

Over time I was able to fit more pieces into the puzzle. The body needs protein. The body needs calcium. Fiber is important for this or that. I still wasn't a whiz in the kitchen, but I was starting to catch on. Eventually I did learn to cook and that, step by step, led me out of the world of processed foods. The more I handled fresh, whole foods, the more I began to distance myself from those seemingly "healthy" products that had once comprised almost my entire diet. I realized that I was no longer eating out of packages or just heating something up, but actually arranging and consuming legitimate true food meals.

When I would wander down the aisles of a supermarket I found myself disenchanted by the slick, provocative packaging of the processed foods, and drawn toward the natural, vibrant colors of the produce section. Friends would invite me over for dinner and, when they pulled out precooked patties from little plastic bags, I would feel disheartened, cheated. "Check out these new vegetarian chicken leg things!" they would exclaim. I couldn't share their enthusiasm when I checked out the ingredients. My head would fill with doubt. "What is going into these products?" I asked myself. "What are these extra ingredients that I don't recognize, these suspicious names I can't pronounce?"

Grocery stores have exploded with a stockpile of soy products, faux meats, imitation cheeses and a wide range of plant-based milks. However, now that we learn more about the effects of processed foods, pesticides, preservatives, and additives, it seems like our best option might be to go back to square one. It might have been better when "health" food was, by default, a D.I.Y. endeavor.

Nutrition is a fundamental part of any diet. The timeless tip "You are what you eat," has never been more relevant than right now. What so many of us consume has been processed and stripped down to the point that the essential vitamins and minerals needed to maintain general health are almost absent, and what's left may be coated in malignant chemicals or pumped full of preservatives. Our "food" doesn't have much food left in it. Sadly, consumers are trapped in the crossfire of big money food producers and have no idea what their bodies truly require to function optimally. Many don't even know the difference between proteins and carbohydrates.

The ability to select and prepare quality whole foods can have a tremendous impact on your physical, mental and spiritual health. Living in ignorance of the current state of food contamination and processing could lead to serious illness or death. Many of the diseases that threaten our wellbeing are preventable. Our choices towards consumption determine who we are and how we live.

....

Now let's put it all together: We're going traveling into a foreign land with the desire to eat healthy and meat-free. By cooking for yourself you are by no means missing out on the culinary culture of the places you travel. You can still try the local cuisines and create your own with the same local ingredients. You can still interact with the community in the marketplace. Go ahead, get out of your comfort zone. Learn a new language, new customs, learn to cook, learn to live. Breathe air, try new food. The further you stray from yourself, the firmer your understanding of who you are becomes – almost like an astronaut looking back at earth to get a better view of his home. Pushing the limit, growing to potential.

This is a book about plant-based whole foods. It's not just for vegetarians. It's a piece of literature that can be used to build a solid food foundation able to support a vigorous lifestyle. Many of the ingredients that appear in the book can help to counteract diseases and maintain healthy body weight as well as aid in digestion, boost energy levels, and create a better state of general wellbeing. It serves as a culinary guide to help incorporate ancient and contemporary ingredients into recipes that reflect a wholesome and healthy diet.

The ancient Mayans and Aztecs understood the benefits of a diet based on plant-derived foods. The principal sustenance of these bygone civilizations was essentially vegetarian (although some small game meat was consumed before the introduction of beef and pigs from Europe in the 16th century). Mexico and Central America are home to hundreds of beneficial plants used for food, beverages, housing, and medicine. From corn and chocolate to chilies and coconuts, this region is rich in flavor. These staple foods, alongside beans, squash, potatoes, yucca, and a variety of seeds and nuts are still extremely prevalent in contemporary Mesoamerican cuisine.

I invite you to share in my appreciation of the great wealth of foodstuffs found in Central America. My hope is that you can use this collection of information and life lessons I've picked up through my travels to help enrich your own journey. At home or abroad we can learn to better ourselves and refine our practices. Our life voyage takes place inside and outside of us, but without quality food as fuel we won't get too far.

Most recipes found here can be completed in any household kitchen and the nutritional information is valuable in any part of the globe. However, this book was made for use on the road, so toss it in your backpack and *let's go!*

Instructions

During my first tour of Latin America I spoke very little Spanish. I ate rice and beans for breakfast, lunch, and dinner almost every day because I didn't know what else was available and much less how to ask for it. As the months fell away I stumbled upon more vegan-friendly options and began to experiment with cooking. Years later I stopped and thought, "Wouldn't it have been cool to have had all this knowledge way back then?" I decided to compile what I'd learned into what you now hold in your hands.

This book almost reads like a Choose Your Own Adventure novel. The various sections are meant to work together to supply you with the most complete information that I've been able to wrangle up. You will find many links from one page to another to help move between recipes and informative data.

When you see words in *italics*, they will usually be either *Spanish* or *indigenous* words, or just special words that I want to *stand out*. When you encounter a word in **bold type** within the text, it will most likely (but not always) refer to parts of the nutritional guide towards the end of the book. Important words like **fiber, protein,** or **vitamins** might prompt you to read more about them in the latter pages of the guide.

The ingredients guide in the back of the book (which contains a lot of **bold** and *italic* words) provides some noteworthy information on many of the ingredients used in the recipes, including their local names and where in the Mesoamerican markets to find them. The lists of available nutrients pertaining to each entry, found at the top of the pages in the ingredients guide, present the nutrients in order, left to right, from the highest to lowest quantity. The only exemptions are the vitamins, listed in alphabetical order. Nutrients with a presence of less than 5% RDI per serving are typically not included.

Please read through each recipe before you attempt to make it to be sure that you have all the proper ingredients, time, and equipment to pull it off. Many recipes require a stove (duh), a blender, a strainer, pots, pans, bowls, a measuring cup, and, of course, a good knife and various spoon sizes. A cutting board wouldn't hurt. Depends on whose house you're in! I use both metric and standard measurements throughout the book-- whichever serves best at the moment and is easiest to communicate while buying foods in the markets.

Speaking of the markets, and of your travels in general, the translations I've included for food items are only a small part of what you'll need to successfully navigate through the rich and colorful region of Mexico and Central America. If you don't already speak Spanish, I highly recommend bringing along a small Spanish pocket dictionary. The more you can communicate, the deeper your trip will take you.

I felt that it would be fun and important to include a few images of certain fruits or vegetables that you have never seen before and may have a hard time distinguishing in the markets. Kevin Hennessy has been kind enough to provide fine quality artistic illustrations of such foods. Of course, if you want to see more or colored photographs, please make use of the nearest internet connection and search engine site.

And since I've just mentioned the internet, let me again restate that I am neither a doctor nor a nutritionist. My suggestions are based on both my cooking and travel experiences. I've spent years living, traveling, and cooking in Central America. The information I provide in this book is meant only as an informative guide and I recommend that those of you who are inclined to continue learning about the art of healthy living employ the vast sea of knowledge available on the World Wide Web to help further your studies. Please feel free to check and crosscheck any data found on these pages and use it to form your own understanding of your body and its daily necessities.

Tips for Travel

As a traveler I believe in packing light. If I'm out on the road for a week, a month, or a year I generally pack the same. I like to walk. When my luggage or backpack becomes too awkward or heavy to allow me to stroll from a bus stop or train station to the center of town... or even town to town... I know I've got too much. I like to think of my bag as a turtle shell. It has everything I need and although it might slow me down a little, it won't stop me. I can take it with me anywhere.

SOME THINGS TO BRING WITH YOU:

Don't over-pack your clothes. Think about where you're going. I recommend starting off with just the basics: A pair of shorts, one or two pairs of pants, two or three t-shirts, a swimsuit, a sweatshirt, a few pair of socks, underwear, good shoes. That should get you through most situations. If you're going to the beach you don't need much. Later, if you plan to hit a colder climate, you can buy new or used clothing to suit the situation. When you leave that climate you can sell or donate the clothes. The whole of Central America is host to numerous weather systems. You will encounter everything. Low-altitude beaches and jungles are typically hot and often humid. Deserts can be both hot and cold. High-altitude mountains can get downright chilly and if you're quite adventurous you may even encounter snow or ice on the taller peaks.

When your clothes get dirty, wash them. Full service laundry facilities are almost always available or you can hand-wash your clothes in a bucket and, if you're lucky, a washboard. Unless you plan on staying in one place for a long time, no one will notice that you've been wearing the same pair of jeans for a month.

Bring something to read. But you don't need to bring the whole library. Two books at a time is a good measure. Many hostels and tourist areas have book exchanges. I've found plenty of gems on book exchange shelves, some mediocre titles, and a few off-the-wall weird books. In my opinion it's interesting to read what the other people around you have been reading. When you finish your books, trade them in for others.

A sewing needle and dental floss. If you plan to be traveling for an extended period, most likely your clothes, shoes, or equipment will start to break down. No worries! Patch it back up! I've found that wax-coated dental floss is the best in that it's tough and versatile. Use it on your teeth or on your tennis shoes! If a strap goes on your backpack, you'll want something a little stronger than standard thread to stitch it back together.

Pack a stainless steel water bottle. Most importantly, by bringing a non-disposable bottle, you'll cut down drastically on the amount of plastic you consume and throw away. Multiply a couple liters of water a day by how many days you'll be traveling. That's a lot of plastic!

Secondly, you can save money. Water is a commodity in Central America. The tap water is not potable. Unless you have an extremely dependable portable filtration system, you will need to buy water. Most hotels and restaurants have big jugs of purified water they use for clients or cooking. Offer up some change to refill your bottle. Many times they'll do it for free.

Keep toilet paper handy. Traveling away from home, you never know what to expect. Always better to keep a roll or a few napkins tucked away for emergencies. Through my experiences in Latin America I was amazed to find that the further south I traveled, the less luxuries were offered to me. There were points where renting a room in a guesthouse would not include sheets, showers, or toilet paper. Those items were to be paid for separately.

Bring copies of your passport and other important documents. Keep them separate from your passport in case one or the other is lost.

Sunscreen and bug repellant. If you're traveling anywhere in the tropics, it's good to have a couple of small bottles of this stuff available. Plan ahead because it's often much more expensive in the tourist zones. If you can't or don't bring these items with you, you can usually find them at a local pharmacy.

Emergency cash. It's a good idea to tuck a few bills away in a secret place. Maybe cut and sew a secret pocket into the waistline of your pants. Just in case. Most of the world now knows about "secret" money belts. They're not so secret anymore, so get creative.

Small stuff. Travel scissors, earplugs, pocketknife, lighter, pens and paper, fingernail clippers, travel flashlight, etcetera.

TAKE CARE OF YOURSELF:

A friend once told me: **Sleep when you're tired and eat when you're hungry.** Put these wise words into play and it will make a world of difference on your journey.
Plan ahead. Never assume that the place you're going or the road that takes you there will be vegetarian friendly. Keep some snacks on hand and eat a decent meal before you board a bus or boat for a long ride.

Drink lots of water. Dehydration can lead to all kinds of problems. Of course if you're taking that long bus or boat ride there might not be any bathrooms on board, so...take that into consideration.

Relax and don't worry. Extra stress creates useless baggage. Be aware of yourself and your surroundings, but don't get aggravated or let down by things you can't change. Take deep breaths and be patient. Positive energy is an essential traveling tool.

Trust your instincts for good and for bad. Your intuition is priceless. Listen to it constantly. If a situation doesn't feel right, get out of it. It's tough to evaluate situations as a foreigner being unaccustomed to a place and its people. Be aware, but also don't miss out on the good times. Some of my best memories and outstanding friendships have been made by taking chances in new and unfamiliar circumstances. Don't be afraid, just aware.

Walk a lot. Stretch and exercise your body as often as possible. Keep the air flowing and the blood pumping. Walking is great for cardiovascular health, to clear the mind, relieve stress, and lets you take in your surroundings at a comfortable and leisurely pace. By walking you'll get a better taste of your surroundings. Wear good shoes. Soft-bodied sports shoes with cushioned soles and good arch support make for happy walking feet. Those are also the most versatile for concrete, dirt, or rocky trails.

RESPECT YOUR ENVIRONMENT:

Remember that there is a world of people around you. Don't take up too much space physically, audibly, or energetically. It's aggravating to have to step over other people's belongings to get to your room or bed and there's nothing worse than being woken up at 3 AM by loud or belligerent chatter. Be aware of others and their needs. Be gracious.

Smile. You'll be amazed at how far this one can take you. Remember that in a foreign land, you're the weirdo. The people you interact with many times have no idea what you're talking about. Be courteous. Be patient. A smile is one of the most disarming tools you have at your disposal. Be thankful for their patience and demonstrate your good intentions.

Be respectful of customs. Remember that you are a guest. You're on vacation and you should enjoy it, but not at the expense of others or their beliefs. Visiting a foreign country is like visiting someone else's home. I've spoken with many foreign friends who have felt sometimes that guests are callous to local customs or practices. It may be wise to observe how others act and interact -- even ask if you're unsure, to avoid insulting your hosts.

BE ADVENTUROUS:

Talk to people. You didn't come all this way to do the same thing you do at home! Hang out with the locals. See the sites. Explore. Get lost. Have fun.

Learn the language. By making an effort to speak the local language you can broaden both your travel and life experience. When locals notice your efforts, you will gain their respect. Don't worry if people laugh at you. Laugh with them. No one learns a language overnight. Take it lightly, but be dedicated and determined. There are downloadable applications like Duolingo that can help you practice, but speaking with locals is your best bet if you really want to learn to converse. Make vocabulary lists of words, topics, and phrases that are interesting or important to you.

Try something new. Be it food, music, games, or arts. Once again, ask yourself why you're visiting this place. You could've stayed at home and watched the travel channel. If you've come this far, go ahead and get your hands dirty. Make your journey a learning experience.

Dance. When you have a chance to get out and get loose, do it. Keep that smile on your face. Share some laughs with the people. Experience what they do for a good time.

LAST BUT NOT LEAST:

Check the exchange rate. If you'll be crossing borders by land, it's always a good idea to check the web for current exchange rates. At the border you'll have the opportunity to change cash. Sometimes one country's currency is of less value or no longer accepted the further you get into the next country. If someone at the border can offer you a decent exchange rate, take it. Of course, it will never be quite what the official rate is, but you won't find that in exchange houses or banks, either.

Regarding robbery. Use your head. Stay away from dark, unpopulated areas. Don't carry more than what you need when you go out. Be aware of your belongings at all times. Carry yourself in a humble, unassuming manner. If something does happen, stay calm. A thief usually just wants your valuables, not to harm you.

Basic Food Prep

A few things to be mindful of when preparing food on the road:

Always use purified water in the kitchen for drinking, cooking, washing, or soaking. Boiling tap water should destroy parasites and remove chlorine, but won't remove heavy metals and other inorganic materials. However, if tap water is the best you've got then go for it. If you plan to boil your water, make sure you have enough time to let the water cool, depending on what you need it for. When making sprouts, soaking grains and legumes, or washing produce that you *don't plan to cook*, it's very important to use the best and cleanest water available.

Always wash your produce, no matter where you are. The edible skins of fruits and vegetables contain high concentrations of vitamins and minerals and should not be discarded when it is possible and logical to eat them. For this reason, always buy organic when there is an option. Most food sold in commercial super markets is not organic. However, organic farmers' markets take place at least one or two days a week in many Mexican, Guatemalan, Nicaraguan, and Costa Rican cities and towns. Many of the fruits and veggies sold by individual independent sellers in the people's markets are organic. If it looks like bugs have been on it it's probably organic. Don't be shy to ask, *"Es orgánica?"*

Even with organic produce, always thoroughly wash your fruits and veggies to get rid of any possible chemical or waste residues, dust, germs, bugs, etc. Produce with inedible skins, like avocados, should still be washed. Remember that when you slice into a fruit or vegetable, the knife first cuts through the outer skin and drags any impurities from outside to the inside.

One of the most important aspects of cooking is doing so in a spacious and comfortable work zone -- but we can't always get what we want. When I was a teenager living in a studio apartment, my half-kitchen boasted about a square foot of counter space, a sink with little to no water pressure, and a tiny four-burner stove that was too small to actually fit four pots onto at once. There was no room to turn around in the kitchen, my head hit the cupboards every time I bent over, and the refrigerator was in the living room. (It's no wonder I felt zero inspiration to cook in those days.) You may likely find yourself in a very similar situation if you're traveling through Central America, amigo. And if that's all you've got...make the best of it.

Assuming, though, that the kitchen you plan to use has more potential, prepare your workspace the best you can. Clear off tables and counter space, wipe everything down, set out the utensils and pots/pans that you'll need, and be sure you'll have enough light to do the job right. These little details can make a big difference in your mood and the outcome of your dish. Don't forget to put on some good tunes! Singing and good vibes add flavor to the food.

If you're a backpacker, you'll likely be using community kitchens in youth hostels. This can work either for or against you. You may find that the kitchen has a lot of traffic and you don't have the ideal time and space to prepare a good meal. Maybe the pots and pans are banged up and there is only one worthwhile knife and it's always in use. As with most things in life, though, a fresh manifestation of a dismal situation blooms when you change your perspective. The community kitchen of a youth hostel is also the perfect place to meet new friends and share a meal. If you can get a group involved in the meal-making you may be able to split the costs, divide the work, create friendships, and have a hell of a good time. A glass of wine might seem a little lonely by oneself, but sharing a bottle and some good laughs with company is a very different story... and a delicious dinner may just be the excuse to make it happen!

That being said, whether you're cooking for yourself or with a group, please be respectful of the space you use and the others around you. Leave the kitchen clean when you're finished and store your leftovers properly. If you need to leave beans or grains soaking or have some other experiment in the works, be sure to label it or let staff know so that it doesn't get thrown out. Try and make yourself and your food compact, taking up as little space as possible so that others can enjoy, too.

And now... let's start making some food!

SPICES AND SUCH

Of course you don't have room in your luggage to carry around an entire grocery store, but there are some spices (*especias*) and basic items that I recommend having on hand at all times. A small plastic bag, less than ⅛ kilo (*un octavo de kilo* or *un medio cuarto*), of each would be fine:

*Salt (*Sal*)
*Black Pepper (*Pimienta Negra*)
*Sugar (*Azúcar*)
*Ground Cumin (*Comino Molido*)
*Chili Powder, without salt (*Chile Molido sin sal*)

That list leaves you well stocked to make a meal out of anything. Now, if you have some extra room, or will be staying somewhere for a while, feel free to pick up the following items as well:

*Curry Powder (*Curry*)
*Thyme (*Tomillo*)
*Dried Oregano (*Orégano Seco*)
*Cloves (*Clavo*)
*Cinnamon Sticks (*Canela en Rama*)
*Bay Leaves (*Hoja de Laurel*)
*Honey (*Miel*) - (Don't forget to close it tight!)

And you'll always want a small bottle of **disinfectant** around for vegetables and leafy stuff. If you don't plan on taking airplanes (or will be checking a bag if you do) I highly recommend bringing your own **knife**. Beat up pots and pans in community kitchens can be dealt with, but a knife that won't cut or has a broken or uncomfortable handle can really ruin your creative cooking experience. Find something you like, treat it right, and it will become your best friend.

The following items can be found most anywhere on your travels. Carry them with you or donate leftovers to hostels or community kitchens.

*Flour (*Harina*)
*Whole Wheat Flour (*Harina Integral*)
*Breadcrumbs (*Harina de Pan* or *Pan Molido*)
*Cilantro Seeds (*Semillas de Cilantro*)
*Baking Powder (*Polvo para Hornear*)
*Baking Soda (*Bicarbonato de Sodio*)
*Corn Starch (*Maizena*)

Small bottles of cooking oil can be found anywhere. It is slightly cheaper to buy it in the larger bottles, but that means either more to carry around or more to leave behind. Olive oil (*aceite de oliva*), however, is not as common and often *not* sold in small bottles. You may have better luck finding olive oil at commercial supermarkets. That's one that you may want to carry with you. Just don't confuse olive oil for general vegetable-based cooking oils (*aceite vegetal*). Olive oil is not recommended for cooking at high temperatures. In the larger markets you may also find peanut oil, coconut oil, sesame oil, or others that can withstand more heat.

GRINDING SEEDS

Most seeds are better absorbed when ground. The body can get to and make better use of the nutrients and vitamins contained in the seeds once they're broken down a little bit. Seeds like flax, sesame, chia, sunflower, or pumpkin can be ground and stored in an airtight container to be quickly used later in shakes, smoothies, salads, or oatmeal. Keep in mind that ground seeds won't last as long as whole seeds so grind small portions at a time and use them often.

You can use a regular blender to grind most seeds. Put enough in there so that the weight holds the seeds down over the blades and allows the blender to tear them up. Make sure that both the blender and the storage jar are completely dry before you place the ground seeds in them. Humidity in either will lead to more rapid spoilage.

If you don't have a blender or the blender you have doesn't seem to be doing the job, use a small coffee grinder. It should work just as well if not better.
Be sure to store your ground seeds in an airtight container.

GARAM MASALA SPICE MIX

Garam Masala is a lively spice mix used heavily in traditional Indian cooking. It adds an instant splash of flavor to any plate but can get out of control quickly. You may recognize its warm, musky, slightly spicy taste in dishes like chana masala or dal fry. Learn to use it wisely or the array of flavor can become overpowering.

Ingredients:
1 TBS ground cumin (*comino*)
1½ tsp ground cilantro seed (*semilla de cilantro*)
1½ tsp ground cardamom (*cardamomo*)
1½ tsp ground black pepper (*pimienta negra*)
1 tsp ground cinnamon (*canela*)
½ tsp ground cloves (*clavo*)
½ tsp ground nutmeg (*nuéz moscada*)

Directions:
Mix everything together and keep it in an airtight container. If certain spices need to be ground, pass the mix through a blender or small coffee grinder.

CURRY POWDER SPICE MIX

Curry powder is a classic that most people are familiar with. Similar to Garam Masala, it can be used in a variety of plates from rice to steamed or stewed vegetables. My favorite is Thai Pineapple Curry!

Ingredients:
2 TBS ground cumin (*comino molido*)
2 TBS ground cilantro seed (*semilla de cilantro molido*)
2 TBS turmeric (*cúrcuma*)
½ tsp ground crushed red pepper flakes (*semilla de chile rojo*)
½ tsp ground mustard seed (*semilla de mostaza molida*)
½ tsp ginger powder (*jengibre en polvo*)

Directions:
Mix everything together and keep it in an airtight container. If certain spices need to be ground, pass the mix through a blender.

VEGETABLE BROTH

A hearty vegetable broth is useful in adding taste and thickness to soups, curries, stews, or just about anything of that nature. It adds a distinct, enriching flavor to your food. And you can make it out of the leftover veggie scraps you would have just thrown away!

Ingredients:
Celery scraps
Carrot scraps
Onion scraps
Garlic scraps
A pinch of salt

Directions:
Ideally, you would have about the same amount of each of these. Well, maybe a little less garlic! And of course you would have washed your veggies before cutting them, so the scraps should be clean. By scraps I mean what you would normally throw out: Carrot tops, celery tops, onion skins, and so forth. If you don't have any scraps, of course you can make the broth with fresh vegetables. If you want, you can throw other vegetables or spices in as well -- try some pepper or bay leaves. You will want about 1 part vegetables to 2 parts water.

Directions:

In a covered pot, simply bring water to a boil with all ingredients in the pot. Lower heat and let simmer, mostly covered, for 1 hour.

This lasts about 5 days in the refrigerator. Extra broth can be frozen and saved for later.

☺Makes about 2 to 3 cups (depending on the amount of veggies) in just over an hour.

RICE MILK

Rice milk is one of the more watery vegan milks.
It's also one of the quickest, cheapest, and easiest to make.

Ingredients:
1 cup uncooked, whole grain rice (soaked in water overnight)
3 TBS sugar (optional)
1 TBS vanilla extract (optional)
Water

Directions:
The rice should be rinsed and soaked overnight in purified water to make it softer, easier to digest, and to activate the nutritious enzymes.

Drain and rinse the rice thoroughly. Dump the rice into a blender and fill the blender a little over halfway with water. Blend.

Strain the "milk" from the blended rice using a tight mesh strainer, cheesecloth, or bandana. Catch the milk in a large pot or bowl. Press all the excess liquid out of the pulp with a spoon. Return the rice pulp to the blender and fill it halfway again with water. Blend and repeat the straining process. Discard the pulp and pour the milk into a pitcher.

If the milk doesn't fill the pitcher, you may need to add more water. This recipe should make at least 1 liter of milk. Mix in the sugar and vanilla (if desired). Refrigerate.

Fresh rice milk should keep 4 to 5 days in the refrigerator.

⊕Makes 1 pitcher (about 1 liter) in about 10 minutes, plus soak time.

SOY MILK

Soymilk is thicker than most vegan milks. It has a distinctly "beany" taste that can be cut by sugar and vanilla. It's great for "milkshakes" or baking.

Ingredients:
1 cup soybeans (uncooked - soaked in water overnight)
2 liters water
5 TBS sugar
3 TBS vanilla extract

Directions:
Drain and rinse the soybeans. Place ⅓ of the beans in a blender with ⅓ of the water. Blend and strain the "milk" from the pulp through a fine mesh strainer cheesecloth, or bandana into a large pot. Push down on pulp with a spoon to help press out all the milk. Toss out the pulp. Repeat with the other ⅔ of beans and water.

Put the pot on the stove and heat milk over medium flame, stirring constantly, for about 10 minutes. Remove from heat and let cool. Stir in the sugar and vanilla. This milk keeps for 4 or 5 days in the refrigerator.

☺Makes 2 liters in about 20 minutes.

ALMOND MILK

Aside from the soak time, this is one of the quickest milks to prepare, although a bit more costly.

Ingredients:
1 cup almonds (soaked in water for at least 8 hours)
1 tsp vanilla extract (optional)
Sugar or honey to taste (optional)
Water

Directions:
Drain and discard the soak water and rinse the almonds.
Place the almonds in a blender and cover with 2 cups of drinking water. Blend on low and then high speed for at least 30 seconds. Pour the liquid through a fine mesh strainer into a pot or medium-sized pitcher. Use a spoon or spatula to press all the "milk" out of the mush. Return the mush to the blender and cover with 3 cups of water. Blend and strain again. Discard the mush.

Stir in the vanilla. If you decide to sweeten the milk you can add honey or sugar. Add a tablespoon or two until you arrive at the desired taste.

Fresh almond milk should last up to 4 days in the refrigerator.

☺Makes 1 pitcher (about 1 liter) in about 10 minutes, plus soak time.

NOTE: Cashew or hazelnut milk can be made by simply substituting the nuts and following the same steps. It has a smooth and silky taste and I find it great for use in desserts.

COCONUT MILK

Who doesn't love coconut milk? The taste is outstanding on its own and adds a delicious creamy taste to curries, desserts, or smoothies. Have you tried coconut ice cream?

Ingredients:
1 mature dry coconut
Water

Directions:
Fresh coconut milk is best made in tropical beaches or lowlands where coconuts grow. If you have access to mature coconuts and a blender, coconut milk is easy to do. Young coconuts are used for drinking. As they grow, the water begins to solidify and create the meat. The meat is needed to make coconut milk, so the older the coconut the better in this case. If you're using dry brown coconuts that have already fallen from the tree, make sure there are no cracks in the inner shell or bad smells. If the coconut is intact and unspoiled, you're good to go.

Strip the tough husk from the shell using a machete, ice pick, screwdriver, backside of a hammer, etc. Once you get down to the shell, brush away any excess fibers or dust. Hold the coconut shell over a bowl and whack it a few times around the circumference with a hammer, backside of a thick machete, or other heavy tool. It should split and any remaining water will fall into the bowl. Save the water.

Break up the two sides of the shell however possible to make it easier to scoop out the hardened meat. Remove the meat using spoons, screwdrivers, paint can openers... whatever works. Watch your fingers. I've drawn blood on a couple occasions trying to extract coconut meat. But don't let that deter you! It's worth a scratch or two.

Place all the coconut meat in a blender and pour in the coconut water and/or purified water, covering the meat by a just a couple of inches. Blend on high for about 30 seconds. Pour the liquid through a fine mesh strainer or cheesecloth into a pitcher and set aside.

Replace the shredded coconut leftovers back in the blender and just barely cover them with water. Blend and strain again, adding to first batch. Toss or compost the coconut mush.

This milk is of a good consistency for cooking. If you would like milk for drinking, it can be watered down. If you desire a sweeter milk, mix in some sugar or honey to taste.

The whole process should take about 30 minutes. The amount of milk made from each coconut varies depending on the amount of meat in the coconut. Generally, you can get about 1½ cups from 1 mature coconut.

COOKING RICE

Cooking rice is pretty basic, but I'll include it just to be handy. I recommend using brown rice whenever possible.

Ingredients:
1 cup brown rice (soaked in water overnight)
3 cups water

Directions:
Bring the water to a boil in a small pot. Meanwhile thoroughly rinse the rice for at least 30 seconds in a strainer. Add the rice to the water, cover and return to boil. Once boiling, lower heat to a minimum and leave just a small gap with the cover for steam to escape. Cook for about 45 minutes *without* stirring.

Check rice periodically to make sure the water doesn't run out. Without stirring, you can use the end of a wooden spoon or something similar to poke down to the bottom of the pot. If you don't see any more water, your rice should be done. Taste a couple grains from the top. Cooked brown rice will be a little chewy, but not too much. If it needs more time, add a little more water, re-cover and cook. Don't let it burn! When the rice is ready, turn off the flame and let the rice sit, covered for 5-10 minutes before serving.

⊕Makes 3 cups in about an hour.

NOTE: When cooking white rice the ratio should be 1 part rice to 2 parts water. White rice will cook faster. If you have time, it's recommended to soak your rice overnight or up to 24 hours before cooking. This activates the enzymes in the rice, elevating the nutritional level, and cuts down on cook time. If you've soaked your brown rice first, you may want to use 2½ cups of water and cook for about 35 minutes.

To add some flavor to your rice you can try cooking it in coconut water, in (or with) coconut milk, with some chopped cilantro, with a little salt, or with some lime wedges. Or combine them all!

COOKING BEANS

Cooking up beans from scratch, although time consuming, is simple. And, of course, almost all of that time is hands off cook time. So there's really no reason not to eat clean, fresh beans! Use this cooking guideline for most dried beans like black, white, pinto, red, garbanzo, bayo, etc.

Ingredients:
½ kilo beans (2 cups - soaked in water overnight)
Salt
Water

Directions:
Soak the beans in water overnight (at least 8 hours). During this time the beans will absorb all the water and double in size, so make sure you cover them at a ratio of 2:1 water to beans.

Drain the water and rinse the beans thoroughly. Place beans in a medium-sized pot and fill it with water about three fingers higher than the beans. Place pot over high heat. Add 1 tsp of salt, stir, and cover the pot. Once boiling, turn down the heat to low and let the beans simmer.

Check the beans every so often over the next 4 hours to make sure they have water. If the water gets low, add a little more. Taste a couple beans after the 4 hours are up. They should be soft and cooked by now. If not, keep cooking.

☺Makes about 6 cups in about 4 hours, plus soak time.

NOTE: Cooking the beans in a pressure cooker will save time and nutrients.

COOKING BLACK BEANS

This is my favorite way to cook black beans. It can be modified as desired. Basically when cooking any kind of beans they need to be rinsed, soaked, rinsed again and cooked for a long time. The rest is just flash for good taste.

Ingredients:
½ kilo black beans (2 cups - soaked in water overnight)
1 chili *guajillo* (seeded)
1 chili *pasilla ahumado* (seeded)
½ white onion (intact)
5 whole cloves
3 cloves garlic (peeled and smashed)
1 stalk *epazote*
½ TBS salt
½ tsp pepper
1 bay leaf

Directions:
Soak the beans in water overnight (at least 8 hours). During this time the beans will absorb all the water and double in size, so make sure you cover them at a ratio of 2:1 water to beans.

Drain the water and rinse the beans thoroughly. Place beans in a medium sized pot and fill it with water about three fingers higher than the beans. Place pot over high heat.

Meanwhile, push the 5 whole cloves into the curved side of the half-onion as if they were little nails. This will allow you to remove the onion and cloves easily after you finish cooking. Smash the garlic cloves with a spoon or the wide side of a knife. Add all the ingredients to the pot, cover, and bring to a boil.

Once boiling, lower heat, leave a slight opening with the lid and let simmer about 3-4 hours. Check beans periodically. When they are completely soft all the way through, they are ready. Remove chilies, onion with cloves, garlic, and bay leaves. Enjoy.

⊕Makes about 6 cups in about 4 hours, plus soak time.

NOTE: You may want to keep the cooked bean water for use in other recipes as a broth. If you have access to a pressure cooker, this will cut your cook time down to about 45 minutes and help your beans retain more nutrition.

FRESH TOFU FROM SCRATCH

This is a simple method for making tofu with common ingredients. It might take one or two tries to get it right, but once you've got it...... .fresh tofu is the best!

Ingredients:
1 cup soybeans (uncooked - soaked in water overnight)
½ cup lime juice (about 4 or 5 limes)
2 liters water

Directions:
Rinse the soybeans and soak them in water for at least 8 hours to overnight.

Drain the beans, rinse them again and blend ⅓ of the bunch in a blender with ⅓ of the water. Filter the "milk" from the bean mush using a tight mesh strainer or cheesecloth, catching the milk in a pot. Press the mush with a spoon to extract all the milk. Save the milk. Toss out the mush. Repeat this step 2 more times with the remaining beans until all of it is blended and pressed.

Heat the soymilk over medium-high heat for 10 minutes, stirring constantly. Raise heat and bring to a boil. Continue to stir. Once boiling, remove from heat and let cool. The milk should cool just enough so that you can stick your finger in without burning it.

When ready, pour in the lime juice, making a circle around the whole pot. Stir 2 times and let the milk sit for 5 minutes, untouched.

Meanwhile, prepare the tofu mold. If you don't have a genuine tofu mold, time to get creative. Find a cube or rectangular-shaped object about the size of your hand. This object will need holes in the bottom to let the water drain out. Try an old Tupperware that you can poke holes into with a knife or nail, or a plastic strawberry or blueberry dish from the grocery store, possibly something similar waiting in the recycling bin. Maybe even the same strainer you used to filter the milk. You can even cut up a cardboard milk or juice container and put holes in the bottom.

You will also need a lid that is *smaller* than the top of the container, as well as a weight and cheesecloth. The lid will need to press down on the tofu to squeeze out the water. The weight (another Tupperware or jar filled with water) does the pressing. If you don't have cheesecloth, a thin, porous material like a square foot-sized piece of t-shirt or a bandana will work for this step.

Line the mold with the cheesecloth, leaving some material sticking out on all sides. Use a large spoon to scoop the milk curds out of the pot and into the cloth-lined mold. If you need to use two molds, fill one and then the other. Once filled, fold the cheesecloth over on all sides, closing the top of the box. Place the lid on top. It will need to be small enough to fit down inside of the mold, but not so small that it lets the sides spill out around it. Press down gently with your hand to squeeze out the water. Place the weight on top of the lid and let it sit, undisturbed, for about 45 minutes. (For softer tofu you can take the weight off after 20 minutes)

Remove the weight and pull the cloth from the mold. Unfold and behold...fresh tofu! Eat it warm or save it for later. Tofu should be refrigerated in an airtight container, covered in cold water. The water should be changed daily. This keeps for 4 or 5 days.

⊕Makes 1 tofu block in about 45 minutes, plus soak and stand time.

***NOTE:** Because we used lime juice to make this tofu, it will have a slightly acidic taste. Once cooked with spices or vegetables, it won't be noticeable. Use a little sugar with it to counteract the acidity.

How to Cure Cashew Nuts

Raw cashews are tainted with a toxic substance found inside their tough shells. This toxin, urushiol, is produced by plants in the cashew family (anacardiaceae), which include poison ivy, poison oak, poison sumac, and even mango. Urushiol causes a nasty, irritable rash on the skin and provokes symptoms leading to possible death if ingested. Therefore, cashew nuts must never be eaten raw. However, heat destroys the toxin, so steamed or cooked nuts are safe to eat.

Cashew nuts are found inside of a hard shell at the end of the cashew apple (page 155). One simple way to cure the nuts is to steam the entire shells in a frying pan. Be sure to do this in a well-ventilated room. You'll need rubber gloves, a nutcracker or tough knife, and a spatula or spoon.

Heat a frying pan with lid over medium-high heat. Once hot, place the whole cashew shells, as many as will fit, around the bottom of the pan and cover. Steam will begin to seep out of the shells. They will brown on the bottoms. Turn and stir them every so often, being careful not to inhale too much of the steam. This steam can irritate the eyes, nose, or throat. Replace the lid when not stirring. When both sides of the shells are thoroughly browned, your cashew nuts should be cured. Remove the pan from heat and let the cashews cool.

Put on the gloves. Either crack the shells with the nutcracker or very carefully break the shells along the crease with a knife. Watch your fingers! A hammer may work, as well, to crack the shells but go easy as it's quite easy to accidentally smash the nuts inside.

The extracted cashew nuts (or pieces) will be safe to eat. If you want to further cure them, you can also toast, steam, or fry the extracted nuts. Enjoy!

Handy Conversion Chart

1 mm (*milímetro*) = 0.039 inch (*pulgada*)
1 cm (*centímetro*) = 0.393 inch (*pulgada*)
1 m (*metro*) = 1.09 yard (*yarda*)
     or 3.28 feet (*pie*)
1 km (*kilómetro*) = 0.62 mile (*milla*)
1 l (*litro*) = 1.05 quarts (*cuartos de galón*)
     or 0.26 gallon (*galón*)
1 mg (*miligramo*) = 3.52 ounces (*onzas*)
1 g (*gramo*) = 0.035 ounce (*onza*)
1 kg (*kilogramo/kilo*) = 2.2 pounds (*libras*)

1 inch (*pulgada*) = 25.4 mm (*milimetros*)
1 foot (*pie*) = 30.48 cm (*centímetros*)
1 yard (*yarda*) = 0.914 meter (*metro*)
1 mile (*milla*) = 1.609 km (*kilómetros*)
1 ounce (*onza*) = 29.57 ml (*mililitro*)
1 cup (*taza*) = 0.24 liter (*litro*)
1 pint (*pinta*) = 0.473 liter (*litro*)
1 quart (*cuarto de galón*) = 0.946 liter
1 gallon (*galón*) = 3.785 liters (*litros*)
1 ounce (*onza*) = 28.349 grams (*gramos*)
1 pound (*libra*) = 0.453 kg (*kilogramo*)

How much? - *¿Cuanto?*
All - *Todo*

Quarter - *Cuarto*
Half - *Medio*

Full - *Lleno*
Empty - *Vacío*

Honey vs. Sugar

Many people are becoming more conscious about the damaging effects of too much sugar in their diet. Natural sugars, like those occurring in fruit, are one thing. Processed sugars, like refined table sugar, are something very different. Overconsumption of refined sugars can affect certain bodily functions, leading to serious health complications like obesity, diabetes, heart disease, and liver problems. However, sometimes a particular recipe or drink calls for a little extra sweetener. What can you use?

A little bit of refined sugar from time to time probably won't do you any harm if you eat a balanced diet and get some exercise. Even within the realm of processed sugars there are levels and methods of processing. Always, the purest is the best. "Unrefined" sugar is kind of a misleading myth. The processes used to convert sugarcane juice into crystallized sugar often do just that -- refine the food, removing valuable nutrients and trace minerals, leaving behind unbalanced glucose in the form of "empty calories." Even brown sugar is usually just bleached white sugar mixed with some molasses extract. The closer you can get to raw sugar cane, the better.

Much of tropical and sub-tropical Latin America uses *panela*, or *piloncillo*, which is one of the purest forms of sugar available. *Panela* is dehydrated sugar cane juice, usually boiled in brass rather than steel. The end product is a dark brown solid block that retains much of the sugar cane's original mineral and nutrient content. *Panela* can be chopped into smaller pieces and liquefied in boiling water or grated and used as granulated sugar.

And what about honey? Table sugar and honey actually contain the same basic sugar units, fructose and glucose. Refined sugar comes from sugar cane, a natural source, and honey is generated by bees using plant pollen. The difference is that to produce granulated sugar many steps are needed, which in the end strip the sugar of most of its mineral and fiber content. Honey is usually just heated before sold to prevent crystallization and yeast formation. If heated minimally it retains more vitamins and digestive enzymes than processed sugars.

Honey generally has more calories than refined sugar, but it's also sweeter. Most of the time less honey is needed to do the sweetening than refined sugar meaning that the caloric consumption may be equal or less, depending on how much is used.

In the end, the two are similar, but honey may have a slight nutritional advantage over processed sugar. When possible, always try to use pure raw cane sugar (*turbinado* or *azucar moreno*) and honey with a low *glycemic index* (less than 55). If you have access to it, go for the *panela*. You'll enjoy the difference in taste and quality.

The Recipes

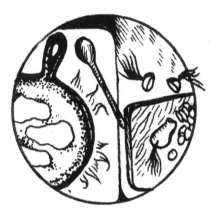

Salsas, Creams & Dips

BUTTER BEAN DIP

This is a wonderful, quick, and easy dip/spread that can go just about anywhere a good hummus or bean dip can.

Ingredients:
2 cups butter beans (cooked)
½ cup olive oil
½ tsp salt

Directions:
If you haven't already cooked the beans, soak them in water for at least 1 hour, drain, rinse, and cook until tender.

Place the cooked beans in a blender. Start blender on low speed and slowly pour in the olive oil. Stop the blender when necessary and move the contents around with a wooden spoon. Blend again and again until a smooth and uniform consistency is reached. Add the salt towards the end and blend (or mix with the spoon) until equally distributed.

Serve with chips, crackers, or as a sandwich spread.

☻Makes 2 cups in about 5 minutes.

CASHEW CHEESE

Cashew cheese is a creamy spread that can be used to replace dairy cheese in recipes that call for some kind of melted cheese like pizzas, nachos, tacos, etc. It's also great with grilled veggies or pastas.

Ingredients:
1 cup cashews
1 large garlic clove (chopped)
1½ TBS lime juice
½ TBS vinegar
½ tsp olive oil
½ tsp salt
¼ cup rejuvelac (page 274) or water

Directions:

Soak the cashews in water for at least 6 hours. Drain and rinse the cashews and place them in a blender along with all the other ingredients. Blend until the mix becomes smooth and uniform, scraping down the sides of the blender with a spatula as needed. Keeps in refrigerator for 4 or 5 days.

⊕Makes 1 cup in about 10 minutes, plus soak time.

CASHEW SOUR CREAM

Here's a quick, simple concoction to take the place of sour cream. It's pretty similar to the cashew cheese, of course. Same same, but different. Try it on a toasted bagel.

Ingredients:
1 cup cashews
Juice of 1 lime
1 tsp apple cider vinegar
⅛ tsp salt
¼ cup water

Directions:

Soak the cashews in water for at least a few hours and up to overnight. When ready, drain and rinse the cashews.

Place the cashews and all other ingredients in a blender and blend on low until completely smooth.

⊕Makes 1 cup in about 10 minutes, plus soak time.

NOTE: *Vinagre al sabor de manzana* is **not** the same as apple cider vinegar -- it's just vinegar with apple flavor. However, true apple cider vinegar can be tough to find in Central America so work with what you've got.

CHIMICHURRI

Chimichurri originated in Argentina as a sauce used atop grilled meat. However, it also works as a dip for bread or chips as well as with grilled veggies or veggie burgers. Try it on a grilled portobello or oyster mushroom!

Ingredients:
1 cup fresh parsley
3 or 4 large garlic cloves (chopped)
2 TBS onion (chopped)
2 TBS dried oregano
1 tsp salt
½ tsp black pepper
¾ cup olive oil
3 TBS vinegar
2 TBS lime juice

Directions:
Dump all ingredients into a blender and pulse repeatedly until a rough but well-mixed consistency is reached. Let stand at least 30 minutes before serving. Keeps a few days in the refrigerator.

☺Makes a little more than 1 cup in about 10 minutes.

OPTION: If there is no blender available, just chop the parsley, garlic, and onion into very fine pieces and mix the chimichurri by hand in a bowl.

CHIPOTLE AIOLI

This cream adds a little zing to sandwiches, nachos, or grilled veggies!

Ingredients:
½ cup soymilk (page 20)
⅔ cup vegetable oil
¼ tsp vinegar
¼ tsp honey
¾ tsp salt
½ tsp lime juice
⅛ tsp mustard
1 fresh or dried chipotle pepper

Directions:
If using a dried chipotle pepper, soak it in water for at least 10 minutes to rehydrate it. Meanwhile, combine all the other ingredients, except the oil, into a blender. Blend on medium speed. Slowly pour in the oil as it blends.

Check the consistency. It should be close to that of sour cream. If it's too watery, add more oil.

If soaking, remove the pepper from the water, cut off the stem and remove the seeds. If fresh, cut off the stem and remove seeds just the same. Add the pepper to the blender and blend until completely absorbed by the cream.

This keeps 4 or 5 days in the refrigerator.

⊕Makes a little over 1 cup in about 15 minutes.

NOTE: Use a vegetable oil that doesn't have a distinct taste. Olive oil, for example, is too strong and makes the aioli bitter. Use apple cider vinegar when available. Canned chipotle peppers can also be used, if need be.

GRAVY

If you ask me, gravy is the foundation of soul food. So rich and savory! Often, gravies are made with chicken or beef stock, milk, and butter, but this vegan recipe will have you reeling.

Ingredients:
1 large onion (diced)
3 large garlic cloves (minced)
½ cup canola oil
¾ cup white flour
¼ cup garbanzo flour
⅓ cup soy sauce
¾ TBS thyme
1 TBS sage
1 tsp fresh or dried rosemary (minced)
1 tsp black pepper
3½ cups milk of choice (thicker is better)

Directions:
Heat the oil in a medium-sized pot over low-medium flame. Add the onions and sauté them for about 3 minutes, stirring often. Mix in the garlic and stir for another minute or so. Next, stir in both flours and the soy sauce. Mix everything together thoroughly and cook, stirring constantly, for another minute. Add the thyme, sage, rosemary, black pepper, and milk. Whisk everything together and bring to a boil, stirring often. Reduce heat and simmer for 7 or 8 minutes or until the gravy has thickened.

Serve over mashed potatoes, burritos, sautéed veggies, or black bean burgers.

⊕Makes around 4 to 5 cups in about 35 minutes.

OPTION: Add sliced button mushrooms after you stir in the soy sauce. Garbanzo flour (*harina de garbanzo*) can be found in most markets. If you're lucky enough to find nutritional yeast it can be used in place of the garbanzo flour.

NOTE: If the gravy becomes too thick after time in the refrigerator, just mix in a little more milk as you heat it up.

GUACAMOLE

Quick and easy, guacamole provides a very healthy snack or addition to sandwiches, chips, or meals.

Ingredients:
2 medium-sized ripe avocados
½ tomato (diced)
¼ small onion (diced)
2 TBS cilantro (minced)
Juice of ½ lime
1 large garlic clove (minced)
¼ tsp salt
¼ tsp black pepper

Directions:
Scoop out the avocado meat from the peel into a small bowl. Add the lime juice and mash the avocado with a fork until it's good and smooth. Add the salt, pepper, and garlic and mix thoroughly. Stir in the tomato, onion, and cilantro. Serve!

☺Makes more or less 1 cup of guacamole in about 10 minutes.

NOTE: Ripe avocados are dark green/black and give just a little when squeezed lightly. Avoid avocados that are too soft or "airy" to the touch. Also avoid avocados that are too hard or bright green.

HUMMUS

Traditionally, tahini (sesame seed paste) is one of the key ingredients used to make hummus.
If you're traveling in rural Latin America tahini may be very hard to come across. This recipe delivers a delicious and simple hummus made with all the more common ingredients.

Ingredients:
2 cups cooked garbanzos (*or* 1 16-oz. can)
2 large garlic cloves (chopped)
½ tsp salt
1 tsp ground cumin
¾ cup olive oil
Juice of 1 small lime

Directions:
Place all of the solid ingredients in a blender. Next add the lime juice and half of the oil. Begin to blend and, being very mindful of the blades, use a wooden spoon to help move the garbanzos around. It's easy to burn out the motor on the blender if you don't pay attention. If the blades stop turning, switch off the blender, move the mix around with the spoon, and give it another go. Don't leave the blender on if the blades get stuck. Little by little keep adding the remaining olive oil. Blend until smooth. If the hummus seems too thick or is difficult to blend, you can add a little warm water (you may even want to consider saving the cooking water from the garbanzos to add to the hummus blend).

☺Makes 2 cups in about 15 minutes.

OPTION: Serve with minced parsley and paprika.

NOTE: Tahini is essentially ground sesame seeds. You can make a quick "tahini" in the same blender with sesame seeds and oil beforehand to mix with your hummus.

MANGO CHUTNEY

Chutney is essentially and Indian dipping sauce. There are many varieties of chutney, often made with the fruits of the season, served with everything from samosas to flat breads.

Ingredients:
2 large mangos (very finely diced)
1 TBS fresh ginger (minced or grated)
1 TBS garam masala (page 17)
½ tsp whole fennel
1 tsp chili powder
½ tsp turmeric
3 TBS *panela* (grated) *or* sugar
2 TBS vinegar
½ tsp salt
1 TBS cooking oil (peanut oil preferred)

Directions:
Over a low flame, heat the oil in a medium-sized saucepan. Stir the garam masala and fennel thoroughly into the oil. Stir in the ginger and move the mix continuously until it becomes quite fragrant, about 2 minutes.

Pour in the mango and stir continuously for one minute. Add the chili powder, turmeric, *panela*, and vinegar. Partially cover and let cook, stirring often, for about 15 minutes. Add the salt and cook, uncovered, for another 2 minutes.

Remove pan from heat and let the chutney sit, covered or refrigerated, for at least an hour before serving.

Serve mango chutney with vegetable cutlets (page 80), samosas, frybread, grilled veggies, toast, or even pancakes.

☺Makes about 1½ cups in about 40 minutes.

NOTE: Panela (aka *piloncillo*) is solidified cane sugar. Alternatively, you can use regular sugar or brown sugar, but you may need to adjust the measurements as the taste will differ some.

MINT & CILANTRO CHUTNEY

This chutney is more fresh and herbal than sweet. It tastes delightful with chips, sandwiches, or samosas on a hot afternoon.

Ingredients:
1 cup fresh mint (lightly packed)
1 cup fresh cilantro (lightly packed)
2 heaping TBS onion (diced)
2 heaping TBS ginger (minced)
1 heaping TBS jalapeño (diced)
1 TBS lime juice
¼ tsp salt
1 tsp sugar
1 tsp whole cumin seed
1 small clove garlic (minced)
1 TBS cooking oil (preferably almond or coconut)
Water

Directions:
Heat up the cooking oil in a small frying pan over low heat. Add the garlic and cumin seeds and stir well. Sauté the garlic and cumin until they brown and become fragrant. Don't let them burn. Remove pan from heat and let cool.

If you haven't already washed your mint and cilantro, do so now and separate the leaves from the stems. Put the leaves in a blender along with the onion, ginger, jalapeño, lime juice, salt, and sugar.

Pulse the blender a few times to chop up all the ingredients. Add the oil mixture and a tiny bit of water. Blend for a few seconds, scrape down the insides of the blender and blend again. If needed, add water little by little until you arrive at a smooth, saucy consistency. This shouldn't take more than ¼ cup of water.

Ready! Serve your mint chutney with samosas, vegetable cutlets, frybread, crackers, tamales, raw or steamed veggies, fried potatoes, on a sandwich, or even as a salad dressing. This keeps for a few days and tastes even better as the flavors steep together.

☺Makes about ¾ cup in about 20 minutes.

OPTION: Add a few chunks of thick, fresh coconut meat to the blender. Mmmm.

NOTE: Every jalapeño is a little different. The spiciness of the chutney is relative to the punch packed in the pepper. You may want to test a couple small pieces of your jalapeño before you add it to the mix in order to determine how *picante* it will make your chutney.

NACHO CHEESE SAUCE

If you've ever felt frustrated with vegan cheeses that don't seem to melt right, if at all, then this "cheese" may be for you! Very similar to a typical nacho cheese sauce.

Ingredients:
2 small potatoes (peeled & chopped)
1 carrot (chopped)
¼ cup cashews
¼ cup garbanzo flour
1 TBS onion (minced)
1 clove garlic (minced)
1¼ tsp salt
½ tsp tumeric
1 TBS lime juice
⅓ cup coconut oil
Water

Directions:
Bring 4 or 5 cups of water to boil in a pot. Add the potatoes and carrot chunks, lower heat a little, and cook for about 20 minutes or until the potatoes and carrot become soft. When ready, drain the potatoes and carrot in a colander and let cool.

In a blender, grind the cashews into a powder.

Place the potatoes, carrot, and all other ingredients into a blender along with 1¼ cup of water. Pulse a few times and then blend the mix until smooth. Serve warm on nachos, over refried beans, with steamed veggies (like broccoli), on a pizza, or anywhere cheese sauce might go.

☺Makes about 4 cups in about 40 minutes.

OPTION: Add a tablespoon of jalapeño (seeded) to give the sauce a little kick!

NOTE: Your nacho cheese is likely to turn somewhat solid in the fridge. Before serving, heat it up with a touch of warm water and it should return to a pourable sauce.

PESTO SAUCE

Pesto sauce is often made with pine nuts. These can be expensive and hard to find in Central America. Try this version using peanuts!

Ingredients:
2 cups fresh basil leaves
⅓ cup peanuts
3 large garlic cloves (chopped)
⅓ cup olive oil
¼ tsp salt
¼ tsp black pepper

Directions:
Heat a skillet or frying pan over medium flame and toast the peanuts (with skins), moving constantly until they brown on all sides. Remove from heat, let cool, and peel off the skins (if necessary).

Place basil leaves in blender, followed by garlic, peanuts, salt, and pepper. Start blender and slowly pour in the oil. Stop the blender, move contents, and scrape down the sides with a wooden spoon or spatula when necessary. Continue blending until smooth.

🕐Makes 1 cup in about 15 minutes.

PICO DE GALLO

A traditional Mexican salsa to accompany burritos, tacos, rice and beans, cactus, and just about anything else you want.

Ingredients:
3 large tomatoes (seeded and diced)
1 medium-sized red onion (diced)
2 jalapeños (seeded and diced)
¼ cup cilantro (finely chopped)
1 small clove garlic (minced)
Juice of 1 lime
1 tsp salt

Directions:
In a medium-sized bowl, mix all the cut ingredients together. Store, covered, in the refrigerator.

☺Makes more or less 1½ cups in about 10 minutes.

RED SALSA

This is a general recipe for salsa roja *to accompany tacos, burritos, tostadas, etc. Get creative with it*!

Ingredients:
3 medium-sized tomatoes
3 *puya* chilies (seeded)
1 clove garlic (chopped)
½ tsp salt

Directions:
In a small frying pan over low-medium heat, roast the tomatoes, turning often, for about 10 to 12 minutes. Add the chilies after the first 5 minutes, turning and flipping them often, as well. The tomatoes will blister and burn in certain areas, losing their skin. This is fine. Try to let them cook a little on all sides. When the tomatoes and chilies are roasted, remove them from the pan and let them cool for 2 minutes.

In a blender, place the tomatoes, chilies, garlic, and salt. Blend until a uniform consistency is reached. Add more salt if desired. Store in an airtight container in the fridge. Keeps for about a week.

☺Makes 1½ cups in about 20 minutes.

NOTE: You can substitute *guajillo* chilies if you don't have *puyas*. Even chipotles or any other red chilies could work. The type, quantity, and even individual chilies will slightly alter the flavor of the salsa. Experiment! Be sure to test the spiciness of the chilies first, however, as all are different and you don't want to overdo it. *Picante* = Spicy! *Muy Picante* = Very Spicy! *Menos Picante* = Less Spicy!

GREEN SALSA

Same same, but different. Salsa roja *uses red ingredients.* Salsa verde *is made with green tomatoes and green chilies (duh). Use it where you please.*

Ingredients:
6 green tomatoes (*tomatillos*)
1 clove garlic (chopped)
⅛ onion (chopped)
1 jalapeño (seeded and chopped)
3 TBS cilantro (chopped)
½ tsp salt

Directions:
Bring 2 or 3 cups of water to boil in a small pot. Once boiling, add the 6 tomatoes. Boil the tomatoes for about 5 minutes. They should become soft but remain green, even if the green fades some. Remove the tomatoes from the water and let cool 2 minutes.

In a blender, place the tomatoes and all other ingredients. Blend until a uniform consistency is reached. Add more salt if desired. Store in an airtight container in the fridge. Keeps for about a week.

☺Makes 1 cup in about 15 minutes.

NOTE: You can use serrano chilies in place of the jalapeños. But be sure to test how spicy the chilies are first. Not all are the same and you don't want to overdo it!

SPICY SESAME SALSA

Creamy salsa with a protein punch! Great for tacos, veggie burgers, or salads.

Ingredients:
1 cup sesame seeds
5 *árbol* chilies
¾ tsp salt
2 TBS cooking oil
Water

Directions:
Begin by toasting the whole chilies (with seeds) in a skillet over medium-high heat. They should become brown but not black. Once toasted remove them from the pan and put the sesame seeds in their place, toasting them until light brown. If the seeds begin to pop and shoot out of the pan, mix in a tablespoon or so of the oil to hold them down. Stir the seeds with a wooden spoon to keep them from burning.

Next, transfer the sesame seeds and chilies (without stems) to a blender. Add salt and any remaining oil and cover ingredients with water. Blend. Use more or less water to arrive at the consistency you desire. For a less spicy salsa, remove the seeds from the chilies before adding them to the blender.

☺Makes 1½ cups in about 10 minutes.

OPTION: This salsa can be made with toasted peanuts in place of the sesame seeds.

SWEET CREAM

This little cream can be used to top off deserts. It's not as thick as whipped cream, but the taste is similar.

Ingredients:
¾ cup soymilk
2 TBS cornstarch
½ cup vegetable oil
¼ cup sugar
⅛ tsp salt
2 tsp vanilla extract

Directions:
Put the soymilk and cornstarch in a blender. Begin blending on low speed and slowly pour in the oil as the mixtures spins. Add the sugar, salt, and vanilla, and blend again for at least 1 minute on low speed. If you want it thicker, add a little more oil. Allow cream to sit in the refrigerator for at least an hour before serving.

This mixture will only keep a few days.

☺Makes 1½ cups in about 10 minutes.

THAI STYLE PEANUT SAUCE

Who doesn't love Thai food? No one that I know. Thai peanut sauce is a delicious combination of sweet, spicy, and creamy. It can be used in many ways, but I really love it with crunchy steamed broccoli.

Ingredients:
1 cup peanuts
2 cloves garlic (minced)
1 jalapeño (seeded & minced)
Juice of 1 lime
4 TBS soy sauce
2 TBS sesame *or* coconut oil
2 TBS sugar
2 TBS vinegar
¾ cup warm water

Directions:
Heat a skillet or frying pan and lightly toast the peanuts, with the skins on, moving constantly. Remove peanuts from heat, let cool, and rub off/remove the skins.

Heat the water. Place all the other ingredients in a blender and pour the water in on top. Blend until smooth, using a wooden spoon to help move contents through the blender if they stick. Add more water if necessary.

Use with Veggies and Tofu with Thai Peanut Sauce recipe (page 114) or with pasta.

☺Makes 2 cups in 20 minutes.

OPTION: You can use peanut butter in place of whole peanuts if you wish. In this case, the blender is not needed. Just add all ingredients to a bowl, pouring the warm water in last. Mix very well with a spoon or whisk.

Salad Ingredients

Contrary to popular belief, salads can be made with more than iceberg lettuce, tomato, and onion. Here is a list of suggested items that can be mixed up and interchanged to create fresh, delicious, and highly nutritious salads according to your taste or preference.

Greens:
Spinach
Chard
Kale
Lettuce
Arugula
Watercress
Chaya
Sorrel

Vegetables:
Celery
Onion
Carrot
Broccoli
Mushrooms (steamed or sautéed)
Beets (baked or shredded)
Cabbage
Okra (boiled or baked)
Radish
Yuca (boiled)
Sweet potato (boiled or baked)
Jicama
Nopal cactus (grilled)
Corn (grilled or boiled)
Zucchini (grilled)

Fruits:
Strawberry
Mango
Grapes
Kiwi
Orange
Apple
Raisins
Cranberries
Avocado

Proteins:
Green beans (raw or boiled)
Beans (any kind-boiled)
Peas (boiled)
Garbanzos (boiled)
Peanuts (raw or toasted)
Almonds
Walnuts
Cashews
Sesame seeds
Pumpkin seeds
Chia seeds
Amaranth seeds (toasted)
Shredded coconut
Tofu (raw, grilled, or herbed)

Herbs:
Dill
Tarragon
Mint
Basil
Cilantro
Parsley
Chepil
Hierba mora
Moringa (fresh leaves or dried powder)

Flowers:
Squash flower
Loroco
Pito
Yucca flower (*Izote*)

Soups

BLACK BEAN SOUP

This Sopa de Frijol Negro *is a hit at parties or potlucks. It's relatively quick and simple but will have people asking how in the hell you made it. It's a common food in parts of Mexico or Costa Rica.*

Ingredients:
4 cups cooked black beans (page 25)
2 TBS vegetable oil
1 onion (diced)
3 large garlic cloves (minced)
2 tomatoes (diced)
1 handful *epazote* (chopped)
2 tsp salt
1 tsp pepper
1 tsp cumin
1 large bay leaf
3 cups vegetable broth (page 18)
Parsley (optional)
Avocado (optional)

Directions:
Heat the oil over medium-high heat in a good-sized pot. Toss in the onions and stir, coating them in oil. Cook the onions about 5-7 minutes until translucent and aromatic. Throw in the garlic and stir continuously for another minute. Stir in the tomatoes and *epazote*. Add the salt, pepper, cumin, and bay leaf and stir constantly for another minute. Pour in the vegetable broth, stir, and turn up heat. Cover and bring to a boil.

Once boiling, add the black beans, stir and return to a boil. Reduce heat and simmer, half covered for 10 minutes.

Remove the soup from heat, let it cool off a little, and remove the bay leaf. Pour half the soup into a blender and blend until mostly smooth. Do the same with the other half of the soup. Garnish with chopped parsley and diced avocado, if desired, and serve!

☻Makes 6 portions in about an hour.

OPTION: Add baked or fried sweet potato cubes to the finished, blended soup. Also try cut, grilled *nopal* cactus. Each creates fantastic flavor combinations with spiced black beans.

BOLIVIAN PEANUT SOUP

I first tried Sopa de Maní *in Merida, Mexico, where a Bolivian friend and her French husband were living at the time. Couldn't get enough! Traditionally, the soup would be served with French fries on top. Your call.*

Ingredients:
1 TBS cooking oil
½ onion, medium-sized (diced)
2 carrots, medium-sized (diced)
2 celery stalks (diced)
1 red bell pepper, small (diced)
3 garlic cloves (minced)
2 tsp salt
½ tsp black pepper
½ tsp dried oregano
¼ tsp chile powder
1 cup peanut butter
2 cups veggetable broth (page 18)
2 cups water (or 4 cups water, no broth)
½ cup cilantro (minced)

Directions:
Heat the oil in a large pot over medium heat. Sauté the onion, celery, carrot, pepper, and spices for about 2 minutes, stirring often. Add the garlic and cook for another 3 minutes, stirring often. Add the water, broth, and peanut butter. Turn up the heat and whisk the peanut butter until it dissolves in the water. Once about to boil, turn down the heat and let the soup simmer for about 10 minutes. Meanwhile, prep the cilantro.

Remove pot from heat and serve hot with fresh cilantro as garnish.

☺Makes 4-6 portions in about 40 minutes.

*OPTION: Substitute parsley for cilantro. Add a half-cup of green peas. No peanut butter?! No problem! Toast about a cup and a half of shelled and skinned peanuts in a frying pan over medium-hot heat. When somewhat cool, transfer the peanuts to a blender and grind them down. Add a little water if necessary. Use this in place of the peanut butter.

CARROT & ZUCCHINI COCONUT CREAM SOUP

This soup is delicious and a great addition to a meal with friends.

Ingredients:
7 large carrots (diced)
3 medium-sized zucchini (diced)
1 large onion (chopped)
2 TBS cooking oil
2 cloves garlic (minced)
1 TBS curry powder
½ tsp salt
A couple pinches black pepper
3 cups vegetable broth (page 18)
2 cups coconut milk (or 1 13-oz. can)
1 TBS honey

Directions:
In a good-sized pot, heat the oil and cook the onions, carrots, and zucchini over medium heat for about 7 to 10 minutes. Cover and stir occasionally. When the onions start to turn brown add the garlic, curry, salt, and pepper. Sauté for 1 minute more. Add the vegetable broth and bring to a boil. Lower heat and simmer 10 to 12 minutes until carrots are tender. Add the coconut milk and bring to a low boil. Turn off the heat and stir in the honey.

Let the soup cool down some and then transfer it little by little to a blender. Only fill the blender about halfway to avoid spitting soup all over the room. Blend soup and transfer to a large bowl or pot. Repeat this step until all the soup has been blended. Reheat slightly, if necessary, and serve hot.

☺Makes 4-6 portions in about an hour.

OPTION: Sprinkle toasted coconut or chopped cilantro on top. Goes well with toasted bread.

GREEN PEA AND GARLIC SOUP

I loved green pea soup as a kid. And I still do. Peas pack a protein punch and pea soup is fun to eat. I used to think it was dragon food.

Ingredients:
2 cups dried peas (soaked in water overnight)
½ onion (diced)
4 cloves garlic (minced)
2 TBS cooking oil
1¼ tsp salt
1 tsp black pepper
½ tsp cumin
4 cups water

Directions:
Drain and rinse peas and set aside in a colander.

Heat the oil over medium-high heat in a good-sized pot. Add the onion and stir often until the onion becomes tender and aromatic (about 2 minutes). Add the garlic and stir for one minute more. Add the peas, pepper, salt, and cumin and stir well for another minute. Add the water and turn up heat. When water begins to boil, turn to low-medium heat and let cook, ¾ covered, for 30 minutes or until peas are soft and cooked through.

Remove pot from heat and let cool for 5-10 minutes. Place half of the soup in a blender and blend until smooth. Do the same with the other half and serve at once!

☺Makes 4-6 portions in about an hour (plus soak time).

OPTION: Use coconut milk. Only add 3 cups of water. Cook peas 20 minutes in the water and then add 1½ cups (*or* 1 13-oz. can) of coconut milk. Stir well and cook for another 10 minutes.

NOTE: If you use fresh or frozen peas, the cook time will be considerably less. Fresh or frozen peas should cook in about 2-3 minutes. In this case, use a little less water.

LENTIL SOUP

Simple, satisfying, and definitely filling. Good before long trips or in cold weather.

Ingredients:
2 cups lentils (soaked overnight)
2 medium-sized potatoes (cut into 1-inch cubes)
1 large carrot (cut into half moons)
1 onion (diced)
4 medium-sized garlic cloves (minced)
2 TBS vegetable oil
1½ tsp salt
1 tsp black pepper
1 tsp ground cumin
1 tsp curry powder
¼ tsp chili powder
Water

Directions:
In a large pot, heat the oil over medium heat. Add the onion and stir well, coating the onion thoroughly with oil. Let cook for 3 to 4 minutes, stirring occasionally until the onion begins to turn translucent and brown on the edges. Add the garlic and stir continuously for another minute. Add the lentils and spices, stirring well. Add 2 cups of water and turn up the heat, bringing water to a boil.

Once boiling, lower heat, cover, and let simmer for 7 minutes. Add 4 cups of water and the potatoes. Turn up the heat and bring water back to a boil. Add carrots, lower heat and let simmer, half-covered for about 12-15 minutes.

Serve with warm bread or tortillas.

⊕Makes 6 portions in about 50 minutes.

Sandwiches

BLACK BEAN BURGERS

Well, there's no quick and easy version of this one, but the work is worth the wait. While you're at it, I recommend making a double batch to freeze or use for a dinner party or some kind of communal eating event... or just for yourself!

Ingredients:
4 cups black beans (cooked & drained, page 25)
½ cup oatmeal (uncooked)
¾ cup breadcrumbs
2 TBS ketchup
1 medium-sized carrot (grated)
½ red onion (sliced into very thin strips)
½ medium-sized zucchini (finely diced)
2 garlic cloves (chopped)
½ jalapeño (seeded & chopped)
¼ cup fresh cilantro
½ TBS ground cumin
½ TBS dried oregano
½ TBS chili powder
½ TBS salt
½ TBS black pepper
2 TBS olive oil
1 cup puffed amaranth
1 TBS cooking oil

Directions:
In a large bowl, mash the black beans with a potato masher until they are turned into complete mush. It's okay if a few whole beans remain. Add the oatmeal, breadcrumbs, ketchup, and carrots. Mix everything together thoroughly. Don't be afraid to get your hands dirty.

Heat the cooking oil in a frying pan and sauté the onion and zucchini for about 5 minutes until they become tender and golden, stirring often. Add them to the mix.

Place the garlic, jalapeño, cilantro, spices, and olive oil into a blender and blend until smooth. Pour contents into the bowl and mix everything together well.

Pour some amaranth out onto a flat, wide plate. Place another empty plate next to the first to collect the finished burgers. Roll out golf ball-sized pieces with the bean mix and then squash them down into hockey pucks. Round and shape the edges of the little patties to create ½-thick discs. One by one, push each side of the patties into the puffed amaranth, coating them completely. Place the finished burgers on the empty plate.

Now they are ready to cook or store. Cook in a frying pan with a bit of vegetable oil over medium heat for about 3 minutes per side until lightly browned (at least 5 minutes per side if they're frozen). It helps to place a lid or another frying pan on top to ensure that both sides and the center become equally cooked.

If you need to stack the patties on top of one another for storage purposes, you can place a piece of plastic between them to keep the burgers from sticking to each other. They can be kept in the fridge or freezer.

That's it! Serve on a tasty toasted burger bun with tomato, avocado, lettuce, and chipotle aioli sauce (page 37).

NOTE: If you don't have any burger buns, try serving the patties over rice. Even better, try them over rice with gravy, steamed peas, avocado, and hot sauce (recipe, page 93). Enjoy!

⊕Makes 6-8 patties in about 40 minutes.

BRAISED BEET & HERBED TOFU SANDWICH

This recipe takes a little time, but it utilizes even the beet leaves and it's fun to make! You should have at least 2 frying pans for this one.

Ingredients:
1 block tofu (page 26)
2 beets with greens
2 tomatoes (sliced)
2 TBS fresh rosemary (minced)
2 TBS fresh tarragon (minced)
2 TBS fresh dill (minced)
4 cloves garlic (minced)
½ jalapeño (minced)
½ cup red wine
¼ cup orange juice
1 TBS dried oregano
½ TBS dried parsley
½ tsp dried sage
⅓ tsp turmeric
½ lime
Salt and black pepper to taste
Cooking oil (preferably coconut)
4 bread rolls (sliced in half lengthwise)

Directions:
In a small pot with lid, mix the wine, orange juice, garlic, jalapeño, rosemary, tarragon, dill, and ¼ tsp black pepper. Turn the burner on to medium heat. Cut the tops off the beets and drop the beets in the pot, rolling them around to coat them thoroughly with the marinade. Place a piece of tin foil over the top of the pot and seal it well. Place the lid on the pot (over the tin foil) and let the beets cook over medium heat for about 45 minutes.

On a wide plate, mix up the oregano, parsley, sage, and turmeric with ¼ tsp of black pepper. Set aside.

Press any excess water out of the tofu block and slice it into 4 slabs. Rub the slabs with the juice of a sliced lime. Press each side of each slab into the herb mix and set aside.

Heat about 2 TBS of oil in a frying pan over medium-high heat. Meanwhile cut the stems off the beet tops. When the oil is hot, sauté the tofu slabs for 2-3 minutes per side. Add more oil to the pan, if necessary.

When the beets are ready, remove them from the pot and cut them into slices, about ¼ inch thick, and set aside. Squeeze the lime juice into a glass and mix it with a little water.

Heat a second frying pan. Once hot, place the beet tops and tomato slices in the skillet. Sprinkle a little salt over them. Pour in about 2 TBS of the lime water and cover the pan quickly so the vapor doesn't escape. Steam the greens and tomatoes for about 1 to 2 minutes or until the greens are soft. Remove from heat.

When the tofu slabs are done, quickly clean off that frying pan and reheat it over medium-high heat. Cut the bread rolls in half and toast each side in the frying pan until slightly browned.

Assemble the sandwiches! Place a tofu slab on each bun, followed by a couple beet slices, tomato slices, and some beet greens. Serve hot and enjoy!

⊕Makes 4 sandwiches in a little over 1 hour.

BREADED EGGPLANT & GRILLED VEGGIE SANDWICH WITH HUMMUS SPREAD

Fresh, flavorful sandwiches made from a rainbow of colors. You may want to try them with a glass of red wine and an orange for dessert.

Ingredients:
8 slices breaded eggplant (page 86, eggplant only)
½ cup hummus spread (page 40)
½ small white onion
1 large red bell pepper (deseeded and cut into thin slices)
2 medium zucchinis (cut into wide, thin, flat strips)
2 large tomatoes (cut into disc slices)
1 tsp salt
1 tsp black pepper
1 tsp dried oregano
1 tsp dried thyme
1 tsp sugar
1 pickled jalapeño (optional, sliced)
4 sandwich rolls (sliced in half)
Handful of fresh spinach (washed)
Olive oil & Cooking oil

Directions:
Begin by preparing your eggplant and hummus spread if you haven't already. Do not cook the eggplant yet.

Rub the bell pepper and zucchini slices in olive oil. Let the excess drain off. Prepare the grill over medium flame and, separately, heat a large frying pan over medium-high flame. Add 2 TBS cooking oil to the frying pan. When the oil is hot, place 2 slices of eggplant in the frying pan. Let them cook, covered if possible, for 4 minutes. Flip them and let the second side cook for 3 minutes.

Meanwhile, rub the pepper and zucchini slices with olive oil and lay them, side by side, on the grill over the flame. If they don't all fit, cook them a few at a time. The flame should not be touching the veggies. Place the half-onion on the grill, cut side up. Let the veggie slices cook for about 2½ to 3 minutes per side and then flip them over with a set of tongs. Let them cook half that time on the other side. Store grilled veggies between 2 plates to keep them warm.

When the eggplant slices are cooked, remove them from the pan and store them between 2 plates to keep them warm. Add 2 more TBS of oil to the pan and, once hot, lay out 2 more slices of eggplant. Cover and let cook as before. Repeat this until all the eggplant slices are cooked. You should have 8 slices at the end.

Wipe out any leftover breadcrumbs from the frying pan with a paper towel and return pan to medium flame. Add 1 TBS cooking oil and let that heat for 30 seconds. Place 4 tomato slices in the pan and sprinkle them each with a pinch of salt, black pepper, oregano, thyme, and sugar. Let them cook for 1 minute, flip them over, and repeat the process on the other side. Cook 1 minute more and remove tomatoes from heat. Add 1 TBS of cooking oil to the pan and repeat entire process with the next 4 tomato slices. You should have 8 in the end.

With the grill on medium-high heat, place the bread roll slices face down on the grill to toast. Meanwhile, cut the cooked onion into thin slices.

Once good and hot, remove bread from grill and begin to build sandwiches:

Place 2 eggplant slices on the bottom half of the bread roll. Next lay out a few zucchini slices, then the red bell pepper slices, followed by the onion slices. Add the sliced jalapeño, if so desired. Cover the veggies with fresh spinach leaves. Spread a generous helping of hummus on the top half of the bread roll. Put the top on the sandwich and get ready to eat!

☺Makes 4 sandwiches in about 1 hour (plus eggplant and hummus prep times, about 1½ hours total).

SIMPLE SANDWICH

This is a quick and easy sandwich I make often while camping or hiking. It's full of flavor and energy and best made with multigrain bread, when available.

Ingredients:
1 bell pepper (stemmed, seeded, and sliced lengthwise)
2 tomatoes (sliced)
1 avocado (sliced)
½ cucumber (sliced)
4 cloves garlic (thinly sliced)
1 cup hummus (page 40)
Bread (sliced into 8 pieces)

Directions:
Spread a generous amount of hummus over a piece of bread. One by one, add some bell pepper, tomato, avocado, cucumber, and garlic slices to each piece of bread. Add another piece of bread on top and you're done. Bon appetít!

⊕Makes 4 sandwiches in about 10 minutes.

Side Dishes

CASSAVA WITH GARLIC & CITRUS

Yuca al Mojo de Ajo is a *Cuban-style dish made with yuca root, citrus juice, onion, and garlic. The exotic taste will hook you.*

Ingredients:
3 good-sized yuca (peeled and cut into 1 inch chunks)
¾ large onion (very thinly sliced)
¼ cup fresh-squeezed orange juice (about ½ of a large orange)
¼ cup fresh-squeezed lime juice (about 2 limes)
6 cloves garlic (minced)
1 TBS fresh cilantro (chopped)
¼ cup olive oil
½ tsp oregano
¼ tsp cumin
Salt and pepper to taste (about ½ tsp of each)
Orange wedges for garnish

Directions:
Chop the yuca into chunks and slice off the thick skin. Put about 7 cups of lightly salted water to boil in a medium-large-sized pot. The yuca has a tough, fibrous cord that runs down the middle. Remove this as you are cutting the root. The cord is nearly impossible to chew. When ready, boil the yuca for about 20 minutes then drain and set aside.

As the yuca cooks, prepare the rest of the ingredients. Squeeze the orange and lime juices into a bowl and mix well. Add the onion, garlic, and cilantro. Place the cooked yuca on a large plate. Pour the juice mix over the yuca.

In a frying pan over medium flame, heat the olive oil, oregano, cumin, salt, and pepper, stirring well, until hot (about 2 minutes). Pour hot oil over the yuca.

Garnish with orange wedges and serve immediately.

⊕Makes 4 servings in about 40 minutes.

CHANCLETAS

This is a modified version of a cute little dish I tried in El Salvador called chancletas *("little sandals"). It's a bit tough to work with the* chayote *in this way, but fun to make and happy to eat.*

Ingredients:
2 *chayote* squash
1 potato (cubed)
2 garlic cloves (minced)
½ cup fresh *hierbamora* (finely chopped)
2 TBS fresh rosemary (minced)
2 TBS fresh dill (minced)
¾ tsp salt
½ tsp black pepper
½ tsp ground cilantro seed
½ tsp ground nutmeg
¼ tsp chili powder
4 TBS olive oil
4 TBS breadcrumbs
1 cup cashew cheese (page 34)

Directions:
Steam the chayote over medium-low heat in a covered pot with about a cup of lightly salted water at the bottom. Turn the chayote every 15 minutes until they are soft, about 45 minutes.

Boil the potato pieces in a small pot for about 10-15 minutes or until soft enough to squash with a fork. Remove the potato pieces and mash them with a fork or potato masher in a separate bowl. Add the oil, garlic, herbs, and spices as well as 2 TBS of the breadcrumbs. Mix and mash everything together well.

Remove the chayote from the pot and let cool. Preheat oven to 350° F (177° C). Cut the chayote in half, lengthwise, following the wrinkles in the squash. With a spoon, carefully scoop out the insides of the chayote leaving the skin intact. This is more difficult than it sounds! Go slowly, delicately. The skin is easy to tear so don't get too close. Separate the thick fibrous pieces from the softer pieces. Add the softer chayote chunks to the potato mix. Mash them with a fork and mix them in with the rest.

Gently refill the hollow chayote cups with the mix. The filling can be big and round and taller than the half-chayote skins. Sprinkle some breadcrumbs, olive oil, and a little chili powder on top. Place *chancletas* on a cookie sheet and bake for about 20 minutes. Top each *chancleta* with a few heaping spoonfuls of cashew cheese and serve hot!

OPTION: If *hierbamora* is not available, any dark green will do. Try *chaya*, *chepil*, sorrel, spinach, or kale.

COWBOY CACTUS AND POTATOES

Start your morning off right. Get some carbs with a kick, some cactus full of vitamins. This plate goes great with hot refried beans and a tall glass of fresh juice.

Ingredients:
½ onion (diced)
4 small potatoes (cut into ¼ disc slices)
2 medium *nopal* cactus pads (cut into ½ inch squares)
1 tsp fresh rosemary (minced)
¾ tsp salt
¼ tsp black pepper
¼ tsp chili powder
3 TBS cooking oil

Directions:
Warm the oil over medium heat in a large frying pan for about 45 seconds. Add the onions and stir well for about a minute and a half. Add the potatoes, salt, black pepper, and chili powder. Stir well and often for about 8 minutes. Add the rosemary and stir well for another 2 minutes. Add the cactus, stir, and turn up the heat a little bit. Stir often for another 12-15 minutes or until the potatoes and cactus are tender enough to eat. Enjoy!

⊕Makes 4 portions in about 40 minutes.

FRY BREAD

These Guatemala-style fritos de harina *are good to accompany a meal or can be taken with you as a travel snack.*

Ingredients:
½ kilo white flour (4 cups)
½ tsp salt
1 heaping tsp baking powder
1 bar margarine (½ cup)
Warm water (about 1 cup)
1 cup cooking oil

Directions:
Mix the flour, salt, and baking powder together in a bowl. Cut the margarine into chunks and add it to the mix. Pour in warm water little by little using your hands to knead the ingredients into dough. The dough should be neither too sticky nor too dry. You should be able to make little balls out of it. If it's too sticky, add more flour. If it's too dry, add more water.

Heat the oil in a frying pan over medium heat. Meanwhile form golf ball-sized units with the dough and then flatten each one out between your hands, making almost a footprint form. Poke a hole or two through the middle of each to keep air from becoming trapped inside. Test the oil by tossing in a tiny piece of dough. If bubbles form around it immediately, the oil is ready. If it smokes, the oil is too hot. Place the bread forms in one or two at a time. Let them fry for a couple minutes on each side and then flip them. Be careful not to let them burn.

Transfer the fried breads to a plate covered in paper towels to absorb the excess oil and allow time to cool. Enjoy!

☺Makes 10 pieces in about an hour.

GRILLED PINEAPPLE & SWEET POTATO MASH

This side dish makes a wonderful accompaniment to a variety of main dishes. Try it with steamed kale, grilled portobellos, rice and beans, breaded eggplant, or even a falafel sandwich.

Ingredients:
2 large sweet potatoes
½ cup coconut milk
1 cup pineapple (cut into 1-inch cubes)
¾ tsp ginger (grated or finely minced)
1 tsp salt
½ tsp black pepper

Directions:
Preheat the oven to 350° F (176° C). Wash the sweet potatoes well and place on a cookie sheet. Pour a little bit of water onto the cookie sheet to create steam in the oven. Place potatoes in the oven and cook for about 1 hour, turning once halfway through. The sweet potatoes should be soft to the touch.

When the potatoes are done, remove them from oven and set aside. Heat a frying pan and grill the pineapple, stirring constantly, for 3-5 minutes or until browned on the outside. Stir in the ginger during the last minute of frying. Remove pan from heat and set aside.

Cut the potatoes into chunks, both lengthwise and widthwise, and toss them into a big pot or bowl. Pour in the coconut milk and mash everything, including skins, together with a potato masher or fork until a universally smooth consistency is reached. Add the salt and pepper and stir well. Add the pineapple and ginger, stir some more, and serve!

☺Makes 4 portions in about 1 hour and 15 minutes.

NOTE: You can use yams in place of sweet potatoes, if desired. They will cook more quickly than the sweet potatoes. Also, if you don't have access to an oven or don't have time to bake, you can boil the sweet potatoes (or yams). However, by boiling you will lose more nutrients than by baking.

MASHED POTATOES (BASIC)

Yes, good old mashed potatoes. I assume you've made them before, but since they're a universal hit I decided to include a recipe. Just in case.

Ingredients:
4 large potatoes
5 TBS margarine
1½ cups milk of choice (the thicker the better)
1½ tsp salt
1 tsp black pepper

Directions:
Bring about 5 or 6 cups of water to boil in a medium-sized pot. Wash the potatoes and chop them up lengthwise and widthwise. Drop the potato chunks in the boiling water and cook for 20 minutes or until they are soft enough to smash with a fork.

Use a large strainer to drain water from potatoes. Return the potatoes to the pot, add margarine and mash with a potato masher. Little by little, add all the milk and keep mashing. Add the salt and pepper and mix well with a spoon until creamy and smooth. Mmmmm. Mashed potatoes.

NOTE: This is just the base for mashed potatoes. If you want to start branching out, add roasted garlic or caramelized onions. Try something new! Or leave it alone. Classic mashed potatoes are pretty dang good on their own.

☺Makes 4-6 portions in about 30 minutes.

NACHOS

Traveling can get you down at times. Nachos pick you back up. These vegan nachos are pretty righteous and guaranteed to put you in a good mood.

Ingredients:
A few handfuls of tortilla chips
1 cup refried pinto beans (page 78)
½ cup guacamole (page 39)
½ cup cashew sour cream (page 35)
½ cup red salsa (page 45)
1 cup nacho cheese (page 43)
½ jalapeño (thinly sliced)
5 heaping TBS black olives (sliced)
2 TBS cilantro (minced)

Directions:
If you have access to an oven, preheat it to 350° F (176° C). Pile the chips on a large plate followed by the beans. Once the oven is ready, place the plate inside and heat the chips and beans for about 10 minutes.

If you do not have access to an oven, separately heat the beans in one frying pan and the chips in another.

Assemble the plate in this order (or whatever order you choose). Chips, beans, guacamole, nacho cheese, sour cream, salsa, jalapeño, black olives, and cilantro. One on top of the other spread out all over the plate. Enjoy!

☺Makes one large plate (4 portions) in about 30 minutes, plus other ingredients prep times.

OKRA A LA MEXICANA

This is a Mexican-inspired okra plate. It's about as simple as they get, but you'll be amazed at how tasty it is!

Ingredients:
¼ kilo okra (sliced into discs)
½ onion (diced)
2 large garlic cloves (minced)
2 large tomatoes (diced)
1 TBS cooking oil
¼ tsp salt
1 tsp chili powder

Directions:
Heat the oil in a frying pan over medium-high heat. Drop in the diced onion and stir until golden brown. Mix in the okra, garlic, salt, and chili powder. Stir well for about 5 minutes. Add the tomatoes and cook, stirring often, for another 10 minutes or until okra is done. That's it.

⊕Makes 4 portions in about 30 minutes.

OPTION: In the last five minutes, add some greenery... spinach, *chaya*, kale, *hierbamora*, etc.

ORANGE GINGER BROCCOLI

Orange-ginger is another classic combination that is widely enjoyed. Round it off with some fresh broccoli and toasted sesame seeds.

Ingredients:
1 large head broccoli (cut into bite-sized pieces)
¾ cup orange juice
1 TBS ginger (minced)
1 clove garlic (minced)
1 TBS sesame seeds (toasted)

Directions:
Steam the broccoli in a hot, covered frying pan with about ½ cup of water for about 5 minutes over medium heat. Remove from pan, drain water, and set aside.

Place the orange juice, ginger, and garlic in the frying pan and simmer over medium heat for about 10 minutes, stirring often. Add the broccoli to the pan and stir well, heating for about 1 minute. Transfer broccoli to a serving bowl and pour remaining orange-ginger sauce on top. Sprinkle with sesame seeds and serve hot.

⊕Makes 4 portions in about 20 minutes.

PICKLED CABBAGE

Curtido de repollo *is a typical quasi-pickled cabbage salad used widely throughout Central America. It is often added to* pupusas *in El Salvador. It can be likened to sauerkraut or coleslaw.*

Ingredients:
1 small green cabbage (cored and thinly sliced, 3 inches long)
2 carrots (shredded)
1 onion (halved and thinly sliced)
1 jalapeño (seeded and minced)
1 TBS oregano
¾ cup white vinegar
Salt to taste

Directions:
Bring 4 or 5 cups of water to boil. Turn off heat, place sliced cabbage in the pot, and let steep for 3 minutes. Thoroughly drain the water and let the cabbage cool.

Place the cabbage in a bowl, add the rest of the ingredients, and mix well. Transfer salad to a glass jar or plastic pitcher with a lid. Cover and refrigerate. The longer it sits, the better it tastes! Use your *curtido de repollo* as a side dish, on sandwiches or burgers, on tacos, or in pupusas.

☺Makes about 5 to 6 cups in about 30 minutes.

OPTION: You can add a clove of minced garlic or a bit of chopped cilantro.

REFRIED BEANS

Take the basic bean-cooking recipe from the front of the book and turn it into this!

Ingredients:
4 cups cooked pinto beans (page 24)
¼ onion (diced)
2 cloves garlic (minced)
1 TBS ground cumin
1 tsp chili powder
2 TBS olive oil
½ cup water
Salt to taste

Directions:
Heat the oil in a large frying pan over medium heat. Add the onion and sauté for about 2 minutes, stirring often. Add the garlic, cumin, and chili powder and cook for another minute, stirring constantly. Stir in the beans and water. When the water begins to bubble, start mashing the beans with a potato masher or a fork. Mash until the beans all uniformly squashed, stirring often. Remove from heat and stir in the salt to taste. Serve hot!

☺Makes 4 portions in about 20 minutes.

STOVETOP PITA BREAD

Warm, fresh pita bread is a treat. It can be used in a variety of ways and packaged for rugged travel.

Ingredients:
1½ cups unbleached white flour
1½ cups whole wheat flour
½ tsp active dry yeast (*levadura*)
1½ TBS olive oil
½ TBS salt
Pinch of sugar
1¼ cup warm water

Directions:

In a small bowl, stir the sugar into about ½ cup of warm water. Once the sugar is completely dissolved, mix in the yeast and set aside for 10 to 15 minutes.

In a large bowl, mix together both flours, the olive oil, salt, and remaining ¾ cup of water. Mix thoroughly, using your hands if you prefer. The resulting dough will still be a little dry.

When the yeast mix has bubbled up some (and the bubbles may be very small), mix it in with the dough. With clean hands, knead the dough into a smooth, soft ball. If the dough is too sticky, add a little more flour. When ready, coat the ball all around with a little olive oil, return it to the bowl, and cover the bowl with a paper towel or napkin. Let the dough ball sit at room temperature for about an hour and a half. During this time the dough should rise and double in size.

When ready, preheat a skillet, preferably cast iron or non-stick, over medium heat. Make medium-sized balls with the dough. You should get 6 to 8 balls out of the mix. Again, if the dough is too sticky, add a little flour.

Thoroughly clean the counter top and sprinkle a good helping of flour over it. Either with your hands, a rolling pin, or a trusty bottle, roll the balls out into 6-inch-wide circles, about ¼ inch thick. Set the circles aside.

Once all are ready, begin to heat them, starting with the first rolled, on the skillet. Heat the pitas, covered, for about 3 minutes per side. They should begin to puff up as they cook. Getting the pitas to puff is a bit of an art, so don't be surprised if they don't come out perfect the first time.

Serve hot with falafel, hummus, salads, salsas, wraps, or whatever you can dream up.

☺Makes 6-8 pitas in about 40 minutes, plus rising time (1½ hours).

NOTE: The water should be warm. If it's too cold or too hot the yeast won't activate.

VEGETABLE CUTLETS

I first tried vegetable cutlets in Agra, India. I was amazed. These tasty little friends will put a smile on your face, I'm sure. They're almost like sautéed samosas.

Ingredients:
1 potato (peeled & chopped)
1 cup garbanzo beans (cooked)
⅓ cup fresh green peas
½ cup carrot (shredded)
3 cloves garlic (minced)
1 jalapeño (minced)
2 TBS cilantro (finely chopped)
1 tsp ginger (minced)
2 tsp ground oregano
1½ tsp salt
½ tsp black pepper
½ tsp turmeric
10 TBS breadcrumbs
2 TBS olive oil
Cooking oil
Mint or mango chutney (pages 41, 42)

Directions:
Bring about 4 cups of water to boil in a medium-sized pot. Add the potato, return to boil, and then turn down the flame and let cook. When the potato is soft enough to mash with a fork, strain out the water and let the chunks dry. Meanwhile steam the peas and prepare the carrot. Pat the peas and carrot with a paper towel or cloth to remove all possible moisture.

In a large bowl, mash the potato and garbanzo together with a potato masher or fork. Add the garlic, jalapeño, cilantro, ginger, oregano, salt, pepper, turmeric, olive oil, and half of the breadcrumbs. Mix everything thoroughly by hand. Add the carrots and peas and finish mixing.

Pour the remaining 5 TBS of breadcrumbs onto a plate and set out another empty plate to collect the cutlets. Form golf ball-sized balls with the mix and then pat them down into oval shaped patties, about a half-inch thick. Press each side of the patties into the breadcrumbs and then set it on the extra plate.

As you are nearing the end of the mixture, prepare a non-stick or cast iron frying pan to cook the cutlets. Heat 1 TBS of cooking oil in the pan over medium heat. Depending on the size of the pan, cook 3 or 4 cutlets at a time for 4 to 5 minutes per side, or until they become golden brown. Drizzle a tablespoon of oil around the pan each time you flip or change the cutlets, gently sliding the cutlets through the oil to coat the cooking side. Repeat this step until all the cutlets have been cooked. Serve hot with mint or mango chutney.

☺Makes 8 cutlets in about 1 hour.

NOTE: If your peas have been bought at a local market and they are dried, they may need to be boiled rather than steamed. Soaking them over night (with the garbanzos) can cut down on the cook time. Otherwise, they may need to be cooked for up to an hour. This can be done as you are preparing everything else, as they are not added until later.

Main Dishes

BEER-BATTERED STUFFED PEPPERS

Chile rellenos *are another favorite. They are often made with cheese, but this version is entirely vegan and utterly delicious. The recipe is a bit elaborate but well worth the effort. You should have a paper bag on hand before you start this.*

Ingredients:
4 Anaheim peppers (*chile poblano*/sometimes called "*pasilla*")
1 cup whole grain rice (uncooked)
¾ cup TVP (*carne de soya*)
1 cup cashew sour cream (page 35)
½ cup fresh basil (chopped)
1 tsp paprika (or chili powder)
Water
Vegetable oil

Salsa:
4 tomatoes
2 jalapeño peppers
2 garlic cloves (minced)
¼ onion (diced)
1 tsp oregano
¼ tsp thyme
1½ tsp salt
½ tsp black pepper
Vegetable oil

Batter:
1½ cup flour
¼ TSP baking soda
¼ TSP baking powder
¼ TSP cornstarch
½ TSP salt
1 cup beer

Directions:
Roast the 4 peppers on either a grill or dry frying pan, turning often, until the skin begins to blister and burn on all sides. Remove the peppers and place them in a paper bag. Tightly close the bag and set it aside.

Meanwhile, bring 3 cups of water to boil in a pot and boil the tomatoes and jalapeños for about 10 minutes. Remove the tomatoes and jalapeños from the water and let them cool. Save the water. When cool, dice the tomatoes and de-seed and dice the jalapeños. Meanwhile, heat 1 TBS of oil in a large frying pan over medium-high heat. Add the onions. Stir frequently.

When the onions begin to become translucent, add the garlic. Keep an eye on the garlic, stirring frequently for about a 1 minute. Don't let it burn. Add the tomatoes and jalapeño to the frying pan and stir. Add the oregano, thyme, salt and pepper, and stir. Add the rest of the water from the pot and bring to a boil. Once boiling, lower the flame, cover, and let simmer.

In a second frying pan, heat 3 TBS vegetable oil over medium-high heat. Add the uncooked rice. Stir well to coat all the rice in oil. Continue to stir frequently for about 5 minutes. Don't let the rice burn. Add the rice to the salsa and stir well. Bring to a boil and then lower flame, cover (leaving a small gap for the steam to escape), and let simmer for about 40 minutes.

In a bowl, prepare the batter. Mix together the flour, baking soda, baking powder, cornstarch, and salt. Add the beer little by little as you whisk the mixture. Set aside. Now take the peppers from the paper bag and peel the thin outer skins off. The heat and humidity of the bag should make them easy to peel. Remove the stems and seeds, leaving the peppers intact with a small hole on top.

After 40 minutes add the dry TVP to the rice mixture and stir well. Cook about 10 minutes more, covered, and then an additional 10 minutes with the lid off. Test the rice and soy. They should be cooked by now. If not, add a little more water to the pan and continue cooking until the rice and soy are tender. Once they're ready, mix in the fresh basil, remove frying pan from heat and let it cool. Clean the second frying pan and add 3 TBS of oil. Heat over medium flame.

Begin to stuff the peppers with the rice mix and cashew sour cream, alternating spoonfuls as you go. Roll the peppers in the batter, one by one, and carefully place them, one or two at a time, into the hot oil. Fry all sides of the pepper until golden brown and remove from heat. Drain excess oil onto a paper towel. Repeat until all peppers are cooked.

If there is any leftover rice mix, lay some out on each plate. Serve the peppers on top of the rice mix. Dab some cashew sour cream over the top of each pepper then sprinkle a little paprika over that. *Así es! Buen provehco.*

☺Makes 4 *chili rellenos* in about 2 hours.

OPTION: Drizzle some chipotle aioli (page 37) over the top of the cooked peppers.

BREADED EGGPLANT WITH PIPIÁN SAUCE OVER RICE

Pipián, *or* pepián, *is a typical dish from southern Mexico and some parts of Central America or South America. We'll use the* pipián *sauce from a later recipe to make a tasty dish with eggplant.*

Ingredients:
1 eggplant
¼ cup flour
½ cup breadcrumbs
3 TBS dried oregano flakes
1 tsp thyme
1 tsp salt
½ tsp sugar
½ cup milk of choice (thicker is better)
1 TBS good quality mustard
Pipián sauce (page 110, sauce only)
4 cups brown rice (cooked)
Cooking oil

Directions:
Begin by preparing the eggplant: Slice the eggplant, unpeeled, lengthwise into ¼ inch thick pieces that resemble sandals. Place a paper towel on a large plate or tray and sprinkle it evenly with some salt. Place 4 or 5 slices, however many will fit, side by side on the paper towel. Sprinkle salt over the eggplant and place another paper towel on top. Sprinkle the top of the paper towel with salt and lay the remaining slices over it. Once again, salt the eggplant and lay a paper towel over the top. Place another plate on top of this to weigh it down and set aside for 1 hour. This process will draw some of the bitterness out of the eggplant.

Meanwhile, prepare and cook the rice if you haven't yet.

When ready, remove the eggplant and rinse with water. Let dry. Meanwhile, mix the breadcrumbs, oregano, salt, and sugar together on a wide, flat plate. Pour the flour out onto a similar plate. Whip the milk and mustard together in a bowl. Place your eggplant all the way to the right side of the counter space and then, moving left, place the flour, milk/mustard, breadcrumb mix, and an empty plate or container. If you're left-to-right inclined, go ahead and lay the whole thing out as a mirror image the other way.

For each slice of eggplant, press both sides into the flour, then pass it through the milk mix, press both sides into the breadcrumb mix, and lay it out on the clean plate. Repeat until all slices are breaded.

Heat 1 TBS cooking oil in a frying pan over medium-high heat. Sauté two slices at a time for about 4 minutes per side. Heat up the pipián sauce at the same time.
On a plate, place 2 slices of eggplant over about a cup of rice. Pour pipián sauce over the eggplant and serve.

OPTION: Pipián with or without the vegetables can be used (according to the recipe on page 108). Alternatively any marinara sauce will do. I also recommend serving the breaded eggplant over couscous or quinoa, when available.

⊕Makes 4 servings in 30 minutes plus dehydration and rice cooking time.

CHANA MASALA

An Indian favorite! Impress your friends with this exotic specialty.

Ingredients:
2 medium-sized onions (finely diced)
1 clove garlic (minced)
1 jalapeño (minced)
2 tsp ginger (minced)
1 TBS ground cilantro seed
2 tsp ground cumin
1 tsp turmeric
½ tsp chili powder
2 tsp paprika
1 tsp garam masala (page 17)
2 tomatoes (diced)
⅔ cup water
4 cups cooked garbanzo beans (page 24)
1 tsp salt
Juice of 1 lime
2 TBS cooking oil
4 cups cooked brown rice (page 23)

Directions:
Heat the oil in a large saucepan over medium-high flame. Add the onions, garlic, jalapeño, and ginger. Stir continuously for about 5 minutes. Add cilantro seed, cumin, turmeric, chili, paprika, and garam masala. Stir well and cook for 2 minutes. Mix in the tomatoes and cook for 1 minute. Add the water and garbanzos. Stir well and let simmer, uncovered, for 10 minutes. Mix in the salt and lime juice. Serve with rice.

☺Makes 6 servings in about 45 minutes.

OPTION: Add toasted or roasted cashews and/or almonds.

CURRIED GREEN BEANS WITH MUSHROOMS

I cooked this up once for a birthday party. Everyone seemed to enjoy it and a few asked for the recipe. Well, here it is!

Ingredients:
⅛ kilo fresh green beans (de-stemmed and chopped)
⅛ kilo button mushrooms (sliced)
½ onion (diced)
2 cloves garlic (minced)
2 medium heirloom tomatoes (cut into chunks)
1 tsp salt
½ tsp black pepper
¾ tsp ground cumin
1½ TBS curry powder
4 TBS cooking oil

Directions:
Warm the oil in a large frying pan over medium-low heat. Add the onion and stir well for about 2 minutes. Stir in the garlic and cook for another minute and a half. Add the beans, salt, pepper, cumin, and curry. Stir well and cover. Let the mix cook, stirring every few minutes for about 12-14 minutes. Cover in-between stirring sessions. Add the mushrooms and stir often for about 4-5 minutes, covering in-between. Stir in the tomato and cook for another 2 minutes. Ready to serve!

⊕Makes 4 portions in about 45 minutes.

CHILI CON "CARNE"

Chili seems to be universally satisfying. Unfortunately, for vegetarians, it's usually a "no-go" due to the meat. Try this hearty version made with soy meat.

Ingredients:
1 cup pinto beans (cooked, page 24)
1 cup red beans (cooked, page 24)
1 cup dried soy crumbles or TVP (*carne de soya*)
1 large onion (diced)
4 cloves garlic (minced)
2 TBS soy sauce
1 red bell pepper (chopped)
1 16-oz. can tomato paste
2 dried chipotle chilies (seeded)
2 tomatoes (diced)
1 jalapeño (seeded & diced)
1 TBS lime juice
1 ½ cups veggie broth (page 18)
½ TBS salt
1 tsp black pepper
1 tsp ground cumin
½ TBS dried oregano
1 cinnamon stick
1 bay leaf
3 TBS cooking oil
½ cup cilantro (finely chopped)
1 Avocado (cut into cubes)

Soy meat marinade:
1 cup veggie broth (page 18)
2 TBS soy sauce
1 tsp salt

Directions:

Your beans should already be soaked and cooked when you start this recipe. It's best to marinate the soy meat at least 2 hours before you begin cooking.

For the soy marinade, pour the broth, soy sauce, and salt into a bowl or Tupperware container and stir thoroughly. Mix in the soy crumbles so that they're evenly coated in marinade. Cover and refrigerate.

Begin making the chili by preparing all your vegetables. Heat the oil in a large pot over medium heat. Add the onion and stir well for about 2 minutes. Add the garlic and stir continuously for another 2 minutes. Add the soy meat and stir for about 3 minutes more. Pour in the 2 TBS soy sauce and stir thoroughly. Move the mix often for the next 2 minutes and then add the bell pepper. Stir well and then add the salt, pepper, cumin, oregano, cinnamon, bay leaf, and chipotle. Stir often for about 3 minutes.

Thoroughly mix in the tomato paste and let simmer for the next 2 minutes. One by one, stir in the tomatoes, jalapeño, and lime juice. Cook for 2 minutes. Now pour in the broth and add the beans. Cover the pot, turn up the heat, and bring the mix to a boil. Once boiling, turn down the heat to low and let the chili simmer, covered, for about 12-15 minutes. Remove from heat and stir in the cilantro while the chili is still hot. Find and remove the cinnamon stick, bay leaf, and chipotle chilies before serving. Add some avocado. Enjoy!

☺Makes 6 portions in about a little over an hour.

OPTION: You can use any kind of beans you want. I actually prefer to pair up the pinto beans with "*frijoles de bayo*" if you can find them. Black-eyed peas work well, also.

DAL FRY

Another Indian specialty. This adaptation uses spices and chilies found in Mesoamerica.

Ingredients:
1 cup dried red or yellow lentils (soaked 2-4 hours)
1 onion (finely diced)
1 tomato (diced)
1 serrano chili (seeded and minced)
6 cloves garlic (minced)
1 tsp ginger (minced)
1 tsp turmeric
¾ tsp salt
4 cups water
1 TBS cilantro (minced)
Pinch of garam masala (page 17)
1 smoked chipotle chili (rehydrated, seeded and minced)
1 tsp ground cumin
2 TBS cooking oil
Cilantro for garnish (chopped)

Directions:
If using a dried chipotle chili, rehydrate it in a cup of water now.

Drain and rinse the lentils. Place the lentils, onion, tomato, green chili, 1 clove of the minced garlic, ginger, turmeric, and salt in a pot. Turn heat to medium-high, pour in the water and stir well. Cover, leaving just a small steam gap, and bring to a boil. Once boiling, lower flame to medium-low heat and simmer for 25 minutes or until lentils are on the verge of being mushy. Use a wire whisk or fork to whip the lentils until the texture becomes smooth and creamy. Stir in the cilantro and garam masala and remove pot from heat.

In a frying pan, heat the oil over medium-low flame. Add the cumin and stir continuously for 2 minutes. Add the remaining 5 cloves of minced garlic and chipotle chili. Stir often for about 3 minutes or until garlic browns. Don't let it burn.

Serve dal fry in a bowl with some of the oil mixture poured on top and garnished with chopped cilantro.

☻Makes 4 servings in about 1 hour (plus soak time).

NOTE: If red or yellow lentils aren't available, brown lentils will work, though they may take longer to cook. If you didn't have time to soak the lentils, they may take up to 45 minutes to cook and need more water. A jalapeño can be substituted for the serrano chili, and the chipotle chili could be substituted for a couple of árbol chilies or any red chilies.

DAN'S LOCO MOCO

My great buddy Dan Landes put this one together one evening as the rest of us stretched out in hammocks on the beach in Oaxaca, Mexico. In that moment we came to know it as the "Osa" plate, named after our boutique hostel there, the Osa Mariposa. Loco moco is a traditional plate from Hawaii made with white rice, a hamburger, and fried egg topped with brown gravy. In Spanish, loco moco means "crazy booger."

Ingredients:
4 black bean burger patties (page 60)
4 cups brown rice (cooked, page 23)
2 cups gravy (page 38)
1 cup green peas (canned or cooked)
2 avocados (sliced)
Cooking oil

Directions:
Heat a large frying pan with about 1 TBS of oil over medium heat. If they'll fit, place 2 burgers in the pan and make sure they get a good coating of oil. If the patties were frozen, put a lid on the pan to create more heat. Begin to heat the rice, gravy, and peas, if needed.

Flip the burger patties after a few minutes and cook the other side until they're good and hot all the way through. Repeat for the remaining burgers.

When all the elements are ready pile some rice up on each plate, followed by a burger, then some gravy with peas scattered over it, and finally a few avocado slices on top. Serve hot and enjoy!

☺Makes 4 portions in about 15 minutes plus cook time.

EGGPLANT AND MANGO SALSA OVER RICE

I cooked this up once for some friends in Guatemala using just about everything we had left in the kitchen. They liked it so I decided to cook it up again for some other friends in Colorado. They liked it, too, so I decided to include it in the book. Now, I hope you like it.

Ingredients:
1 large eggplant (cubed and dehydrated)
1 medium-sized onion (thinly sliced)
3 large yellow mangoes (thinly sliced)
3 large tomatoes (diced)
2 large cloves garlic (minced)
1 large carrot (shredded)
1 tsp salt
1 tsp ground cumin
½ tsp black pepper
½ tsp thyme
2 TBS cooking oil
½ cup almonds (sliced or chopped)
½ cup cilantro (minced)
2 cups brown rice (cooked, page 23)
Water

Directions:
Prep the eggplant about 1 hour before you start cooking:

Cut eggplant into 1-inch cubes, leaving the skin on. Sprinkle some salt on a large plate or platter and lay the eggplant cubes over it, close together, but not on top of each other. Sprinkle a little more salt on top of the eggplant and cover with a paper towel. If all the eggplant won't fit on the first plate, repeat this step again, sprinkling salt over the paper towel, adding the eggplant, more salt, and another paper towel. If needed, repeat a third time until all eggplant is accounted for. Place a book, another plate or some type of weight on top of the pile. This step will draw the liquid and bitterness out of the vegetable. Leave, untouched, for 1 hour. In the meantime, prep all your veggies.

Over medium flame, heat the oil in a large saucepan or wide-bottomed frying pan. Add the onions and stir often for about 4 minutes. Add the garlic and stir well for another minute. Add the eggplant, salt, pepper, cumin, and thyme. Turn up the heat a little, stir well, and cover for 3 minutes. Stir in the mango and tomato. Cover, lower heat a little, and let cook, stirring occasionally, for 10 minutes.

Meanwhile, toast the almonds over medium-high heat in a skillet or frying pan. Move them often so they don't burn. When they become dark brown on all sides, remove them from the pan and set aside.

Stir the shredded carrot into the salsa and cook, uncovered, for another 5 minutes. Remove pan from heat. Serve hot over rice, garnished with chopped cilantro and toasted almonds.

☺Makes 4 portions in about 45 minutes (plus eggplant dehydration and rice cooking time).

NOTE: If using large red mangoes, use only 2. The mango and eggplant portions should be equal.

FALAFEL BALLS

A traditional Mediterranean staple. A feel good food for just about any time, anywhere.

Ingredients:
1½ cup garbanzo beans (soaked overnight)
½ medium-sized onion (chopped)
½ cup parsley (chopped)
3 garlic cloves (chopped)
1 TBS flour
1 tsp salt
1 tsp black pepper
½ tsp ground cumin
½ tsp ground cilantro seed
½ tsp chili powder
¼ tsp baking powder

Directions:
Thoroughly mix all ingredients together in a large bowl. Now you will need to grind the mix down. Most blenders can handle this if you do a little at a time. Some blenders can handle it all at once. If you're unsure about your blender, or don't even have one, pull out the ol' potato masher and get to mashing (and in this case it wouldn't hurt to mince, rather than chop, the onion, parsley, and garlic).

When your mix is ready, let it sit for about 15 minutes in the refrigerator while you prepare a small pot with cooking oil. The smaller the pot the better because you're going to be deep-frying the falafel. Put at least 2 or 3 inches of oil in the pot and heat over medium heat.

Take out the falafel mix and begin to make little golf balls. Squeeze all possible liquid out of the balls as you're forming them. Test the oil by tossing in a tiny piece of falafel mix. If it sinks immediately, the oil is too cold. If bubbles appear around the mix, the oil is ready. Cook 3 or 4 balls at a time until they are dark golden brown. If need be, roll the balls around in the oil every 30 seconds to ensure that all sides get cooked. Place cooked falafel balls in a metal strainer or paper towel to allow any excess oil to drain.

Add your falafel balls to a sandwich or salad. Be creative. Traditionally you would wrap them up in pita bread (page 78) with hummus (page 40), lettuce, cucumber, tomato, onion, and a tahini dressing.

⊕Makes 10 balls in about 45 minutes.

GALLO PINTO

This is your typical Central American rice and beans dish. It's easy to make and provides complete and balanced protein. Gallo pinto *basically means the spotted or "painted" rooster, which your imagination may recognize in the plate of mixed up beans and rice. Add an avocado for some essential fats.*

Ingredients:
4 cups brown rice (cooked, page 23)
2 cups red beans (cooked, page 24)
2 TBS cooking oil
1 medium-sized onion (diced)
2 cloves garlic (minced)
1 tsp ground cumin
1 tsp ground cilantro seed
Salt and pepper to taste
Fresh cilantro for garnish (chopped)

Directions:
Heat oil in a large frying pan over medium heat. Add onion and sauté until transparent. Add the garlic and sauté, stirring frequently, 3 to 5 minutes until onion starts to brown. Add cumin and cilantro, mixing well. Add beans and rice, mix well and let cook until mixture is equally heated. Remove from heat and add salt and pepper to taste. Add fresh cilantro as garnish, if desired.

OPTION: You can garnish with *pico de gallo* (page 45) instead of cilantro. Try adding a little vegetable broth or bean broth when you add the beans and rice to the pan to give it some extra moisture and flavor. To make *gallo pinto* Costa Rican style, substitute red beans for black and add a couple tablespoons of Worcestershire sauce (typically not vegan) or Lizano sauce.

⊕Makes 4 portions in about 20 minutes.

GARBANZO AND ASPARAGUS IN COCONUT CREAM SAUCE

This plate provides plenty of rich, savory taste along with a truckload of nutrients.

Ingredients:
1 cup garbanzo beans (soaked in water overnight)
8-10 thick asparagus shoots (about 2 cups)
½ onion (thinly sliced)
4 large garlic cloves (minced)
½ tsp ginger (minced)
1 jalapeño (minced)
1¾ cup coconut milk (*or* 1 14-oz. can)
1 TBS soy sauce
2 TBS cooking oil
1½ tsp salt
1 tsp black pepper
1 tsp ground cumin
½ cup vegetable broth (*or* ½ cup water)
½ tsp orange zest (grated or minced orange peel)
20 large mint leaves (minced)
4 cups brown rice (cooked, page 23)

Directions:
Soak, rinse, and cook the garbanzo beans according the cooking guide on page 24. However, remove them from heat after 1 hour, drain, and set aside. If you're using canned garbanzos, skip this step.

In a large pan, heat the oil over medium-high flame. Add the onion and sauté for about 3 minutes, stirring often. Mix in the garlic and ginger and let cook for 1 minute. Add the jalapeño and stir for another minute. Mix in the coconut milk and soy sauce and bring nearly to boil. Add the salt, pepper, and cumin and stir well. Toss in the garbanzo beans. Stir, cover, reduce heat, and let cook for 10 minutes.

Make use of those 10 minutes to chop the asparagus shoots into 1-inch sections. Add the asparagus and vegetable broth. Turn up heat and bring to a boil. Stir well, reduce heat, cover, and let simmer for another 10 minutes.

Check the garbanzos and asparagus. If each are nearly cooked (tender), add the orange zest, cover, and cook for 5 minutes more. Stir in the mint leaves and remove from heat. Scoop a cup of brown rice onto each plate and serve a cup or more of the hot stew on top.

☻Makes 4-6 portions in about 1 hour, plus garbanzo cook time (1 hour).

HOT CAKES "A LA OSA"

This is an adaptation of a pancake recipe I got from a Mayan woman in the jungles of Guatemala. She used chocolate and oatmeal in hers. This was the hotcake standard at Osa Mariposa in Oaxaca.

Ingredients:
3 cups flour (ideally half unbleached white and half whole wheat)
⅓ cup sugar
1 TBS baking powder
1 TBS baking soda
2 TBS ground flax seed
1 ~~TBS~~ salt PINCH
A pinch of cinnamon
2 TBS vinegar
2 TBS vanilla
1 ripe plantain (peeled and sliced)
Margarine or vegetable oil
3 cups milk of choice

Directions:
Mix all the dry ingredients together in a large bowl. Leave a crater space in the center to later pour in the wet mix.

Heat a skillet and have the wet ingredients, including plantain, ready to go. Melt 1 TBS of margarine in the pan while mashing the plantain into it. Add the vinegar and vanilla and about a cup of the milk. Whisk all the ingredients together and pour them, little by little, into the dry mix. Keep whisking the dry and wet ingredients together so they don't clump up. Meanwhile, stir in the remaining milk.
Once the mix is ready, evenly pour a very large spoonful back into the skillet. If you're not using a cast iron or non-stick skillet, you may need to add a bit of margarine or oil before pouring out each cake to keep it from sticking. Cook over medium heat until all the bubbles have burst. Flip it over and cook for another couple minutes. Et voilà! Hot cakes!

☺Makes 8-10 pancakes in about an hour (less if you only cook a few pancakes and store the rest of the batter). The batter keeps about 4 days in the refrigerator.

NOTE: If you can't get a hold of a plantain, a regular banana will do just fine. The plantain just gives a little more flavor and body to the pancakes.

INDIO VIEJO

Indio Viejo is a traditional Nicaraguan dish. The name is derived from an old legend that states that as foreign invaders began to appear in Nicaragua the locals began to call this favorite food "Old Indian" in hopes to dissuade invaders from commandeering and eating it. Traditionally, it would contain beef or native animal meat. I used portobello mushrooms in this recipe.

Ingredients:
½ kilo corn flour (*masa harina*)
1 small yellow onion (diced)
3 cloves garlic (minced)
3 tomatoes (diced)
1 red bell pepper (diced)
1 cup fresh mint (chopped)
3 marinated portobello mushrooms (page 111)
2 tsp salt
1 tsp ground cumin
½ tsp ground black pepper
2 tsp sugar
1 tsp *achiote*
1 bitter orange
4 TBS cooking oil (preferably coconut)
Water

Directions:
The portobello mushrooms should be marinated before you begin this recipe.

Heat the oil in a good-sized pot over medium heat. Add the onions and stir well. Add the garlic, mint, and tomatoes and stir often for about 10 minutes. Meanwhile, in a large bowl, mix about a liter of warm/hot water into the corn flour. Whisk the flour and water thoroughly until you arrive at a uniform consistency.

Begin to sauté the portobellos in a frying pan according to the directions on page 111. This should take around 10-15 minutes. When the caps are ready, remove them from the frying pan and slice them into thin strips about 1½ inches long.

Add the wet *masa* to the pot, whisking it into the mix. Stir in the salt, cumin, black pepper, sugar and *achiote* and continue mixing. Add about another ¾ liter of water to the pot and stir everything well. Let the stew cook for about 10 minutes, stirring often so the corn flour doesn't form clumps.

Extract the juice from the orange and stir it into the stew. Add the portobello mushrooms and cook for another 5-7 minutes, stirring often, then remove from heat.

Garnish with mint sprigs. This dish is typically served with rice and fried plantains.

⊕Makes 6 portions in about 1 hour, plus time to marinate.

NOTE: You can substitute spearmint (*hierba buena*) for mint (*menta*). Also, if you can't find bitter orange, you can substitute the juice of 1 lime with that of half of a regular orange (about 1 cup). *Achiote* is a bright red spice used to color foods. You can substitute paprika if *achiote* is unavailable.

LENTILS AND RICE WITH CARAMELIZED ONIONS

I tend to cook a pot of this just for myself to last the week. Of course, it's good to share with your friends, as well. Tons of protein, carbs, and fiber to help you through the day.

Ingredients:
1 cup brown rice (soaked 8 hours)
¾ cup brown lentils (soaked 8 hours)
3 cups water
1 cup vegetable broth (or water)
1 TBS curry powder
1½ tsp salt
1 tsp ground cumin
½ tsp black pepper
½ tsp chili powder
1 cinnamon stick
½ onion (sliced thinly)
1 TBS cooking oil
Parsley (or cilantro) to garnish

Directions:
Rinse and soak the rice and lentils separately in water for 4-8 hours before cooking. Drain and rinse when ready.

Bring the 3 cups of water to boil in a large pot. Add the rice, return to boil, then lower heat and cover almost completely. Let rice cook for 10 minutes. Add lentils, veggie broth, and spices. Stir well. Add the cinnamon stick. Let simmer, 95% covered, for another 45 minutes or until rice and lentils are thoroughly cooked.

While the rice and lentils are cooking, go ahead and caramelize the onions. Heat the oil in a pan over medium-high heat. Add the onions and stir well, coating them completely with oil. Lower the heat to medium. Cover the pan but stir the onions every so often, letting them brown but not burn. Sprinkle some water (or broth) in from time to time if the onions seem to be drying out. Sprinkle a pinch of salt in, as well. As they onions become softer, you will need to stir them more often. The caramelization process should take 15-20 minutes.

Check the water level of the rice and lentils often. Don't let them burn. You can make a little hole in the mix with the end of a wooden spoon to see if there is sufficient water at the bottom. If the water starts to run out and the rice and lentils still aren't cooked, add a little more water. Repeat until they're done. Serve in bowls topped with onions and chopped cilantro.

⊕Makes 4 servings in about an hour (plus soak time).

MANGO GINGER TOFU

I first made this recipe under the guidance of Vegan with a Vengeance and later adapted it to fit more common Central American ingredients.

Ingredients:
1 pound (½ kilo) firm tofu (page 26)
3 TBS cooking oil (coconut preferably)
2½ TBS fresh ginger (minced or grated)
2 cloves garlic (minced)
½ jalapeño (seeded & minced)
3 medium-sized mangoes (peeled & sliced into strips)
½ cup vegetable broth (page 18)
3 TBS honey
Juice of 1 lime
½ cup orange juice
⅛ tsp ground cinnamon
⅛ tsp ground nutmeg
⅛ tsp ground cloves
⅛ tsp ground black pepper
Dash of salt
1 red bell pepper (seeded & cut into strips)
1 tsp red pepper flakes
¼ cup raw or toasted cashew nuts (optional)
4 cups cooked brown rice (page 23)

Directions:

First you'll need to marinate the tofu for at least 2 hours. So, start by making the marinade:
Heat the oil in a good-sized frying pan over medium-low heat. Add the ginger, garlic, and jalapeño and sauté, stirring often, for 5 minutes. Add the slices of 1 mango and let cook for another 5 minutes, stirring often. Pour in the broth and honey and bring to a boil. Once boiling, reduce heat and let simmer, covered, for about 30 minutes.

Uncover the pan and stir in the lime juice, orange juice, cinnamon, nutmeg, cloves, salt, and black pepper. Remove marinade from heat and let cool for 5 minutes.

Meanwhile, drain and press the tofu. Cut the block into 4 thin slabs. Slice those 4 slabs in half diagonally - as triangles. You should have 8 triangles now.

Pour the marinade into a blender and blend until smooth. Transfer the marinade to a square Tupperware-style container. Slide the tofu pieces into the marinade, making sure they're well-coated on all sides. Fit them all in, cover the container, and place it in the refrigerator for 2 (up to 8) hours. (If Tupperware isn't available try zip-loc bags)

When the tofu is done marinating, remove it from the fridge and preheat the oven to 375° (190° Celsius). Place the tofu triangles on a flat cookie tray. Pour a little marinade over the top, saving most in the container. Bake tofu for 20 minutes.

Flip tofu and drizzle a little more marinade over the top. Coat the bell pepper and remaining mango pieces in the rest of the marinade and add them to the tray. Bake for another 15 minutes.

If you're using raw cashew nuts, take this opportunity to toast them lightly in a skillet of frying pan.

Remove tray from oven. Serve tofu and veggies over rice and accompanied with steamed greens like kale, chard, or broccoli. Sprinkle a few red pepper flakes and the toasted cashews over the top. Enjoy!

☺Makes 4 servings in about 1 hour and 40 minutes, plus time to marinate.

MEGA CARIBBEAN MASH-UP

Drawing from some sazones *I experinced while living in Eastern Guatemala, I came up with a little stew that makes you feel like you're eating on a little Caribbean island. Maybe you are!*

Ingredients:
(Stew)
1 onion (diced)
1 *chayote* squash (cut into half-inch cubes)
4 cloves garlic (minced)
1 red bell pepper (seeded and cut into half-inch squares)
2 medium carrots (cut into quarter circles)
1 TBS ground cumin
2 tsp salt
1½ tsp black pepper
2 cups vegetable broth (page 18)
3 cups black beans (cooked, page 25)
1 jalapeño (minced)
1 cup fresh cilantro (chopped)
2 TBS cooking oil
4 TBS shredded coconut

(Mash)
4 ripe plantains
4 tsp ginger (minced)
4 cloves garlic (minced)
2 tsp fresh sage (minced)
2 tsp fresh rosemary (minced)
2 cups coconut milk (page 22) *or* 1 16-oz. can

Directions:

In a large pot, heat the oil over medium-high flame. Stir in the onions and move often for about 3 minutes or until they are tender and beginning to brown. Add the chayote, stir well, and cover. Let cook, stirring occasionally, for about 10 minutes. Add the garlic, bell pepper, carrots, cumin, salt, and black pepper. Stir well, cover again, and cook for 5 minutes.

Add the vegetable broth, cover halfway, and bring to a boil. Uncover, add the black beans and jalapeño. Stir well and cook for 2 minutes. Add the cilantro, stir well, and cook for 2 more minutes. Remove pot from heat.

To make the mash, peel the plantains and slice them into discs. In a pot, or even in a frying pan, mash up the plantains with a potato masher of fork. Heat the frying pan over medium-high heat.

Place the plantain mash in the pan and pour in the coconut milk. Mix everything together well with a wooden spoon. Add the ginger, garlic, sage, and rosemary. Cook, stirring continuously, for about 3 minutes. Remove from heat.

To serve, spread out a portion of plantain mash over a plate, leaving a depression in the center, like an upside-down Frisbee. Pour out a portion of the stew into the middle and top it off with a sprinkling of shredded coconut.

⊕Makes 4-6 portions in about 1 hour.

NOTE: Ripe plantains are yellow with mostly blackening skin. The blacker the skin, the sweeter the fruit, but beware of mushy or moldy plantains. These are no good.

MÜESLI

Müesli is a great breakfast bomb. It's full of fiber, protein, sugars, antioxidants, and vitamins. Not to mention it tastes good and is simple to prepare.

Ingredients:
½ kilo rolled oats
2 cups milk of choice
6 strawberries (sliced)
2 bananas (sliced)
1½ cup grapes (halved)
1 TBS pumpkin seeds
1 TBS chia seeds
1 TBS toasted amaranth
1 TBS ground moringa
1 TBS honey

Directions:
Mix the oats and milk together in a bowl. Mix in the sliced fruits. Let mixture sit covered in a refrigerator overnight. The flavors and sweetness of the fruits will melt into the oats.

When it's ready to eat, scoop out some muesli into a bowl and top it off with a tablespoon or so or each of the remaining ingredients. Mix it up and enjoy!

☺Makes 4 servings in about 10 minutes (plus overnight in the fridge).

NOTE: This recipe is completely open to your own personal preferences. Change the fruits, change the seeds, etc. Some people experience bloating or gas when eating müesli for the first time. This can be a result of the high levels of insoluble fibers in the oats. Once the body adjusts to these fibers, usually after a few days, the gas should subside. If not, try drinking a glass of water before eating the muesli. Also try drinking ginger, mint, or *epazote* tea before and/or after your meals.

Cooking the oatmeal also lessens the probability of gas (see following recipe). When available, you may want to try the same ingredients for a breakfast with cooked quinoa in place of the oats.

OATMEAL BREAKFAST (COMPLETE)

I eat this every morning. Every day. No joke. Ask anyone. I love it.

Ingredients:
1 cup rolled oats
2 TBS raisins
2 TBS dried cranberries
2 TBS raw or toasted pumpkin seeds
2 TBS shredded coconut
1 TBS sunflower seeds
2 TBS ground flax seed
2 TBS ground chia seed
1 TBS ground moringa leaf
1 tsp cinnamon
Water

Directions:
Bring 2 cups of water to a boil in a medium-sized pot. Add the oats and turn down heat to medium-low. Allow oatmeal to cook 3 to 5 minutes or until most of the water is absorbed.

Scoop the oatmeal into a bowl and thoroughly mix in all the other ingredients. If the oatmeal is too dry, add a little warm water or milk of your choice. Chew well!

⊕Makes 2 portions in less than 10 minutes.

OPTION: Add fresh fruit! Try bananas, blueberries, strawberries, raspberries, or mango. Maybe add some almond butter or coconut oil.

SIMPLE VEGGIE PASTA

There is so much that can be done with pasta. Here is a basic recipe. Please adapt and experiment with it. Ever tried hummus pasta? Pretty good.

Ingredients:
300 grams dry spaghetti noodles
1 large onion (diced)
2 large garlic cloves (minced)
2 zucchini (cut into thin quarter discs)
12-15 button mushrooms (sliced)
4 Roma tomatoes (diced)
1 large carrot (shredded)
Handful of cilantro (minced)
Salt
1½ tsp ground black pepper
1 tsp ground oregano
½ tsp dried thyme
Olive oil

Directions:
Bring about 6 to 7 cups of water to boil in a large pot. Stir in 1½ TBS of salt and 1 TBS of olive oil. Once boiling, add spaghetti and turn heat down to medium-high. Let cook for about 20 minutes or until noodles are soft and ready. Drain.

Meanwhile, in a large frying pan, heat 4 TBS of olive oil over medium heat. Add the diced onions and allow them to cook for about 3 minutes, stirring frequently. Stir in the garlic and cook for another 3 minutes. Add the zucchini, pepper, oregano, and thyme. Stir well and cover half way, letting mix cook for about 5 minutes. Stir in the mushrooms and cover again. Let mix cook for about 4 to 5 minutes. Stir in the tomatoes and let cook for another 4 minutes. Add the shredded carrot and about ¾ TBS of salt and mix well. Cook for about 3 to 4 minutes more, stir in the cilantro, and remove from heat.

Serve spaghetti with a healthy helping of veggies on top.

☻Makes 4 servings in about 45 minutes.

PESTO PASTA WITH MUSHROOMS

I'm not sure if I'm remembering correctly, but wasn't there a Greek or Roman god named Pesto?!

Ingredients:
8 ounces dry spaghetti noodles
8 cups water
1 TBS salt
3 TBS olive oil
8 ounces button mushrooms (sliced)
3 tomatoes (chopped)
2 cups pesto sauce (page 44)
Salt and pepper to taste

Directions:
In a large pot bring the water to a boil, together with 1 TBS of salt and 1 TBS of the oil. Once boiling, slowly stir in the noodles until they are completely covered in water and not making clumps. Reduce heat to medium and let the pasta cook until it is soft, but not overdone (*al dente*). Strain pasta and run cold water over it.

Meanwhile, in a frying pan over medium-high heat, add the other 2 TBS of oil. When ready, toss in the mushrooms, stirring often, and let cook, covered, for 5 minutes. Next, add the tomatoes, stir well, and cover. Remove lid and stir often for about 3 more minutes or until mushrooms are about done. Add the pesto sauce and mix everything together well. Lower heat and cook for another minute, stirring often. Add the noodles and mix in well with the pesto sauce, stirring constantly for a minute or two. Add a little more oil if the mix is too dry.

Add salt and pepper to taste and serve with toasted garlic bread or breaded eggplant (page 86, eggplant only).

☺Makes 4 servings in about 35 minutes.

PIPIÁN WITH CAULIFLOWER AND POTATOES

Pipián, or pepián, is a typical dish from southern Mexico and some parts of Central America or South America. It is usually served with a big chunk of meat. The sauce is similar to mole and equally versatile. This veggie recipe stands good on its own, but you could "beef" it up with tofu or store-bought milanesa de soya if you desire something more "meaty."

Ingredients:
(Pipián sauce)
4 tomatoes
2 green tomatoes (*miltomates* or *tomatillos*)
½ onion (chopped)
1 *guajillo* chili pepper (seeded)
1 *pasa* chili pepper (seeded)
2 cloves garlic
1 cinnamon stick
4 TBS sesame seeds
4 TBS hulled pumpkin seeds
1 tsp salt
½ tsp black pepper

(Veggies)
1 head cauliflower (*coliflor* - cut into 1 inch chunks)
2 potatoes (cut into large chunks)
1 cup green beans (*ejotes*)
1 carrot (grated)
1 cup cilantro (finely chopped)
4 cups brown rice (cooked, page 23)

Directions:
In a large frying pan over medium-high heat, toast the red and green tomatoes, whole, turning often, for 5 minutes. Add the chili peppers, cinnamon, sesame and pumpkins seeds and toast everything, stirring often, until golden brown.

Transfer the toasted ingredients from the frying pan to a blender and blend with about 1 cup of water. Blend until smooth. Pour the liquid from the blender back into the frying pan and bring to a boil over medium-high heat. Stir in the salt and black pepper.

Once the mixture is boiling, add the cauliflower, potatoes, and green beans. Stir well and bring back to a boil. Reduce heat and simmer, mostly covered for about 20 minutes. Add the carrot and cilantro and simmer, mostly covered, for another 10 minutes or until veggies are cooked. Serve over the rice.

⊕Makes 4-6 portions in about an hour.

OPTION: Use *chayote* in addition to, or in place of, the other vegetables.

MARINATED & GRILLED PORTOBELLO CAPS

Use these rich, tasty mushrooms in place of meat with a dinner dish or even in a sandwich or salad.

Ingredients:
4 medium-sized portobello mushrooms
1 cup red wine
1 TBS olive oil
2 TBS soy sauce
2 TBS balsamic vinegar
2 cloves garlic (chopped)
Salt and pepper to taste

Directions:
Mix the wine, oil, soy sauce, vinegar, and garlic together in a bowl. Rinse off the portobello caps in clean water and place each one in a separate zip-lock bag. Pour in enough marinade to coat the mushroom and seal the bag. Flip it over a few times to ensure that the marinade covers the whole mushroom. If no bags are available use a bowl or something that will allow the mushroom caps to soak, covered in the marinade. Let the caps soak in the refrigerator 8 hours or overnight, turning once or twice during that time.

When the caps are ready to be cooked, remove them from the marinade and drain any excess liquid. Prepare the grill, or frying pan if no grill is available. Lightly sprinkle the caps with salt and pepper and place them on the grill. Cook both sides over medium-high heat, without burning, for about 10 minutes per side. Serve whole or sliced.

⊕Makes 4 servings in 30 minutes, plus time to marinate.

OPTION: Try drizzling cooked portobellos with chipotle aioli (page 37) or chimichurri (page 36).

HIBISCUS FLOWER TACOS

Taquitos de Jamaica! *This is a delicious and different dish that I first tried in Oaxaca, Mexico. The flowers provide a fibrous, meaty texture with a unique taste that's perfectly balanced by the guacamole and tortillas. Colorful!*

Ingredients:
2 cups dried hibiscus flower (*flor de jamaica*)
¼ onion (diced)
2 cloves garlic (minced)
6 green tomatoes (*tomatillos* - diced)
1 serrano chili (seeded and diced)
½ tsp salt
¼ tsp black pepper
1 cinnamon stick
1 TBS vegetable broth (page 18)
2 to 3 cups high-heat cooking oil
Water
1 cup guacamole (page 39)
1 cup cashew sour cream (page 35)
1 cup spicy sesame salsa (page 47)
At least 12 fresh corn tortillas
½ head of lettuce (chopped into thin strips)

Directions:
Boil the hibiscus flower in 5 cups of water over medium heat for about 20 minutes. Strain the flowers over a bowl or pan, separating and saving the water (you can use the water to make hibiscus tea: page 121).

As the flowers are draining, heat 1 TBS of oil in a large frying pan over medium-high heat. Add the onion and stir well. Add the garlic, chili, and tomato and stir again. Stir frequently so the mix doesn't burn.

The tomatoes should begin to change color and soften up after about 5 or 6 minutes. Go ahead and add the flowers, salt, pepper, cinnamon stick, and broth. Sauté for another 6 to 7 minutes, stirring often, and then remove from heat.

Heat about half an inch of oil in a smaller frying pan over medium-high heat. Make sure the tortillas are warm and flexible so they don't break. Roll the flower mix into the corn tortillas, pinning them shut with toothpicks or wood splinters, if available. If not, no worries. Just put the open side down first so the hot oil can seal it.

Fry each taco for about 3 minutes per side or until golden brown. You can fry multiple tacos at a time. Remove the tacos from the oil and drain any excess liquid over a paper towel. When cool enough, remove the toothpicks.

Lay out a bed of lettuce on a plate and place a couple tacos on top. Dab some guacamole and drizzle some spicy sesame salsa on top of each taco. Ready to serve!

⊕Makes 12 tacos (6 servings) in about 1 hour, plus guacamole and salsa prep time.

OPTION: Serve with red or green salsa. Use spinach and arugula mix in place of lettuce. You can substitute a serrano pepper for the jalapeño.

VEGGIES AND TOFU WITH THAI PEANUT SAUCE

If you're like me, you can appreciate many types of food from all parts of the globe. Some of your favorites might be hard to find when you're on the road. Just in case you've been dreaming of some Thai style veggies... here you go.

Ingredients:
¼ small head red cabbage (sliced thinly)
¼ small head green cabbage (sliced thinly)
2 large carrots (cut into half moons)
1 small head broccoli (chopped into bite-size florets)
¼ cup water
2 cups Thai-Style Peanut Sauce (page 49)
2 TBS cooking oil
Tofu (cubed) *and/or* breaded eggplant (pages 26 and 86)
2 cups brown rice (cooked, page 23)

Directions:
If you haven't already cooked the rice, start now.

Prepare the vegetables.

Heat a frying pan over medium-high flame with the 2 TBS cooking oil. When ready add the tofu or eggplant. If tofu, stir often until the cubes begin to brown on all sides. If eggplant, cook each side for about 5 minutes.

Meanwhile, heat a separate frying pan also over medium-high flame. When ready, place the veggies in the pan, mix well, add the water, and cover. Let veggies cook in the steam, stirring occasionally, for about 3 minutes. Add the peanut sauce to the veggie mix, stir well, and cook for another 2 minutes. Remove from heat and leave covered. The veggies should be cooked, but slightly crispy.

Serve the veggies over the rice, topped with the tofu or eggplant.

⊕Makes 4 portions in 30 minutes.

VEGGIE STIR-FRY

Don't let the long list of ingredients fool you. Stir-fries and quick, easy, and tend to hit the spot.

Ingredients:
1 onion (sliced thinly)
1 small head broccoli (chopped)
1 cup green beans (cut in half)
3 medium-sized carrots (sliced lengthwise, about thumb-length)
1/4 head green cabbage (thinly sliced)
1 cup button mushrooms (sliced thinly)
1/2 cup mung bean sprouts
3 large cloves garlic (minced)
1 tsp ginger (minced)
3 TBS soy sauce
2 TBS cooking oil
1 tsp ground cumin
1/2 tsp salt
1/2 tsp black pepper
Dash of red pepper flakes (optional)
1/2 cup peanuts (roasted)
4 cups brown rice (cooked, page 23)

Directions:
Make sure all your ingredients are cut and prepped before you start cooking. There's not much time to cut-as-you-go with this one.

Heat the oil over high flame in a frying pan or wok, if available. Before the oil starts to smoke, toss in the onion and stir well, coating with the oil. Next, throw in the broccoli and green beans. Keep stirring. Don't let the veggies burn. Add the carrots and cabbage. Keep stirring. Add the salt, pepper, cumin, and soy sauce. Stir well. Add the mushrooms. Stir, stir, stir.

If you haven't already roasted your peanuts and you're good at multi-tasking you better get to that right away. Heat another frying pan, dump the peanuts in and keep stirring both the peanuts and the veggies. If you're not good at multi-tasking and you only have one pan or one burner, well, you should've roasted the peanuts beforehand.

Cook the veggies until they are tender, but still somewhat crispy. Add the sprouts, stir well, and remove pan from heat. Serve immediately with brown rice.

🕐Makes 4 portions in about 30 minutes.

OPTION: You can substitute lentil sprouts or any other sprouts if you can't get mung bean sprouts. The beauty of stir-fry plates is that they are so versatile. If you find snow peas or sugar snap peas, I recommend using them in place of the green beans. You may also want to try squash, chayote, deep-fried tofu, spinach, *chaya*, or eggplant. Any veggies might work. Not all veggies on the ingredients list may be easy to find at one time in the Central American markets. Use what you can get to.

Drinks

CHAMPURRADO

This is a hot, rich, delicious, chocolaty beverage that will fix you right up on a cold day. You may encounter it throughout your travels in cooler regions of southern Mexico.

Ingredients:
¼ cup corn tortilla flour (*masa harina*)
2 cups milk of choice (the thicker the better)
⅓ cup grated or chopped Mexican chocolate
⅓ cup grated or chopped *panela*
1 stick cinnamon
2 cups water

Directions:
In a large pot, warm about 2 cups of water and lower or turn off heat. Add the corn flour little by little whisking it in with the water. Add the milk, chocolate, *panela*, and cinnamon stick.

Bring to a boil and then reduce heat, simmering for 10 minutes, uncovered, until chocolate and sugar are completely melted and dissolved. Stir occasionally. Serve hot.

☺Makes 4 servings in about 20 minutes.

NOTE: These ingredients can be found at any Mexican market. *Panela* (aka *piloncillo*) is solidified cane sugar. Alternatively, you can use regular dark chocolate and brown sugar, but you may need to adjust the measurements as the taste will differ some. Another option would be to substitute cinnamon for about a ¼ tsp of ground star anise.

CHILATE

Basically just horchata with cacao, but you'll love the twist.

Ingredients:
1 cup white rice (uncooked)
1 cup raw cacao beans
1 large stick cinnamon
Water
4 TBS sugar
Ice

Directions:
Mix dry ingredients, except sugar, together in a bowl. Add mixture to a blender and grind into a rough powder. Transfer mixture back to bowl and mix in about 1 liter of water. Let mixture stand for 15 minutes.

Stir mixture and pour through a strainer into a pitcher. Add sugar (to taste) and ice. Serve cold.

☺Makes 4 servings (4 cups) in about 20 minutes.

CHIA FRESCA

This energetic drink is sold often in the markets, but it's also easy to prepare if you want make it yourself. For the recipe we'll use lime, but chia seeds added to any juice of choice will work the same way. Get creative.

Ingredients:
2 TBS chia seeds
Juice of 1 lime
Water

Directions:
Mix the chia seeds, lime juice, and water together in a glass. Stir well. Let sit 20 minutes for the chia seeds to absorb some water. Go ahead and drink!

The chia becomes very gelatinous. This is beneficial for your digestive system.

⊕Makes 1 glass in 1 minute (plus absorption time).

COLIBRÍ JUICE

Experimenting with fruit juices is a ton of fun in Central America. There are so many flavors to play with... like a box full of crayons. This is a mix we came up with at Osa Mariposa that has become one of my favorites. Colibrí = *Hummingbird.*

Ingredients:
Juice of 3 oranges (1 cup)
3 strawberries
½ banana
Ice

Directions:
Drop the banana and strawberries into a blender with the orange juice. Blend thoroughly and serve over ice. Heck, you can even blend the ice if you want a smoothie!

⊕Makes 1 glass (1¼ cups) in about 2 minutes.

HIBISCUS ICED TEA

Popular in Mexico, agua de jamaica *is a refreshing afternoon tea or to accompany a dinner with friends. The recipe makes a full pitcher. It is known in Central America as "rosa de jamaica."*

Ingredients:
1 cup dried hibiscus flowers (*flor de jamaica*)
8-10 cups drinking water
1 stick cinnamon
6 whole cloves
Sugar to taste

Directions:
Plan ahead by letting the dried hibiscus soak in about 2 cups of drinking water for 2 to 3 hours, until the water turns dark red. Afterwards, in a separate pot bring 6 cups of water to a boil with the cinnamon and cloves. (If you don't have time to let the flowers soak, you can boil them with the cinnamon and cloves.) Once boiling, lower heat and let simmer 5 minutes. Remove from heat, uncover, and let cool.

Strain both the hibiscus water and boiled water into a pitcher. If the pitcher is made of plastic, please be sure that the boiled water is quite cool. Add sugar to taste, usually about 6 tablespoons, and mix well. You may need to add another cup or two or water if the taste is too strong. Serve cold.

⊕Makes 2 liters in about 20 minutes (plus soak time).

OPTION: The cinnamon and cloves are optional. You may want to try adding ginger or lime as well.

HORCHATA

Horchata is a famous Mexican classic. It's basically flavored rice milk. Often, fruit and nuts are added to the drink. Delicioso!

Ingredients:
2 cups whole grain rice (uncooked)
3 cinnamon sticks
Sugar to taste (about 4 TBS)
1 tsp vanilla extract
Water
1 cup cantaloupe (cut into small cubes)
½ cup walnuts (broken into small chunks)

Directions:
Place the rice and about 2 cups of water in a blender and blend for about 30 seconds. Pour all the contents of the blender into a large bowl and add 4 more cups of water and the cinnamon sticks. Let the mixture stand for about an hour.

Remove 1 cinnamon stick (2 if they're very large) and pour the rest of the mix back into the blender. Blend again for another 30 seconds. This time pass the mixture through a strainer as you pour it back into the bowl or into a pitcher. Thoroughly stir in the sugar and vanilla. Add the melon and walnuts.

Serve horchata cold over ice. This keeps 3 to 4 days in the refrigerator.

☺Makes 1½ liters in 15 minutes, plus soak time.

OPTION: White rice will also work in this recipe.

HORCHATA DE JÍCARO

A Honduran version of horchata with jícaro seeds and toasted peanuts.

Ingredients:
2 cups white rice (uncooked)
1 cup dry *jícaro* seeds
½ cup skinned peanuts
1 stick cinnamon
Water
Sugar to taste
Juice of 1 lime
Ice

Directions:
Mix dry ingredients, except sugar, together in a large bowl.

Transfer the mixture to a heated skillet or frying pan and toast until lightly browned over medium-high heat, stirring constantly so it doesn't burn (about 10 minutes). Remove from heat and let cool 3 to 5 minutes.

Add toasted ingredients to a blender and grind them into a rough powder. Transfer the powder back to the bowl and add 6 cups of cold water. Stir well. Let the mixture stand for about 15 minutes.

Stir again and pour the mixture through a strainer into a pitcher. Add sugar and lime juice to taste. (I recommend 3 TBS sugar and ¾ of the lime juice)

Serve cold over ice.

⊕Makes 5 servings (5 cups) in about 40 minutes.

MORNING ENERGY JUICE

This is what I usually start my day with. It gives a good kick and helps activate the brain.

Ingredients:
Big handful of fresh, clean spinach
1 medium-sized carrot (chopped)
1 stalk celery (chopped)
1 *nopal* cactus pad (de-spined and chopped... only use half if it's big)
1 tsp fresh ginger (minced)
2 TBS fresh aloe vera gel (optional)
Juice of 4 oranges (about 1½ cups)

Directions:
Place all the ingredients together in a blender and pulse a few times. Once the mix is fairly well chopped up, go ahead and blend on high speed until the ingredients are liquefied.

It's important that all your ingredients are well washed. I like to start by stuffing the spinach in the bottom of the blender and then piling everything else in on top. The weight pushes down on the spinach and the juices help pull the chunkier ingredients down into the blades.

Depending on the juice output from the oranges you may need more or less to bring your drink to the desired consistency. If the oranges run out, you can substitute water or coconut water.

A normal kitchen blender won't "juice" the ingredients. There will still be plenty of tiny chunks, but these are beneficial to your digestive system as "roughage" to scrub down your insides and slow the passage of the liquid, allowing for a longer absorption period.

☺Makes 3 cups in about 5 minutes.

*OPTION: Try adding a big spoonful of spirulina powder, moringa powder, or chia seeds to boost the nutritive level. Maybe even add a few beet chunks.

*NOTE: The aloe vera gel is obtained from a fresh leaf. Leaves can be bought in the markets whole. Cut about a two-inch section from the leaf. Cut away the outer skin and dump the clear gel into the blender. The green skin is inedible, but the gooey side of the skin can be usefully rubbed on cuts, rashes, or sunburns before you throw it out.

PROTEIN POWER MILK SHAKE

This shake is delicious and filling. It's good to have before a long hike or bus ride. The recipe makes about 2 cups. Modify it at will.

Ingredients:
1 banana
1 disc slice pineapple (chopped)
1 disc slice papaya (chopped)
2 cups milk of choice
1 TBS chia seed
1 TBS ground flax seed
2 TBS shredded coconut (or coconut oil)
1 TBS honey or agave nectar
Handful raw cacao beans (about 8)
2 TBS peanut butter

Directions:
Load the blender up with the ingredients in more or less the order that they appear. Blend. Enjoy. Add ice cubes if you wish.

⊕Makes 2 servings (3½ cups) in about 10 minutes.

NOTE: Add a scoop of protein powder, if you have access to it, to boost the protein levels. Try isolated pea protein or hemp protein if you want something vegan.

PLANTAIN PORRIDGE / *ATOLE DE PLÁTANO*

This is actually a hot drink similar to a thick milkshake. It's sweet, filling, and hits the spot on a cold morning.

Ingredients:
2 ripe plantains
5 cups water
1 cup milk of choice
1/2 cup sugar
1 cinnamon stick
Pinch of salt
Pinch of black pepper

Directions:
Bring the water to a boil while you prepare the plantains. Wash the plantains thoroughly. Make a cut in the skin of each, one side only, from top to bottom. Next slice the plantains, with skin on, into disks about 1 1/2 inches thick.

Mix the sugar into the water until it is completely dissolved. Add the cinnamon stick and the plantain chunks and boil over medium-high heat for 10 minutes. Lower heat and remove plantains, leaving the water, and place them in a bowl. Use a fork to help remove the skins. Discard the skins and place the plantain chunks in a blender. Add the milk to the blender and blend until smooth. Return the mixture to the pot with the water. Add the salt and pepper and stir well. Turn up heat until the *atole* begins to boil and then lower heat some and let simmer, stirring often, for another 10 minutes.

Makes 4-6 servings in about 45 minutes.

NOTE: Ripe plantains are yellow with mostly blackening skin. The blacker the skin, the sweeter the fruit, but beware of mushy or moldy plantains. These are no good.

SWEET CORN PORRIDGE / *ATOLE DE ELOTE*

This is a typical hot drink made in Central America, especially in colder regions. It warms both the body and soul.

Ingredients:
4 ears corn
1/2 cup *panela* (chopped)
1 large cinnamon stick
Water

Directions:
Boil the ears of corn in about 5-6 cups of water for 30 minutes. Turn off heat and remove corn, saving water, and let cool. When good and dry, slice the off the corn kernels and place them in a blender with 1 cup of the boiled water. Blend until smooth. Leave the rest of the water in the pot.

Reignite the stove and bring the water back to a boil. Break or chop the *panela* into small pieces and dissolve them into the boiling water. Toss in the cinnamon stick. Add the blended corn and stir well. Once the *atole* returns to a boil, lower heat and let simmer, stirring often, for 10 minutes. Serve hot.

Makes 4 servings in 45 minutes.

NOTE: These ingredients can be found at any Mexican market. *Panela* (aka *piloncillo*) is solidified cane sugar. Alternatively, you can use regular brown sugar, but you may need to adjust the measurement as the taste will differ some.

REJUVELAC

Rejuvelac is a high protein, fermented liquid believed to aid in digestion and energy production. It can be added to your veggie juices or taken on its own if you enjoy the pungent taste. Rejuvelac is made from grains, typically wheat, rye, oats, barley, or quinoa. For this recipe we will use wheat berries to make 1 gallon of liquid.

Ingredients:
¾ cup wheat berries
Water

Directions:
Thoroughly rinse grains. In a pot or jar cover grains with sufficient water and let them soak for 8 to 12 hours. They should expand in size.

Pour the grains out into a strainer, discarding the water. Rinse them well and allow excess water to drain. Allow the grains to dry out for about 20 minutes and then return them to the jar.

Leave the grains in the jar for about 24 to 36 hours away from direct sunlight. They should begin to sprout during this time. Rinse and drain the grains 2 or 3 times during the sprouting process. Either leave the grains in the jar as you rinse and drain them or transfer them to the strainer. Make sure no standing water remains in the jar when you finish or the sprouts may spoil.

Once sprouted (24 to 36 hours), add 1 cup of the sprouted grain to a blender with 2 cups of drinking water and blend for a few seconds. Pour the contents into a one-gallon container. Add enough drinking water to fill the container. Cover the mouth of the container with a paper towel or screen to keep bugs and dust out. Let the liquid stand at room temperature at least 24 hours. It should begin to ferment. Longer fermentation makes stronger rejuvelac. Too much time will spoil it.

Strain the liquid into another container or jar. It should have a fermented aroma and taste slightly sour. If it tastes too bland or spoiled, something went wrong.

Add rejuvelac to your juices or smoothies. It can be stored up to four days in a refrigerator. Cover it loosely with a cloth or paper towel, but don't put a tight lid on it.

NOTE: Since rejuvelac needs some warmth to ferment, it's best made in hot or controlled climates. The fermentation process won't work in the cold. However, direct sun should also be avoided.

TAMARIND ICED TEA

Fresh tamarind pulp is sold in most markets. It looks like dark brown chocolate chunks in a plastic bag. The pulp can be used to make delicious and refreshing iced tea called agua de tamarindo. *You may also find the whole seed pods (coffee-colored), which you would then need to crack open and take the pulp out yourself.*

Ingredients:
A small handful (about ½ cup) tamarind pulp
Water
3 TBS sugar (optional)

Directions:
Place the tamarind pulp, seeds and all, into a jar or container and cover with a cup or two of purified water. Let the water and pulp sit 6-8 hours or overnight.

With your clean hands, mash up the tamarind pulp in the water, separating the pulp from the seeds, until it is almost completely liquefied. Pour all the liquid through a strainer, saving the water in a jar or pot. Little by little, mix water in with the tamarind concentrate, checking the taste until you arrive at a consistency and flavor that you enjoy. Mix in sugar to your liking. Chill and serve cold, always stirring first.

⊕Makes about 1 liter in about 10 minutes (plus soak time).

NOTE: Any extra tamarind concentrate can be refrigerated or frozen for later.

TEPACHE

Tepache is a fermented Mexican drink made from the pineapple rind. It's delicious, refreshing, and sweet with a kick! Like kombucha? Try tepache!

Ingredients:
1 large pineapple
1 kilo *panela*
1 stick cinnamon
3 whole cloves
8 cups drinking water

Directions:
You will need a bottle or small-mouthed jar for this one - something that can hold about a gallon of liquid (think something like a milk jug). Next, you're probably wondering what *piloncillo* is. *Piloncillo*, or *panela*, is unrefined cane sugar. It's the juice from crushed sugar cane, boiled down, poured into molds, and sold as solid blocks. You will need a kilo, so check the weight of the blocks you find.

Before slicing the pineapple you can prepare the water. In a pot or bowl, heat up about a gallon of water (around 3¾ liters). It doesn't need to boil. Break up and dissolve the *piloncillo* into the water, stirring well. Let the water cool.

Wash the pineapple thoroughly. You will include the rind. Remove the stalk and slice the pineapple first into discs and then chop up the discs. Stuff all the pineapple chunks into the jar. Add the cinnamon stick and the cloves. Pour in the sweetened water.

The water should at least cover the pineapple, if not more. Close off the opening of the jar with a folded paper towel or napkin and secure it with a rubber band. Do not put a lid on the jar. Leave the jar in a warm place out of direct sunlight and let sit, undisturbed, for 2 days. The liquid will begin to ferment. You should see bubbles forming in the bottle during that time.

On the 3rd day, transfer the liquid to another container and discard the pineapple. Cover the container again with a paper towel and let it sit for another 24-36 hours.

The *tepache* should now be ready to drink. Serve it nice and cold, over ice.

*NOTE: Since *tepache* needs some warmth to ferment, it's best made in hot or controlled climates. The fermentation process won't work in the cold. However, direct sun should also be avoided. *Panela* (*aka piloncillo*) is solidified cane sugar. Alternatively, you can use regular brown sugar, but you may need to adjust the measurements as the taste will differ some.

Desserts

STUFFED PLANTAIN BALLS

Plátano Relleno is a dish I first ate in Guatemala. I've since seen it in a couple other places, but because I learned how to make it there I'd like to give them the credit. These are sweet and delicious fried plantain balls with black beans in the center.

Ingredients:
2 ripe plantains
3 cups water
1 stick cinnamon
3 TBS sugar
3 TBS breadcrumbs
1 cup cooked black beans (page 25)
½ cup vegetable oil

Directions:
Bring the water to a boil with the sugar and cinnamon. Peel and cut the plantains into chunks and toss them into the water. Return to a boil and then lower heat and cook for about 5 minutes. Remove plantains from water and let drain in a colander.

Put the black beans in a blender with a little water. You'll want to purée them, but not turn them into a soup. The consistency should be pasty but not too dry, like wet refried beans. Add water little by little until you get there.

Now that the plantains have cooled down, mash them together adding the breadcrumbs. When you arrive at a smooth enough consistency with minimum lumps, roll the mash out into golf ball-sized pieces. Now it gets tricky. The balls will need to be flattened out and topped with beans. This can be done in your hand or on the counter or on a cookie sheet. It can get sticky! Try to flatten the balls out uniformly, about palm-sized or more. Place a heaping tablespoon of beans in the center of the plantain "pancake." Then slowly and skillfully re-roll the mash, making a bean-stuffed ball (similar to making a samosa or dumpling). Repeat until you run out of mash and beans.

Heat the oil in a small frying pan or pot over medium-high heat. Meanwhile, if you have any leftover breadcrumbs you can roll the balls in it. This step is not necessary, but could help to keep the balls from breaking apart in the oil or from sticking to themselves if you plan to store them.

Check the oil by tossing in a small chunk of mash. If it bubbles instantly, it's ready. Place two or three balls, or however many will fit comfortably, into the oil. If they are not completely submerged by the oil, they will need to be turned every couple minutes so that they cook evenly on all sides. When the balls turn a light, golden brown color they are done. Remove them from the pan and drain the excess oil in a paper towel, napkin, or colander.

⊕Makes about 6 stuffed plantain balls in about 45 minutes.

FRIED PLANTAIN WITH SWEET CREAM

Fried plantains are pretty common in Mexico and Central America. They are often served with a sweet cream made from condensed milk. This recipe uses a vegan sweet cream.

Ingredients:
2 large, over-ripe plantains
½ cup sweet cream (page 48)
Canola or high heat cooking oil

Directions:
Measure about ½ an inch of oil into a large frying pan an heat over high flame. Peel the plantains and cut them lengthwise into slices about ¼ inch thick. Test the oil by throwing in a fingernail-sized chunk of plantain. If it bubbles immediately, it's hot enough. Carefully lay the plantain slices, side by side, in the frying pan. If they don't all fit, save some for the next round. Let the plantains fry until they are dark brown on the underside. Flip them over with a spatula or fork and repeat the process on the other side.

When both sides are thoroughly cooked, remove the plantains and lay them on a clean cloth or paper towel to soak up any excess oil. Place the plantains on a plate, drizzle the sweet cream over the top, and serve hot!

⊕Makes 4 portions in about 15 minutes.

NOTE: Ripe plantains are yellow with mostly blackening skin. The blacker the skin, the sweeter the fruit, but beware of mushy or moldy plantains. These are no good.

CHIA CHOCOLATE PUDDING

This rich, tasty pudding makes a great vegan dessert for any party. It's quick and easy to make.

Ingredients:
2 cups soymilk
5 TBS ground chia seed
½ cup sugar
⅓ cup ground dark chocolate
¼ TBS chili powder
½ tsp ground cinnamon
5 TBS crushed cacao beans
1 tsp vanilla extract

Directions:
In a small pot whisk the ground chia into the soymilk until it's completely dissolved. Mix in the sugar and chocolate. Place the pot over medium heat and whisk constantly until the mixture thickens, about 7 to 10 minutes. When the mixture begins to bubble, turn off the heat and mix in the cacao chunks and vanilla extract.

Pour or spoon the pudding into small bowls or shallow glasses and chill in the fridge for at least one or two hours before serving. The pudding should thicken considerably in that time.

☺Makes 4 servings in about 20 minutes, plus chill time.

NOTE: If you can't find ground chia in the markets you can grind your own in a blender. The chia takes the place of cornstarch to thicken the pudding. The crushed cacao seeds can also be achieved in a blender. Place the whole seeds in and pulse until they're broken down into small bite-sized chunks.

SWEET STEAMED SQUASH

I first ate this at a border crossing in between El Salvador and Guatemala and couldn't wait to try it at home. Try using a round winter squash like acorn or pumpkin. If you're in the Central American region and craving something sweet, ask for dulce de ayote.

Ingredients:
1 medium-sized winter squash (any kind)
⅛ kilo *panela or* 5 TBS brown sugar
1 large cinnamon stick
3 cups water

Directions:
Wash the squash thoroughly. Some types of squash are very difficult to cut into. It may be easier to smash it on the concrete or crush it with a big rock or hammer. Once the squash is open you can continue to break it into pieces by hand or with a knife. Go for about 2-inch chunks. Separate the seeds from the squash.

In a large frying pan or wide-bottomed skillet bring 3 cups of water to a boil. As the water is heating, chop the *panela* into pieces and add it to the water. Stir the *panela* (or sugar), helping it to dissolve. Add the cinnamon stick. When the water is boiling, add the squash chunks, skin side down. Lower the flame to medium heat.

After about 30 minutes, flip the squash pieces to skin side up. Check the water. The idea is to boil all the water out of the pan without burning the squash. When the water is gone, the squash should be ready. You should be able to cook it, skin side up, for another 15-20 minutes. After that check the squash for tenderness. If it's cooked all the way through, eat it! If not, add a little water and keep cooking. The squash should be quite soft on the verge of mushy. The skin is edible and highly nutritious.

When ready, remove the cinnamon stick and serve! Enjoy!

☺Makes 4-6 servings in about 1 hour.

*OPTIONS: You can leave the seeds in and cook them together with the squash. They are edible and nutritious. You may also want to add sweet potatoes to the mix. However, they cook more quickly so add them after the first 20 or 30 minutes.

*NOTE: These ingredients can be found at any Mexican market. *Panela* (aka *piloncillo*) is solidified cane sugar. Alternatively, you can use regular brown sugar, but you may need to adjust the measurements as the taste will differ some.

Curious Fruit
Introduction to the Nutritional Information Guide

Isn't it amazing to behold all the colors, shapes, and sizes of the many different fruits and vegetables, roots and flowers that abound on this planet? I love food. I love plants. I find it extremely interesting and enjoyable to search for new types of plant-based food in the places that I visit. Some edibles are so strange and unique, often found only within minute sectors of the globe. Dragonfruit, durion, ice cream beans. Even foods we find at home still astonish me, more so when I learn about the nutritive components they possess. Blackberries, raspberries, rainbow chard -- nature has provided us with a kaleidoscope of delectable options when it comes to edible vegetables.

The fun part for me, aside from actually eating them, is learning about them. I met some college girls once in Zacatecas, Mexico, who invited me out to the *discoteca* one night. We danced and laughed and had a good time... well into the wee hours of the morning. This was during my first month in Mexico and I could barely fumble my way through a handful of Spanish phrases. Butchered, really, would better describe how I handled the language. We communicated through gestures and body language more than anything else. Somehow, though, as the night wore on we found ourselves discussing religion and politics. But that's another story for a different day.

The following afternoon we sat lazily on the couch, recovering from the late night, when one of these young women asked me if I would like some "tuna." I reminded her that I was vegetarian and I didn't eat seafood. She laughed and repeated, a little slower this time: "No, silly... do you want some tuuuunaa?" Yes, I did understand her, but no, I didn't want some tuuuuunaa. I repeated that I was vegetarian. She didn't remember? "I don't eat fish, girl." More laughter. "No, not fish, you fool. Tuna! Do you want some or not?" Woman, we're having a serious communication breakdown here. (You have to imagine how this conversation was taking place: about ninety percent improvisational sign language and ten percent Spanish)

"No, no fish, thanks."

"What? What fish!? Tuna! You know, tuna?"

"No, I don't know."

Finally the girl gets fed up. Wait, gringo. Wait here. She goes to the kitchen and returns immediately with a small green grenade looking thing. "Tuna! It's a fruit. It comes from the cactus. Now do you want one or not?"

Needless to say, I had never eaten "tuna" before. She showed me how to peel it and spit out the seeds. A delicious fruit. I was glad it eventually occurred to her to go get one from the kitchen. The watery melon-like taste won me over instantly. I was a fan. If I were to have encountered this divine fruit in the United States, it would've been called a "prickly pear." Who knew?

So get ready. You're going to find plenty of unidentified edible objects in the markets. Of course, you will probably recognize the majority of the fresh food, but not all of it - and if you don't speak Spanish, you could find a massive headache quickly developing inside your skull.

"*Disculpa amigo*, did you say you want a half kilo of *tuna* or *atún*?" What?!

Meet the Ingredients
Nutritional Information Guide

This section of the book is intended to help you locate and recognize many of the ingredients used in the recipes. Throughout Mexico and Central America, most of these can be found in the local markets. Each entry includes the Spanish and sometimes regional names of the foods, where in the market to find them, what nutritive properties they possess, and how to prepare them. Using this guide should provide you with enough information to maintain a well-balanced and completely nutritious plant-based diet while traveling.

Some of the foods listed here are not used in the recipes, but I recommend trying them if and when you come across them. Many of these are fruits, since Central America is home to myriad exotic fruits of exquisite taste packed full of essential nutrients and vitamins. Of course, if you've never seen them before, you may not know what you're looking at, much less how to eat it. When in doubt, check for photos on the internet.

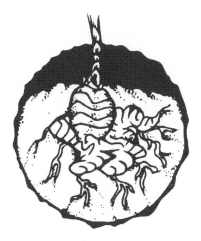

Roots/Underground

BEETS / *BETABEL* (*Mexico*) REMOLACHA (*Central America*)

HIGH IN: Fiber, Folates, Manganese, Phosphorus, Vitamin C, and Antioxidants.

ALSO CONTAIN: Magnesium, Copper, Iron, Sodium, Potassium, and Protein.

Beetroots are very high in glycine betaine, a phytochemical compound that can help in lowering homocysteine levels in the blood. Homocysteine is a highly toxic metabolite (produced by metabolism) that can cause clotting of blood platelets and lead to blood vessel damaging atherosclerotic-plaque formations. Beets could lower the risk of heart disease.

Beets are high in **fiber** as well as betacyanin, the pigment that gives them their rich purple-crimson color. The pigment is believed to be a strong cancer-fighting agent. Between the fiber, betacyanin, and **antioxidants** beets are found to be very effective in preventing colon cancer.
A good amount of the daily-recommended intake of folates can be found in beets. Folates are essential in the synthesis of DNA and can reduce the risk of birth defects. Beets and beet juice both help to remove toxins, clean the bloodstream, produce energy, cleanse the colon, and stimulate the liver.

Beet tops actually contain a larger amount of **nutrients** than the roots. The stems and leaves are richer in iron, calcium, and **vitamins** A and C.

HOW TO EAT BEETS: Betabel or *remolacha* can be found in the vegetable stands of just about every market. Try and find bunches with the leaves still intact. Beets can be eaten raw or cooked, but in raw form they retain more nutrients.

A big chunk of raw beet can be tough to chew and leaves strong slightly unpleasant aftertaste. Try shredding it into a salad with other veggies or into a sandwich. If you prefer it cooked, try steaming or baking instead of boiling.

Beet juice is easy to make. Blend up beet chunks in a *licuadora* with some purified water. If the flavor is too strong on its own, mix it with carrots or apples. "*Vampiro*" is a popular mixed-vegetable juice that contains beets, typically sold at the juice stands in the markets.

CARROT / *ZANAHORIA*

HIGH IN: Vitamins A and K, Fiber, and Potassium.

ALSO CONTAINS: Vitamin B6, C and E, Niacin, Folates, Manganese, Calcium, Sodium, and Copper.

Carrots are famous for supporting eyesight. They are very rich in beta-carotene, a powerful **antioxidant** that the body converts to **vitamin** A. Vitamin A can help slow down the degeneration of optical nerves and, along with vitamin E, can aid in maintaining healthy skin, muscles and hair.

Potash succinate, a **nutrient** found in carrots, may have antihypertensive qualities meaning that it can be useful in lowering high blood pressure. Carrots are high in antioxidants, especially *falcarinol*, which can fight cancer by destroying the pre-cancerous cells in tumors. Carrots are believed to reduce the risk of a wide range of cancers including lung, mouth, throat, stomach, intestine, bladder, prostate, and breast.

Traditional Chinese medicine states that the antioxidants in carrots are better absorbed if the root has been slightly cooked. Some research shows that boiling or steaming carrots whole before slicing allows the carrot to release a much higher quantity of beta-carotene. Unfortunately, the vitamin C can be destroyed by the heat.

Carrots have been eaten for centuries and are believed to be beneficial to the spleen and stomach, provide energy, relieve stress, treat both diarrhea and constipation, trigger the production of white blood cells, clear out unwanted mucus and phlegm, counter the negative effects of smoking, remove tapeworms, and boost sex drive. Daily consumption of carrot juice is said to rid the body of infections and keep the skin fresh, hydrated, and healthy.

HOW TO EAT CARROTS: Zanahoria are sold at any vegetable stand in the markets. The green tops are edible and quite nutritious. They can be boiled, sautéed, or blended into a juice. The same goes for the carrots. Toss them in a salad, a sandwich, a juice, or just eat them raw like a rabbit would. Try them in a soup or shredded over a veggie and rice dish.

CASSAVA / YUCA

HIGH IN: Vitamin C, Manganese, Potassium, Fiber, and Folates.

ALSO CONTAINS: Thiamin, Magnesium, Copper, Vitamin B6, Niacin, Riboflavin, and Phosphorus.

First, let's make the distinction between yuca and yucca. The yuca we are talking about here, also known as cassava, is an edible root vegetable. Yucca, on the other hand, is an ornamental plant grown in warm climates. Cassava, or yuca, is a low-cost staple starch vegetable for at least a quarter of the world's population. It is rich in carbohydrates, **nutrients**, and **fiber** making it a valuable source of food energy.

Yuca root contains high levels of a phyto-compound called *saponins*, which act as natural steroids and can help reduce inflammation of the joints. *Saponins* are also responsible for regulating the balance of intestinal flora by stimulating friendly flora and inhibiting the growth of others. These phyto-compounds also improve the absorption of **vitamins** and **minerals** as well as block and flush out toxins.

The high level of manganese in yuca also aids in the process of joint repair. Yuca is said to be able to break up mineral and inorganic deposits, preventing the calcification leading to kidney stones, gallbladder stones or the calcification of joints. It can also help in conditions like an inflamed prostate.

HOW TO EAT CASSAVA: Yuca can be found at most markets in the vegetable sections. Sometimes you'll need to ask, as certain *yuca* growers come to the market to sell strictly *yuca* and they may be by themselves in the entrance ways or between stalls.

Yuca contains some anti-nutrients and natural toxins that are destroyed through cooking. The root should be boiled for 15 to 20 minutes before consumption.

NOTE: Some similar roots you may want to try are: *ICHINTAL*, in Central America. This is the root of the *Chayote*, or *Güisquil*, plant. *QUEQUISQUE*, most commonly found in Nicaragua. *ÑAME*, found further south in Coasta Rica and Panama. All three look almost identical, taste much like *yuca*, and can be prepared the same way.

GARLIC / *AJO*

HIGH IN: Manganese, Vitamins B6 and C, Selenium, Calcium, Phosphorus, and Copper.

ALSO CONTAINS: Protein, Thiamin, Fiber, Iron, Potassium, Zinc, Riboflavin, and Magnesium.

Garlic has a long history of culinary and medical use. Its strong taste, scent, and nutritional potency have made it a staple of some sort in almost every culture. Garlic has a very high **vitamin B6** content protecting blood vessels and cells from inflammation and oxidative stress. It is also rich in vitamin C, aiding to the general wellbeing of the immune system and maintenance of the body.

Garlic contains organic *thiosulfinites*, which, when activated by crushing or cutting, can form *allicin*. *Allicin* reduces cholesterol formation, decreases blood vessel stiffness, blocks platelet clot formation, and reduces the overall risk of coronary heart disease and stroke. It is also found to have anti-bacterial, anti-viral, and anti-fungal activities. Thus, *allicin* can help prevent and fight off occurrences like the common cold.

Garlic cloves are used as a remedy for infections, chest problems, digestive disorders, and fungal infections such as thrush. A few cloves of mashed garlic in water can be used as disinfectant because of its antibacterial properties. It has been used to treat certain symptoms in AIDS patients.

Among many other uses, garlic can help treat acne when applied topically to the affected area. It works as a mosquito or insect repellent when placed in the vicinity or applied to the skin. It can be helpful to rid animals of ticks, fleas, and other parasites. Garlic can be used as a garden pesticide when a few cloves or extracts are mixed in water with pepper and a bit of soap. A concoction of garlic juices in water with vodka and rosemary can be used as a scalp and hair lotion. Garlic combined with lemon extracts, water, and apple cider vinegar can be applied as a face cleanser. It can treat a cough or sore throat and is even considered to be an aphrodisiac. Last but not least, the juice from crushed garlic cloves can be used as glue. In China, cut cloves have been used to mend broken glass or porcelain.

The health benefits are best utilized when garlic is taken raw. It can be very effective as a healing agent and general antibiotic as, curiously, it doesn't destroy the healthy bacteria in the body. Some say that it's best to let crushed garlic sit about ten minutes before consuming for all the germ-killing properties to become fully activated. If you are taking garlic to treat an illness, it is best not to stop as soon as the illness subsides, but to continue for about a week or so afterwards.

HOW TO EAT GARLIC: Ajo can be found all over the markets. It is sometimes sold in groups with a few heads (*cabezas*) braided together. These are typically the small clove variety. Others are sold as solitary heads or even by the single clove (*diente*).

When cooking, if it's not so important to get the garlic flavor into the oil, wait until the last 2 or 3 minutes of cooking before adding the garlic as to avoid destroying many of its beneficial properties.

GINGER / *JENGIBRE*

HIGH IN: Vitamin B6, Magnesium, and Manganese.

ALSO CONTAINS: Potassium, Iron, Vitamin C, Phosphorus, and Niacin.

Ginger root contains anti-viral, anti-toxic, and anti-fungal properties. It acts as an antihistamine and can help in the treatment of allergies. It also has anti-inflammatory properties and can aid in the treatment of rheumatoid arthritis, osteoarthritis, and various other muscular disorders.

Ginger contains special enzymes responsible for catalyzing the **proteins** in your food, thus aiding in digestion and the prevention of cramps. The ancient Greeks were accustomed to eating ginger or drinking ginger tea after large meals to ease the digestive process. Ginger is widely used to calm an upset stomach or relieve intestinal bloating and gas. It is also good to treat the feelings of nausea, particularly seasickness, morning sickness, and motion sickness.

Due to its promotion of mucus secretion, ginger protects against the development of ulcers and can quiet a cough or sooth a sore throat. It contains many health benefiting essential oils, like gingerols, which improve digestion and have anti-bacterial action that keeps the intestines clean. Ginger can also be used to treat diarrhea, lower cholesterol levels, and prevent blood clots.

HOW TO EAT GINGER: Jengibre can usually be found in the vegetable sections of the markets. If you don't see it, ask. The roots are of an earthy yellow color and sometimes grow like small, deformed hands or twisted little trees. You can buy the size you want. Ask to break off a smaller piece if you don't see what you're looking for.

The ginger peel is edible. Some don't like the taste and it can add a bitterness when used in cooking. If you choose to peel it, the easiest way is just to scrape it with the side of a spoon.

RADISH / *RÁBANO*

HIGH IN: Vitamin C, Potassium, Folates, and Fiber

ALSO CONTAINS: Vitamins B6 and K, Manganese, Calcium, Copper, and Riboflavin.

Crispy little radishes likely have roots in China or the Mediterranean. The word radish actually comes from the Latin *radix*, precisely meaning "root." They are mentioned in ancient Chinese, Greek, and Egytian texts. Europeans brought them to the Americas and they are cultivated, now, all over the world. Crunchy and peppery, radishes, root veggies of the Brassica family, are cousins to cabbage. They can be found in a variety of shapes, sizes, and colors.

Although most people in the United States might recognize radishes as small, round, bright red vegetables with crisp white interiors, radishes can actually be pink, grey, green, yellow, white, purple, and even black. They can be round or long and tubular. The roots, greens, flowers and seeds can be eaten raw, cooked, or pickled. Daikon is a long, white winter radish common in many Asian countries.

Radishes have been used traditionally to treat kidney stones, bad skin, and intestinal worms. They contain powerful detoxifying agents such as the antioxidant flavonoids zeaxanthin, lutein, and beta carotene, able to reduce biliruben levels in the body, therefore protecting it against jaundice. One serving of radishes provides about a quarter of the daily recommended intake of vitamin C, backed by a healthy chunk of insoluble fiber, responsible for scrubbing and regulating the body's digestive and excretory systems. Radishes have antibacterial and antifungal properties that help supply chemical compounds to dry skin, helping to hydrate, treat skin disorders, and sooth rashes. They regulate blood pressure, relieve congestion, and prevent respiration problems like asthma or bronchitis.

Radishes have been used in the treatment and prevention of colon, kidney, prostate, ovarian, oral, stomach, and intestinal cancers. They contain isothiocyanates, compounds that protect the body and blood by causing apoptosis, or progammed cell death, in cancerous cells leaving them unable to regenerate.

Insect bites, bee stings, or mild swelling can be treated with a topical application of radish juice. The root also helps to clean the kidneys, sooth sore throats, prevent illness, relieve constipation, and maintain healthy body weight.

HOW TO EAT RADISHES: Red *rábano* are often sold in bunches in the fruit and vegetable sections of the markets. Other types of radish may be available, including *nabo* and other types of turnips.

SWEET POTATO / *CAMOTE*

HIGH IN: Vitamins A, B6 and C, Manganese, Fiber, and Potassium.

ALSO CONTAINS: Vitamin B5, Copper, Magnesium, Niacin, Thiamin, Riboflavin, Phosphorus, Protein, and Calcium.

Sweet potatoes would mostly likely turn up on any list of the top ten foods highest in **vitamin** A. Some studies show that the tubers offer four to six times the daily-recommended intake of this essential vitamin. Sweet potatoes owe much of their bright orange color to beta-carotene, which the body easily converts to vitamin A. An abundance of this vitamin provides support to eyesight and helps decrease wrinkles in the skin, protect against the effects of aging, and cure skin conditions like acne, sun damage, cold sores, and psoriasis.

Vitamins A and C are both powerful **antioxidants**. They help to flush out potential disease starters and fortify the immune system and body tissues. One sweet potato contains well over half of your vitamin C needs. These vitamins have a strong anti-inflammatory effect on the body that can help provide relief to people suffering from asthma by decreasing congestion in the nasal passage, lungs, and bronchi. They can alleviate joint pain and symptoms of rheumatoid arthritis. The water from boiled potatoes can be applied topically to ease joint pain.

Sweet potatoes are a great source of potassium, a **nutrient** essential to maintaining the fluid and electrolyte balance in the body's cells, normalizing blood pressure, and lowering the risk of heart attack and stroke. Potassium deficiency can lead to muscle cramps and greater vulnerability to injury. People who exercise a lot or lead a high-stress life should make sure to include plenty of potassium in their diet.

The leaves of the potatoes are edible and extremely nutritious. The skins of the potato should be consumed as well as they are rich in vitamins and **fiber**. Yellow or orange skins provide more beta-carotene and purple skins are loaded with *anthocyanins*, powerful antioxidants.

HOW TO EAT SWEET POTATOES: Camotes are found in the vegetable sections of the markets. They are about the size of a fist or two, orange or purple, wrinkly, and pointy at the ends. The skins can be peeled or left on. The potato can be cut into chunks and boiled, left whole and baked, or steamed as a whole or in pieces. Cooked sweet potato can be mashed and many people enjoy making sweet potato fries.

TURNIP / *NABO*

HIGH IN: Vitamin C.

ALSO CONTAINS: Fiber, Manganese, Potassium, Vitamin B6, Copper, and Folate.

Turnips are not unbelievably nutritious vegetables, but they are common in the markets and add a little bite to your salads. A cup of them would contain almost half of the daily-recommended intake of **vitamin C**, however. Vitamin C is water-soluble and it is important to maintain sufficient stores in the body, especially if you are in a hot climate and sweating more than normal. Vitamin C is lost when your body loses water. Iron absorption is increased by the presence of vitamin C, which is important because iron is another water-soluble victim lost to sweat and urine.

Turnips come from the same family as radishes (*rábanos*). Both have a slightly acidic peppery taste. Turnips are traditionally eaten cooked while radishes are not, but either can be eaten in the raw or cooked state.

Turnip greens are edible and provide a great source of **vitamin K** and **antioxidants**. They are actually more nutritious than the root.

HOW TO EAT TURNIPS: Nabos come in various shapes and sizes. Some look like large white carrots and others are round and purple-ish, like an onion. The larger they are, the more bitter the taste, so if you intend to eat the *nabo* raw, go for the smaller size. They can be used in salads or cooked, seasoned and served on their own. The peppery taste adds a kick to sandwiches or even in stir-fry plates. *Nabo* and *rábano* are more or less interchangeable. Larger turnips can be steamed to make them more palatable.

YAM BEAN / *JÍCAMA*

HIGH IN: Vitamin C and Fiber.

ALSO CONTAINS: Potassium, Manganese, Iron, Magnesium, Copper, and vitamin B6.

The yam bean's greatest qualities are its **vitamin** C and **fiber** content and its crisp, refreshing taste on a hot day. There's not much else to it. Of course it does contain small amount of other vital minerals and slipping a few more of those into your diet definitely won't do you any harm.

Yam bean, probably better known as *jícama*, is very common in Mexico. It is sold on street corners and beaches, pre-cut, and served with chili powder, lime, and salt, if you wish. It has a high water content, so is helpful in keeping the body hydrated. One yam bean can provide you with about forty percent of your vitamin C needs and about a quarter that of fiber for one day. Yam bean contains *oligofructose inulin*, a zero-calorie, sweet, inert carbohydrate that does not metabolize in the human body, making the root an ideal snack for diabetics and dieters.

Yam bean is also known to help strengthen and support the structure of capillaries, thereby reducing the risk of capillary damage or fragility. It contains elements that help lower *homocysteine* levels in the body, reducing the risk of heart disease and high blood pressure.

HOW TO EAT YAM BEAN: Jícama can be found in the vegetable sections of the markets. It is a spherical off-white root about the shape of a beet. It can be peeled, sliced, and eaten raw. It adds a tasty crunch to salads.

Fruits

AVOCADO / *AGUACATE*

HIGH IN: Fiber, Vitamins C and K, Folate, and Potassium.

ALSO CONTAINS: Vitamins B5 and B6, Omega 6, Copper, Niacin, Riboflavin, Magnesium, Manganese, Phosphorus, Zinc, Iron, and Thiamin.

Avocados are packed full of **nutrients** that people sometimes forget are important, like **essential fatty acids.** The human brain is about 60% fat. Many of the vitamins the body needs to function properly are fat soluble, meaning that a little fat in the diet is necessary for them to be absorbed. Fat helps build cell walls and form hormones. Most naturally occurring, plant-based fats are good for you and help ward off diseases. Diets deficient in essential fats can lead to severe mental and physical illness. Avocados contain monounsaturated fats, which help boost metabolism and reduce cravings. In moderation they are not known to cause excess weight gain. So don't fear the fat!

Avocados are rich in **antioxidants, fiber, vitamins,** and minerals. Avocado flesh has the ability to nourish the skin with essential vitamins to make it glow. Its oil contains strong anti-inflammatory and antibacterial properties that help in the quick healing of wounds and cuts. It also prevents some skin conditions, scarring, and acne breakouts.

The *tannins,* anti-inflammatory and antioxidant agents found in the fruit, can help to calm and sooth intestinal walls and reduce ulcers. They are also able to eliminate the decomposition in the intestines that can cause bad breath. Avocados are a good source of potassium, which helps regulate blood pressure levels and help prevent the risk of kidney stones by reducing calcium excretion in the urine.

HOW TO EAT AN AVOCADO: Aguacates are sold in the fruit and vegetable areas of the markets. They are pear shaped and dark green, almost black when ripe. A good avocado should give a little when you squeeze it. If it's too hard, it not ready to eat.

Aguacates are good on just about anything. Sandwiches, tacos, pasta, rice, etc. They are even good in smoothies and add a rich, creamy texture. In Mexico a milkshake made with avocado is common. Of course, they are the key ingredient in guacamole (page 39).

BANANA / *PLÁTANO* (Mexico) *BANANO* (Central America)

HIGH IN: Vitamins B6 and C, Fiber, Manganese, and Potassium.

ALSO CONTAINS: Magnesium, Folates, Riboflavin, Copper, Niacin, Phosphorus, and Protein.

Bananas are probably most famous for their potassium content. Potassium, along with normalizing PH and blood pressure, suppresses the exertion of calcium in the urine. Calcium, a water-soluble **nutrient**, is essential for strong bones and teeth. Deficiency in this nutrient, caused by insufficient intake or loss through sweat and urine, can lead to osteoporosis or other serious conditions.

Simple sugars are found in bananas like fructose and sucrose, which are broken down easily in the bloodstream, provide instant energy and revitalize the body. They make a great pre or post workout snack.

Bananas are rich in **vitamin** B6 (pyridoxine), which helps in brain stimulation and energy conversion. B6 also works with B12 and folate to reduce *homocysteine* levels in the blood. High quantities of this **amino acid** in the body have been linked to heart attack. The fruit also contains small amounts of the amino acid *tryptophan*, known for creating stable moods.

Bananas are thought to be useful in soothing upset stomachs, treating ulcers, providing relief from hangovers, lessening premenstrual symptoms, easing headaches, and in the treatment of neuritis and anemia.

HOW TO EAT BANANAS: Plátanos or *bananos* are sold in the fruit and vegetable areas of the markets. You can by them by piece or by weight. Ripe *plátanos* are completely yellow and not to be confused with *plánato macho*, which is really plantain. Eat them plain or blend them up in a smoothie.

BLACKBERRY / *MORA*

HIGH IN: Vitamins C and K, Manganese, and Fiber.

ALSO CONTAINS: Copper, Folate, Vitamins A and E, Potassium, Magnesium, Zinc, Iron, and Niacin.

Whereas all berries are nutritionally beneficial, blackberries have been dubbed the "king of berries." *Anthocyanins* are the **antioxidant** pigments that give blackberries their extremely dark color. These pigments are present in all berries, contributing to their red, purple, or blue hues but blackberries have one of the highest concentrations, making them a powerful disease-fighting food. Blackberries have a high Oxygen Radical Absorption Capacity (ORAC), meaning they can are very effective in warding off free radical cells in the body that can lead to cancer and other complications. The berries are also packed full of vitamin C and ellagic acid, other antioxidant powerhouses. Blackberries are considered one of the top antioxidant foods.

Blackberries are a great way to refuel after a workout. They have some potassium and contain a low-calorie sugar substitute called *xylitol*, which absorbs more slowly than sugar and does not contribute to high blood sugar levels.

Blackberries have are rich in *tannins*, which can help tighten tissue, relieve intestinal inflammation, and help reduce hemorrhoids and stomach disorders. Blackberries may protect against esophageal, breast, cervical, and colon cancers.

HOW TO EAT BLACKBERRIES: Moras are a treat. Take them where you can get them. They may not always be available in the markets, but sometimes on the street corners or small shops. Wash them good and eat them as is or add them to granola, oatmeal, or yogurt. Great in smoothies!

__NOTE:__ Also keep your eyes open for *frambuesas* (raspberries) and *arándanos azules* (blueberries).

CASHEW APPLE / *JOCOTE MARAÑÓN*

The cashew apple is another fruit that has little nutritional information available. It is very fragile and spoils quickly, so is not exported or eaten outside its cultivation area. Native to Brazil, the cashew apple is the "fake fruit" from which the cashew nut hangs. The cashew tree now grows in tropical zones around the world and the cashew nut is a valued cash crop for many countries.

The cashew apple is used often to make a sweet, rich juice. It is said to be an excellent source of vitamin C and is used in some areas to treat flu. The raw fruit has a sweet and slightly sour taste. It is known as brain food to some cultures as it's said to strengthen cerebral activities.

The cashew nut comes enclosed in a hard shell that hangs from the bottom of the fruit. This shell contains toxins that must be neutralized before the nut can be consumed. For information on preparing cashew nuts to eat, see page 27.

HOW TO EAT CASHEW APPLES: Jocote marañón can be found in the fruit and vegetable sections or entryways of the markets. They are about the size, shape, and color of thin red, yellow, or orange bell peppers. A greyish bean shaped cashew nut shell will be attached to one end. The flesh of the *marañón* is of a creamy white color and looks something like vanilla pudding.

The fruit is delicious and can be eaten as is. Once washed, the skin is edible. There is no seed inside. The flesh can also be blended with water and sweetened, if desired, to make a juice.

ALSO TRY THE "MALAY APPLE!" Native to Southeast Asia, this fruit is related to cashew apples only in shape and sometimes in name. It is not of the same family. The "Malay rose apple" is commonly referred to in Latin America as *marañon japonés*. In Nicaragua it is known as *manzana de agua* and in Guatemala as *pera china*. It has also been referred to as the "mountain apple."

The Malay rose apple is a delicious crimson red fruit that takes the shape and size of a pear, but the inner flesh is sweet and appears crisp and white like snow. It can be eaten raw or stewed with cloves and cinnamon to make a creamy dessert. Try adding citrus fruit like oranges into the mix.

DRAGON FRUIT / *PITAYA*

HIGH IN: Vitamin C, Fiber, Calcium, and Phosphorus.

ALSO CONTAINS: Potassium, Magnesium, Iron, Thiamin, and Riboflavin.

Dragon fruit is one of the most eye-catching tropical fruits. The bright red or pink balls (about the size of a mango) with light green scales are hard to miss. Dragon fruit is often displayed in season with a few sliced fruits placed atop a pile of ripe ones. The inner flesh is usually white or purple and full of tiny black seeds. To the untrained eye it may look more like a toy than food.

Dragon fruit is delicious. Its outward appeal and intoxicating flavor make it a hot item when it's available, but not cheap. Native to Central and South America, the fruit is now cultivated all over the world. It is a member of the cactus family and bears fruit more or less often depending on climate.

Being extremely rich in **vitamin** C, dragon fruit is a powerhouse of **antioxidants**. It boosts the immune system and aids in the general cleanup of the body. One of its highlights is the ability to neutralize and expel toxic substances and heavy metals.

The **fiber** and **minerals** found in dragon fruit help maintain a healthy digestive tract, strong bones, good memory and eyesight, balanced blood sugar, and normalized blood pressure.

HOW TO EAT DRAGON FRUIT: Pitaya is not always available. It's a treat when you find it and worth trying if you've never had it. More often than not it is available in the early summer months. Look for bright red, pink, or sometimes yellow fruits about the size of an orange. The fruit is slightly oblong and bears flashy green flap-like scales. It almost looks like a flying fireball.

Pitaya can be cut in half and the flesh scooped out to eat raw. It can be made into a creamy dessert or drink or a fancy topping to any fruit salad.

GRAPES / *UVAS*

HIGH IN: Vitamins C and K.

ALSO CONTAIN: Copper, Potassium, Thiamin, Riboflavin, Vitamin B6, Manganese, and Fiber.

Grapes are little health promoting bombs full of vital phyto-nutrients, **antioxidants** and **vitamins**. The simple sugars in grapes provide you with instant energy and their chemical make-up does wonders for your body.

Resveratrol, a powerful antioxidant, is plentiful in red grapes and has been found to protect against colon and prostate cancers, coronary heart disease, Alzheimer's, degenerative nerve disease, and viral or fungal infections. *Resveratrol* reduces susceptibility of blood vessel damage and increases the production of nitric oxide, which causes the relaxation of blood vessels, preventing clots and allowing for lower blood pressure. *Resveratrol* is concentrated mostly in the grape's seeds and skin.

Red grapes also contain *anthocyanins*, another class of antioxidants that have anti-allergic, anti-inflammatory, anti-microbial and anti-caner properties. Green grapes contain antioxidants in the form of *catechins*, a form of flavonoid *tannins*. Both red and green grapes contain adequate levels of vitamin C.

Grapes are said to increase moisture in the lungs and combat asthma. Pure, ripe grape juice when taken in the morning is said to cure migraines. The fruit is also believed to overcome constipation, treat indigestion, settle irritated stomachs, lower the risk of breast cancer and bring down bad cholesterol levels.

HOW TO EAT GRAPES: Uvas are found in the fruit and veggie sections of the markets. They are usually sold in bags by the kilo or half kilo. Be sure to wash grapes well before eating.

Uvas are delicious alone or with oatmeal, fruit salad, yogurt, or granola. The seeds are edible and highly nutritious. When dried to make raisins (*pasas* or *pasa uvas*) the iron level is increased.

GRAVIOLA / *GUANÁBANA*

HIGH IN: Vitamin C.

ALSO CONTAINS: Fiber, Vitamin B6, Riboflavin, Copper, and Potassium.

Graviola fruit is native to Southern Mexico, Central America, the Caribbean Islands and the jungles of South America. It is also known as *guanábana, soursop, prickly custard apple* and *Brazilian paw paw*. The fruit is now cultivated in tropical and subtropical regions worldwide and used to make juices and sweeteners for desserts. Graviola extract has and continues to undergo testing for its medicinal properties.

One of the most intriguing aspects of the fruit is its supposed ability to hunt down and destroy cancer cells without harming healthy cells. Many studies have been conducted on laboratory animals, but human data is still lacking. Tests show positive results against 12 different types of cancer, including breast, colon, prostate, lung, and pancreatic cancers. It is believed to have potential in fighting multidrug-resistant tumors.

Graviola has diuretic, antibacterial, and antifungal properties. Fresh juice is believed to promote the curing of liver ailments when taken on an empty stomach. It has been shown to lower blood sugar levels and may be helpful to combat diabetes. The juice is also said to have anti-depressive qualities and has been used to treat dysentery and scurvy. A concoction made from the crushed seeds can be used as a skin astringent or to drive off bed bugs or lice.

HOW TO EAT GRAVIOLA: Guanábana can be found at some fruit stalls in the markets of Southern Mexico and Central America. It is a large, green, oblong fruit, sometimes the size of an American football, with tiny spikes or bumps all around. It has white flesh with inedible black seeds.

The pulp can be eaten as is or blended with water to make a delicious juice. It is sweet and slightly sour. The juice can be frozen to make popsicles or used as a sweetener when cooking.

GUAVA / *GUAYABA*

HIGH IN: Vitamin C, Fiber, Folate, and Potassium.

ALSO CONTAINS: Vitamin A, Copper, Manganese, Magnesium, Niacin, Vitamins B5 and B6, Thiamin, and Phosphorus.

Guava is sometimes regarded as a super-fruit because of its intense **vitamin** C levels. It can hold up to four times the vitamin C of oranges. A few guavas can provide you with over six times the daily-recommended intake of this crucial vitamin. Among other things, vitamin C is required for collagen synthesis. Collagen is the main structural protein in the body responsible for maintaining the integrity of blood vessels, skin, organs, and bones.

Guavas have one of the highest concentrations of **antioxidants** among plant foods. Flavonoids like beta-carotene are found in abundance, especially in the red-orange fruits, known to protect from lung and oral cavity cancers. They are also believed to be anti-aging immune system boosters. The cancer-fighting agent lycopene is also present in guava. Lycopene consumption is associated with significantly lower risk of prostate cancer and has been shown to inhibit the growth of breast cancer cells.

Guava fruit and seeds are known to normalize bowels and help cases of both diarrhea and constipation. The astringents at work have both disinfectant and antibacterial properties as well as the power to enhance skin texture and tighten loosened skin or muscles. There is also a significant amount of vitamin A present in guavas that is very beneficial to skin, eyes, and mucus membranes. Guavas are said to have more potassium than bananas. A medium-sized guava for lunch could be enough nutrition until dinner.

In many countries guavas are prescribed to people suffering from cough or cold. The fruit has the ability to disinfect the respiratory tract, throat, and lungs and inhibit further microbial growth. It can also expel excess mucus and support quick recovery.

HOW TO EAT GUAVAS: Guayabas can be found in the fruit and vegetables sections of the markets. They are about the size of limes and typically of a yellow or reddish color. The inner flesh is light yellow or pink. *Guayabas* come in many colors, but the more red or orange the color, the more nutritious the fruit.

Guavas can be eaten whole. The seeds are hard, but edible. They contain a good dose of **fiber** and **protein**. Guavas also make great juice, but its recommend to spoon out the seeds first in this case.

ALSO TRY "CAS" GUAVA! Cas is another class of guava typically found in Costa Rica. It is green and quite sour. Popular in juices or shakes the *cas* has other names outside of Costa Rica such as *guayaba ácida* (Guatemala), *guayaba de agua* (Panama), *guayaba del Choco* (El Salvador) and *guayaba montes* (Mexico).

RED MOMBIN / *JOCOTE*

The mombin fruit appears evasive when it comes to nutritional data. Not much information is available about the fruit. However it is widely available in the Mexico and Central America Zone. It carries many names and can be referred to as *jocote, ciruela española* (Spanish plum), purple mombin, hog plum, or *sineguela*.

Jocotes are of a mottled red or green color. The taste between the two colors varies a little. They are about the size of a very small plum and have a bittersweet, tart, refreshing taste.

The fruit is rumored to have diuretic and antispasmodic qualities and can heal sores in the mouth or skin. It is said to be high in potassium, **vitamin** C, and calcium.

HOW TO EAT RED MOMBINS: Jocotes are usually sold in bags or trays in or around the markets. They are mostly of a spotted green or red color with light yellow flesh and a large central seed. The fruit is about the size of a golf ball and the skin is edible if well washed. The seed can be discarded.

LIME / *LIMÓN*

HIGH IN: Vitamin C.

ALSO CONTAINS: Fiber, Calcium, Iron, Potassium, Copper, Vitamins A, B6, and E.

Limes are a very good source of vitamin C. They do contain other **nutrients** and **vitamins**, but in much lower quantities. However, that doesn't mean that limes aren't a great addition to your daily diet.

Lime juice and oil are very beneficial for the skin when consumed orally or applied topically. It keeps skin shining, rejuvenates the cells, protects from infections, and reduces body odor. The fruit is full of vitamins and *flavonoids*, which act as **antioxidants**, antibiotics, and disinfectants. When applied externally, the acids of lime juice scrub out dead cells, help cure rashes, bruises, and dry skin.

The *flavonoids* found in limes also help to stimulate the digestive system and increase the secretion of digestive juices, bile, and acids. Even before eating or drinking limes, the scent makes your mouth begin to water. It is customary in some countries to have a pickled lime with meals to aid in the digestive process.

Once inside the body, the antimicrobial acids of lime juice wash down the walls of the intestines and excretory tract, eliminating toxins and damage-causing free radicals from the system. It can help prevent the development of kidney stones and urinary infections or disorders. The juice can even help treat peptic and oral ulcers.

Limes can help cure swollen or infected gums, treat cases of tonsillitis, relieve pain from insect bites or stings, prevent gout, alleviate respiratory problems, lower fatigue, and combat rheumatoid arthritis, diabetes, and certain types of cancers. A few drops of lime juice mixed with water can be used as an eyewash in case of infection.

HOW TO EAT LIMES: Limones shouldn't be confused with lemons. In Spanish, lemons are *limas*. But we are talking about good old green limes here. *Limones* can be found in the fruit and vegetable stands at the markets. They are sometimes sold by the kilo in plastic bags on the streets. If you're lucky you might find a lime tree near to you and you can pick them for free. Just be courteous and ask permission first if it's on someone's property.

Limes can be made into *limonada*, a refreshing drink for a hot day. It's recommended to drink warm lime water daily, first thing in the morning, to aid in digestion and the creation of enzymes. It helps to stimulate the liver and alkalize the body.

Limes can be squeezed over your food. The juice can be used in cooking or marinating. The peel is edible and full of nutrients. It can be grated and used in or on top of certain dishes for an added "zest." Lime juice is an essential ingredient in many tropical cocktails as well!

LYCHEE / *LITCHI*

HIGH IN: Vitamin B6 and C, Copper, and Fiber.

ALSO CONTAINS: Potassium, Folates, Riboflavin, Niacin, Phosphorus, Manganese, Magnesium, and protein.

Lychee is a small tropical fruit native to southern China and Southeast Asia. The name, from Chinese, means 'gift for a joyful life'. It bears bright pinkish red skin with sweet, translucent white flesh and a dark central seed. The flesh has the consistency of a grape.

Lychee fruit has an incredible amount of **vitamin** C. A diet high in vitamin C can help the body build up resistance to sickness, infectious agents, and disease. Lychee also contains a low molecular weight polyphenol called *oligonol*, which may have potent **antioxidant** and anti-influenza virus actions. *Oligonol* also helps improve blood flow to organs and protect skin from harmful UV rays. Lychee is a good source of B vitamins and copper.

The high levels of vitamin C and other antioxidants found in lychees makes it a strong counter-cancer food. It is believed to prevent the growth of cancer cells and has flavonoids in the pulp that are particularly helpful against breast cancer. The fiber in the fruit also aids in digestion and protects against cancers in the digestive tract.

Small but powerful, lychee fruit is said to increase the energy levels of the body, improve fluid flow throughout the body, enhance the feeling of well-being, help in the absorption of beta carotene and other fat soluble **nutrients**, prevent blood clots, and reduce the risk of heart attack or stroke.

HOW TO EAT LYCHEE: Litchis are sold when available. They are not commonplace in many markets, but are sold where and whenever possible during the season. In some areas they grow year round, but you're most likely to find them in early summer. *Litchis* are about the size of a small kiwi with rough, bright pinkish red skin that looks almost like alligator scales. The skin can be peeled away and the white pulp eaten raw. The seed can be discarded.

Similar to the lychee is the **longan**, or *longana* in Spanish. It has a smooth, earthy yellow skin but the pulp is close to that of the lychee. Its seed is larger and the fruit is sometimes called dragon's eye in Asia for its reptilian resemblance when opened a certain way.

MAMMY APPLE / *MAMEY*

HIGH IN: Vitamins A, B6 and C, Fiber, Copper, Manganese, Iron, and Folates.

ALSO CONTAINS: Riboflavin, Niacin, Thiamin, Potassium, Calcium, Phosphorus, Protein, Selenium, and Zinc.

Mamey is a curious fruit. It comes the *sapotaceae* family, which also lays claim to the *chico zapote* (*sapodilla*), star apple, green sapote, and *abiu*. The skin of the *mamey*, or mammy apple, is coarse, almost like light tree back or sand paper, but it guards an intoxicatingly sweet, rich, orange meat. The moist flesh of the mammy apple fruit is often used in milkshakes or scooped directly out of the peel with a spoon to eat on its own. It is exceedingly high in **vitamin** C and **fiber**. One mammy apple can support your vitamin C needs for the whole day. The orange color is owed to high levels of beta-carotene.

The mammy apple contains an **antioxidant** poly-phenolic compound called *tannin*. *Tannins* have potential anti-inflammatory, antiviral, anti-bacterial, and anti-parasitic effects. They can be helpful in the treatment of diarrhea, dysentery, bleeding, hemorrhoids, acid reflux, and irritable bowel syndrome. The seeds from the fruit can be ground into a paste and applied to the skin to relieve insect stings or bites.

Mammy apples are good for producing energy and are believed by many to be an aphrodisiac.

Chico zapote, or *sapodilla*, is a close relative of *mamey*. Both are native to southern Mexico and Guatemala. The sap from the chico tree is called *chicle*, a word traced back to the Nahuatl term *tziktli*, meaning "sticky stuff." For centuries this organic latex had been cooked and chewed by ancient Mayans and Aztecs and eventually became the base ingredient for modern day chewing gum. This fruit is very popular now in India, Thailand, and other Southeast Asian countries where it goes by the name of *chicu*.

HOW TO EAT MAMMY APPLES: Mamey are seasonal fruits sold in the vegetable areas of the markets or special stands at the right time of year (usually spring). The name *mamey* is used in Mexico, but in most of Central America the fruit is known simply as "*zapote.*" They are about the size of one or two fists, tan to earth-colored, round or oblong with rough skin. The inside of the fruit is dark orange and has a long black seed in the center. *Mamey* can be eaten as is or it makes a delicious shake with your milk of choice. The pulp is a little too mushy to be used in a fruit salad but can be puréed and cooked to make a sweet sauce to pour over a complimentary dish.

Other fruits of the family you shouldn't miss are the **sapodilla** (*chico zapote*)- a smaller version of the *mamey* with white flesh that tastes like a pear dipped in brown sugar syrup; the **star apple** (*caimito*)- round, about the size of a kiwi with dark purple skin, milky whitish-purple flesh and a bittersweet taste; and the **loquat** (*níspero*), that appears almost like a peach and very sweet to taste.

The skins of these fruits are inedible. Slice them in half and scoop out the insides.

MANGO / *MANGO*

HIGH IN: Vitamins A, B6 and C, and Fiber.

ALSO CONTAINS: Vitamins E and K, Copper, Potassium, Thiamin, Riboflavin, Folate, Iron, and Niacin.

Each mango fruit is a pretty well balanced capsule of **vitamins** and **nutrients**. A mango can supply you with just about a full day's worth of vitamin C. It has a good amount of prebiotic **fiber**, the kind that helps feed friendly bacteria in the digestive system. Mangos contain bioactive ingredients and enzymes that contribute to enhancing the appetite, soothing the stomach, and improving digestion. They are also rich in B6, a vitamin required for the production of *GABA* (Gabba-Amino Butyric Acid) hormones that regulate nerve impulses in the brain. Vitamin B6 may also help to alleviate the symptoms of PMS.

Mangos are high in natural sugars, however, they are low in glycemic load, meaning that they don't affect blood sugar. Mangos are helpful in maintaining a healthy weight. Their fiber helps lower cholesterol and cut excess pounds in overweight persons and their starches, which are converted to sugars, aid to weight gain in persons who are trying to bulk up.

Mangos are a good source of vitamin E, which helps boost sex drive by triggering sex hormones. They have also been used in Chinese medicine to make a tonic known as yin, used to treat bleeding gums, anemia, cough, constipation, nausea, fever, seasickness, and weak digestion.

The inside of a fresh mango peel can be applied to the skin to treat acne. Left on the skin for 10 minutes and then washed off, the juices help to open clogged pores and rejuvenate cells.

HOW TO EAT MANGOS: Mangos seem to always be in season somewhere, but you're most likely to find them from April to July. During that time mangos are sold in the fruit and vegetable stands at the markets and all over the streets. You might be able to just pick them from the trees.

There are a few types of mango. The most common are the small yellow mango and the big green and red mango. They have different tastes and textures, but all are sweet and delicious.

One of the easiest ways to slice a mango is to cut the sides off, parallel to the flat, wide seed. You can cut the inside flesh from these sides into squares without cutting all the way through the skin. Bend the piece inside out and bite off the squares! Then cut off the skin from the piece that contains the seed. Slice or bite off the remaining flesh there.

CUCUMBER TREE FRUIT / *MIMBRO*

The cucumber tree, or *bilimbi*, originated in Southeast Asia. It now grows in hot tropical zones all over the world, but is not very tolerant to cold or heavy winds. Its fruit is small, sour, and cucumber shaped, hence the name. It is a close relative of the *carambola*, or star fruit.

Cucumber tree is also known as tree sorrel and its leaves have some medicinal value. They are used to treat venereal diseases, eye problems, cough, inflammation, insect bites, and skin conditions. The fruit is most often it is used in cooking but can be eaten raw, though it's quite sour.

HOW TO EAT CUCUMBER TREE FRUIT: Mimbro, or *mimbra*, is generally found in the markets of Nicaragua and Costa Rica. It is a small green cucumber-shaped fruit about the size of a pinky finger.

Mimbro can be cooked to take the place of tomatoes or tamarind in certain dishes. It is often used in curry and even salads. Cut into thin slices and mixed with cucumber, red onion, vinegar and cilantro, or tarragon leaves and left to sit for half an hour, the *mimbro* will lose some of its sourness and gain a little sweetness. It can be used as a relish over rice and beans.

At a party? When drinking straight rum shots, try using *mimbro* dipped in salt as the chaser.

NONI FRUIT / *NONI*

HIGH IN: Vitamin C, Niacin, Iron, and Potassium.

ALSO CONTAINS: Vitamin A, Fiber, Calcium, Sodium, and Protein.

Originally native to Southeast Asia and the Polynesian Islands, noni is now cultivated in tropical regions worldwide. It has been used medicinally for centuries and has finally gained a little fame in western markets.

Noni is typically used to make juice. Fermented noni juice is said to treat and prevent a wide number of diseases and conditions including cancer, Alzheimer's, ulcers, insomnia, nausea, migraines, diarrhea, anxiety, nervousness, menstrual cramps, diabetes, constipation, depression, and liver diseases. Noni juice is said to cure acne and aid in skin beautification.

Some studies state that noni juice has the ability to activate serotonin receptors in the brain and body. Serotonin is a brain neurotransmitter for controlling hunger, sexual behavior, temperature regulation, mood, and sleep. Deficiency has been linked to obesity, insomnia, depression, and migraine headaches.

Noni fruit contains 17 **amino acids** (including all 9 essentials), vital **nutrients** and **vitamins** as well as *iridoids* and *anthraquinones*. *Iridoids* are a class of secondary metabolites that have potential antioxidant, anti-inflammatory, anti-cancer, antimicrobial, neuro-protective, cardio-protective, and purgative properties. *Anthraquinones* have antibiotic properties useful to inhibit tumor growth and proliferation.

Noni has been used for centuries in the Polynesian Islands to treat skin sores, ringworm, scalp infection, gout, intestinal worms, arthritis, vomiting, insomnia, colds, respiratory ailments and digestive disorders. It is believed to help treat certain sexually transmitted diseases such as gonorrhea and syphilis. The juice can be used a shampoo that adds luster to hair and treats hair dryness and head lice.

HOW TO EAT NONI: Noni is not as common in the markets as many other fruits are. Finding it may require some asking around. Many families have noni plants on their property, kept for personal use. You may find it in the entryways or specialty item areas of the markets.

Noni is a pear shaped fruit of a light green color, like a honeydew melon, about the size of a kiwi. Its skin is warty with black spots. The skin is thin and the pulp inside is of a similar color and full of tiny dark seeds. The entire fruit is edible, but doesn't taste or smell good. Noni is usually fermented and made into a juice. To learn how to make noni juice, see page 273.

ORANGE / *NARANJA*

HIGH IN: Vitamin C.

ALSO CONTAINS: Fiber, Folate, Potassium, Vitamin A and B6, Calcium, Copper, and Magnesium.

Oranges are famous because they pack a potent punch of **vitamin** C, a powerful **antioxidant** that boosts the immune system and helps rid the body of cancer-causing free radicals. Oranges also contain alpha and beta-carotene antioxidants that protect cells from damage and preserve the body's valuable mucus membranes. Antioxidants may lower the risk or symptoms of rheumatoid arthritis.

Another antioxidant prevalent in oranges is naringenin, a citrus bioflavonoid that has anti-inflammatory properties and has been shown to reduce oxidant injury to DNA in some studies.

Oranges provide energy and boost immunity. They have been found to cure colds, lower the amount of mucus secretions from the nose, aid in dental health, support proper brain development, clear the skin, treat respiratory disorders, and balance cholesterol levels.

HOW TO EAT AN ORANGE: Naranjas are available in the fruit and vegetable stands at the markets. Fresh squeezed orange juice is usually sold in the markets or on the streets. Orange juice is best consumed when the fruit has been freshly squeezed as the vitamin C levels diminish rapidly once exposed to open air.

Jugo de naranja (orange juice) retains vitamin C, but many of the fruits beneficial nutrients are found in the white fuzz and the fibrous pulp. To maximize the health benefits of oranges, eat them whole.

PAPAYA / *PAPAYA*

HIGH IN: Vitamins A and C.

ALSO CONTAINS: Folates, Fiber, Potassium, Vitamins E and K, Thiamin, Riboflavin, and Calcium.

Papaya, or *paw paw* as it's sometimes called, is quite rich in **vitamin** C. It contains almost twice that of an orange. Vitamin C, like A, is a powerful **antioxidant** necessary in maintaining optimum health. Antioxidants help defend the body from disease-causing chemical reactions and can aid in slowing down the general aging process.

One unique ingredient in papaya fruit is a proteolytic enzyme called *papain*, which works as a digestive agent helping to break down **amino acids** (proteins). Papain can be used to treat ulcers, acid reflux, digestive disorders, and destroy intestinal parasites. Much more papain can be found in the skin and fruit of the unripe green papaya. This concentration of papain, present in the white liquid latex secreted by the cut papaya, can remove warts or skin tags and can be effective in treating blood or fat stains in clothes. Papaya extracts have been injected into spinal discs and pinches nerves to speed up recovery.

Eating papaya alone for a couple days can have a useful tonic effect on the stomach and intestines. It helps treat internal infections by breaking down pus and mucus. Papaya is known to settle feelings of nausea and motion or morning sickness. In addition to papain, papaya also contains carpaine, which has tumor fighting potential.

In general, eating papaya, especially 15 to 20 minutes after meals, makes for better digestion, prevents bloating and symptoms of chronic indigestion. It can lower inflammation in the body and alleviate the pain of arthritis or sports injuries. Its juices support muscle recovery and renewal and can help replenish beneficial bacteria in the intestines after treatment with prescription antibiotics.

Papaya seeds are edible and have medicinal properties. They have a spicy pepper-like taste and are high in protein and fat. Compounds found in the seeds can kill intestinal parasites and expel worms. A couple tablespoons of papaya seeds alone or with honey on occasion can help keep your system clean. The papaya flesh and skin can also be used to treat skin sores or wounds.

HOW TO EAT PAPAYA: Papaya is found in the vegetable sections of the markets. The fruits vary from the size of a fist to the size of a head. They are typically long, round, and slightly pointed at one end. Ripe papayas are orange/yellow in color and are a little bit soft to the touch. Check for spots that are too soft or moldy. Unripe papayas are green and hard.

Ripe papayas can be cut and eaten as they are or used in salads, juices, or milkshakes. Green papayas can be eaten raw if you enjoy the taste, or cooked in a curry or stir-fry. The skins of both are edible and contain much vitamin C and other nutrients. Wash the outside thoroughly if you intend to eat it the skin. The seeds can be used in salads.

PASSION FRUIT / *MARACUYÁ*

HIGH IN: Vitamins A and C, Fiber, Potassium, and Iron.

ALSO CONTAINS: Riboflavin, Niacin, Magnesium, Phosphorus, Copper, Protein, and Folates.

Passion fruit is as delicious as it sounds. The small grenade shaped globes are full of small crispy seeds and a sweet, intoxicating gel. Passion fruit is extremely high in **vitamin** C and gives a great immune system boost. Vitamin C and other phyto-chemicals found in passion fruit are able to reduce or inhibit cancer cell growth and help the body function at its optimal level.

Passion fruit seeds are very rich in dietary **fiber** and contain notable amounts of **protein**. The fiber is essential in removing cholesterol from the body and protecting the mucus membrane of the colon by decreasing exposure time to toxic substances.

The **antioxidants** available in passion fruit are both water and fat-soluble, meaning that the body can store them for both short and long term use. Some of these antioxidants work as natural antihistamines, helping relieve asthma, allergies and inflammation. The fruit is high in vitamin A, an antioxidant that also supports eyesight and skin cells.

Passion fruit contains somniferous properties that provide overall relaxation and help produce restful and sound sleep when taken before bed.

HOW TO EAT PASSION FRUIT: Maracuyá are available in a few different colors, but yellow and purple are the most common. They are round or egg shaped with a tight shell. When tapped with a finger, they sound hollow. *Maracuyá* fruits can be cut open with a knife or broken and peeled with bare fingers. The inner jelly and seeds are all edible and can be spooned or slurped out as you desire. *Maracuyá* makes delicious juice.

In some of Central America, passion fruit is known as *granadilla* or *pasionaria*. In Nicaragua it may be referred to as *calala*.

PINEAPPLE / *PIÑA*

HIGH IN: Vitamin C and Manganese.

ALSO CONTAINS: Fiber, Vitamin B6, Thiamin, Copper, Folate, Magnesium, and Potassium.

Pineapple is an excellent source of **vitamin** C. It also contains an enzyme called bromelain that helps breakdown and metabolize **proteins**. Bromelain has anti-inflammatory, anti-clotting, and anti-cancer properties. The enzyme is beneficial to many health problems such as rheumatoid arthritis, heartburn, and acid reflux. It is also credited with the ability to speed up the recovery process of surgeries and injuries including cuts, sprains, bruising, and swelling.

Pineapple, or *anana*, is rich in dietary **fiber**. Its fiber, roughage, and **nutrients** work well to clean and protect the digestive system and rid the body of intestinal worms or parasites. Pineapple is also said to aid in building strong bones, removing plaque from artery walls, treating anemia, curing throat infections and bronchitis, and in relieving bloating, constipation, or nausea.

Manganese is found in large quantities in pineapple. This trace mineral is needed by the body to build bones and connective tissues. Vitamin C helps in the body synthesize collagen, which is fundamental in maintaining healthy skin, blood vessels and organs. Pineapple is packed with antioxidants that keep diseases and illness at bay.

HOW TO EAT PINEAPPLE: Piñas are sold by various sizes in the fruit and vegetable stands of the markets. A ripe pineapple will be mostly yellow on the outside and smell sweet on the bottom. Hard, green pineapples won't have much taste.

Piñas can be sliced widthwise and then cut up like a pie and eaten as a snack, or you can slice all the skin off, dice up the fruit, and use it in cooking or with salads. Try chilled pineapple slices. The skin and/or fruit can be used to make a delicious fermented drink called *tepache* (page 130).

POMEGRANATE / *GRANADA*

HIGH IN: Vitamins C and K, Fiber, Folates, and Copper.

ALSO CONTAINS: Potassium, Manganese, Thiamin, Vitamins E, B5 and B6, Phosphorus, Protein, Riboflavin, Magnesium, Zinc, and Iron.

The pomegranate is a strange and beautiful fruit. Within its rose-colored rind are tiny tooth-sized juicy balloons that hold a dark red, translucent liquid and little tiny seeds. These seedpods, about the shape of a kernel of corn, are completely edible and highly nutritious.

Like most fruits, pomegranate has a considerable amount of **vitamin** C, an **antioxidant** that helps the body develop resistance against infectious agents by boosting the immune system. It has a higher concentration of vitamin K, necessary to maintain healthy bones and cardiovascular system. A polyphenolic antioxidant called punicalagin is found in abundance in pomegranates. It is said to lower the risk of heart disease significantly. Regular consumption of the fruit can help reduce plaque levels in the arteries, avoid clumping of platelets, and the unnecessary formation of blood clots.

Pomegranates are believed to slow down the enzymes that break down cartilage, therefor leading to less deterioration and possible relief from symptoms of arthritis. They are also said to slow down or prevent Alzheimer's disease and be very effective against prostate and breast cancers.

Both the seeds and juice are considered a tonic for the heart and throat, but the seeds in particular are high in soluble and insoluble dietary **fibers** that are very beneficial to the human body. The juice may also inhibit viral infections and have antibacterial effects against dental plaque. Along with fiber, the seeds contain valuable oils, micronutrients, and some **protein**.

HOW TO EAT POMEGRANATES: Granadas can be found in the fruits and vegetable areas of the markets. They are about the size of a large onion or grapefruit with rose-red skin and a little crown on top. The inner flesh is light yellow and the clumps of seedpods are of a dark, clear red.

The easiest way to separate the seeds from the rind is to first cut off the crown. Next slice the rind 5 or 6 times around from top to bottom without cutting all the way through. Submerge the pomegranate crown side down in purified water and let it sit a couple of minutes. Then begin to break apart the rind and separate the skin from the seeds. The seeds should sink while the rind and pulp floats. Remove the pieces of skin and rind with a spoon or strainer and then pass the rest through a strained to separate the water from the seeds pods.

The seeds are edible raw and can be chewed and swallowed along with the juice that surrounds them. You may choose to spit out or discard them, but you will miss out on many of the nutritional benefits of the *granada*.

PRICKLY PEAR / *TUNA*

HIGH IN: Vitamin C, Magnesium, and Fiber.

ALSO CONTAINS: Potassium, Calcium, Copper, Riboflavin, Vitamin B6, and Phosphorus.

The kiwi-shaped fruits that grow off the tips of the *nopal* cactus pads are called prickly pears. Hench the plant itself is sometimes referred to as the "prickly pear cactus." The fruits are green or dark red in color and are covered by a thick, tough skin full of small black dots that look like moles. They taste something like a melon.

Prickly pears have been receiving much attention from the athletic community. They are commonly juiced and used as a sports beverage for their rejuvenating properties. The fruit is sometimes referred to as a resistogen because it helps the body develop resistance against stress and physical or mental exertion. Prickly pear has the ability to provide athletes with more energy and allow them to push themselves for a longer period of time. The nutritional benefits reduce post-workout muscle soreness and speed the recovery of the muscles.

Prickly pears contain 17 **amino acids**, including the 8 essentials. They are a great source of **fiber** and **vitamin** C and are packed full of antioxidants and disease fighting flavonoids. Prickly pears are also said to be very effective to help lose weight. The high levels of magnesium and taurine can be very beneficial to brain and heart health. The cactus fruit is also believed to lessen the symptoms of a bad hangover.

HOW TO EAT PRICKLY PEARS: Tuna can be found in the fruit and vegetable sections of the markets. In some areas it is not available year-round and is less common to encounter south of Mexico.

Tuna fruit comes in a green or red variety. They are kiwi-sized fruits with thick, smooth skin covered in medium-sized black dots. The skin can be broken and peeled away like an orange leaving a crisp pulp full of small seeds. The seeds are edible, but hard. They can be chewed up and swallowed or spit out if desired. *Tuna* is often used to make juice by blending the peeled fruits with a little bit of water and sugar and then pouring the liquid through a strainer to separate the juice from the seeds. It is very refreshing and great in cocktails.

RAMBUTAN / *RAMBUTÁN*

HIGH IN: Vitamin C, Fiber, Potassium, and Iron.

ALSO CONTAINS: Vitamin A, Calcium, Magnesium, Zinc, Copper, Phosphorus, and Niacin.

Rambutan is a close relative of lychee. It shares the same size and strong pinkish red color, but the rambutan is covered in long, thick dark red hairs that protrude from the skin. The name rambutan comes from the Malay language meaning 'hairy'. The inner white pulp of the lychee, rambutan, and longan are very similar in taste and texture.

Like lychee and so many other tropical fruits, rambutan is very high in **vitamin** C. It is also a great source of fiber and potassium as well as iron, which helps control the oxygen levels in the body. The vitamin C helps the iron to be absorbed by the body. Traditional medicine in Malaysia and Indonesia has employed the fruit for hundreds of years to treat diabetes, high blood pressure, and other ailments. Consumption of rambutan can help kill intestinal parasites, treat diarrhea, cleanse the body, and boost the immune system. Parts of the fruit can be used to cure fever.

Rambutan seeds are said to be both beneficial and toxic. The fruit has one central seed about the size of an almond. The general consensus is that cooked or roasted seeds are safe. They are sometimes ground up and used as an alternative to peanut butter. The seeds are said to make skin healthier and softer, help reduce body fat, and stimulate hair growth.

HOW TO EAT RAMBUTAN: Rambután is called *mamón chino* in the southern half of Central America. In some areas it is sold year-round and found in the fruit stalls of the markets. Most likely you will see *rambután* for sale in the late spring or early summer months. The fruit is a vibrant pinkish-red color, about the size of a kiwi with long flimsy spines surrounding it. The sweet inner flesh is crystal-white and has a texture similar to that of a grape. The skin can be peeled away like an orange and discarded.

STAR FRUIT / *CARAMBOLA*

HIGH IN: Vitamin C and Fiber.

ALSO CONTAINS: Copper, Potassium, Folate, Vitamins A and B5, Magnesium, and Calcium.

Star fruit is another eye catching tropical fruit. Normally it grows to about the size of a small potato, but the strange yellow fruit is comprised of five long ridges that come together at each end, giving it the shape of a football. When the fruit is cut widthwise into slices, the slices come out in the shape of stars.

Star fruit is rich in **vitamin** C and **antioxidant** phyto-nutrients called flavonoids. These ingredients make the fruit a powerful cleanser able to ward off cancer and disease-causing free radicals and help the body function at its optimal level. The fruit also has antimicrobial activities found to be effective against E.coli and various bacterial infections in the stomach. The waxy skin is rich in tannins that support the process of regulating the digestive system.

B-complex vitamins are found in star fruit that help the body in metabolizing and synthesizing processes. Vitamin A and calcium are found in small doses, which help maintain healthy skin, eyesight, and strong bones. Star fruit is high in copper, an essential mineral for the creation of new cells.

Star fruit is good for hormone regulation and can be used to increase urine output, suppress cough, and clear the respiratory tract of phlegm, mucus, or other liquids. The dietary **fiber** it possesses helps protect the mucus membrane of the colon from the absorption of toxic substances.

HOW TO EAT STAR FRUIT: Carambola can be found throughout most of the year in the fruits and vegetable areas of the markets. It is a greenish yellow fruit in the shape of a football with long, high ridges running lengthwise down its sides. *Carambola* can be eaten whole, the seeds spit out, or cut into slices and used as garnish on a plate of food or fruit salad. They make great juice or even nice decorations the rim of a cocktail glass.

STRAWBERRY / *FRESA*

HIGH IN: Vitamin C and Manganese.

ALSO CONTAINS: Fiber, Folates, Potassium, Copper, Magnesium, and Iron.

Strawberries are delicious anytime, anywhere. They are a very potent source of **vitamin** C. A cup of strawberries can provide you with way more than the recommended daily intake of this important health-promoting vitamin.

Strawberries are a good source of potassium, helping to maintain electrolyte balance in the body and regulate blood pressure, thus lowering the risk of heart attacks and stroke. They contain small amounts of iodine and are found to increase memory function and support the nervous system. They also contain certain phyto-chemicals called *anthocyanins* and *ellagic acid* that have potential ability to fight cancer, slow the aging process, and lower inflammation in the body.

The copper and iron found in strawberries aid in red blood cell formation. The **fiber** helps the body absorb more nutrients from your food. Rubbing a slice of raw strawberry on the teeth is said to remove tartar and strengthen the gums.

HOW TO EAT STRAWBERRIES: Fresas are sold in the vegetable and fruit sections of the markets. They are usually offered in plastic containers or small plates covered in plastic wrap. In the height of the season you may find them in open bins, sold by weight. *Fresas* make a great addition to salads, they are good with breakfast cereal, and tasty in juices or milkshakes.

Vegetables

BELL PEPPERS / *PIMIENTO*

HIGH IN: Vitamin C, Vitamins A, B6 and K, Folates, and Fiber.

ALSO CONTAINS: Manganese, Potassium, Thiamin, Copper, and Phosphorus.

Bell peppers have been cultivated for some 9000 years. Native to Mexico and Central America, they can now be found in almost every corner of the globe. China is currently the world's largest producer of bell peppers.

These sweet, crunchy peppers are members of the nightshade family, which also includes potatoes, tomatoes, and eggplant. Unlike other peppers, they contain a very minimum amount of capsaicin, the phytonutrient that controls the heat in hot peppers. Capsaicin is believed to have anti-cancer and anti-inflammatory properties. It has been shown to reduce bad cholesterol, control diabetes, and even provide a measure of pain relief. Some studies have shown that capsaicin can boost metabolism and suppress appetite.

Although bell peppers can be seen and eaten in a variety of colors, they're all essentially the same pepper. The green, yellow, orange, or red hue determines the stage of maturity. As the pepper ripens, the nutritional properties change. Green peppers are high in chlorophyll, a powerful plant pigment able to keep the body healthy and energetic. Yellow peppers feature more luetin and zeaxanthin carotenoids, both known to protect the eyes from damaging sun rays and ward off age-related vision problems. Orange bell peppers have more alpha-, beta-, and gamma-carotene, fat-soluble **antioxidants** responsible for the orange or red colors in plants. Red bell peppers boast more lycopene and astaxanthin, disease-fighting antioxidants believed to combat cancer-causing free radicals and cardiovascular disorders.

Bell peppers actually contain 30 different kinds of carotenoids, all aiding in cellular activity and protection. Their vitamin C content is vastly superior to that of oranges, the highest concentration found in the red variety. Peppers are a great source of vitamin E, essential in maintaining healthy, attractive skin and hair.

HOW TO EAT BELL PEPPERS: Pimientos can be found in the fruit and vegetable sections of the markets. They should be washed thoroughly under cold water before use. Any color (*verde, amarillo, naranja, rojo*) can be eaten raw or cooked. The red variety, eaten ripe and raw, provides the most nutritional benefits. Look for *pimientos* that have fresh green stems, vibrant colors, and soft smooth skin. Bell peppers are best cooked for short times at low temperatures.

BROCCOLI / *BRÓCOLI*

HIGH IN: Vitamins C and K, Folates, and Manganese.

ALSO CONTAINS: Fiber, Vitamins A and B6, Potassium, Phosphorus, Riboflavin, Magnesium, Calcium, Iron, and Protein.

Broccoli is extremely rich in **vitamins** C and K. It is also a great source of potassium and calcium. Vitamin K works with calcium to create and maintain a healthy bone structure. Vitamin C helps the body absorb calcium and iron. Iron aids in the production of red blood cells and transports oxygen throughout the body. Potassium and calcium help in muscle growth and function.

Broccoli contains sulforaphane, which doesn't do any good in terms of flatulence, but helps the body get rid of Heliobacter pylori, a bacterium that increases the risk of gastric cancer. The unique combination of antioxidant, anti-inflammatory, and pro-detoxification components in broccoli may help obstruct the growth of cancers such as breast, cervical, prostate, ovarian, bladder, and colon.

Carotenoid lutein is found in broccoli and can help prevent degeneration of the eyes and blindness. Vitamin A and beta-carotene in broccoli also helps support healthy vision. Carotenoid lutein can help fight against heart attack and stroke by preventing the thickening of the arteries.

Eating broccoli pushes fiber and roughage through the digestive system, aiding to the digestive process, regulating the absorption of sugars and nutrients and scrubbing the walls of the digestive track. A balanced diet rich in broccoli can help prevent arthritis, premature aging, high blood pressure, ulcers, osteoporosis, atherosclerosis, heart attack, diabetes, and Alzheimer's disease.

HOW TO EAT BROCCOLI: *Brócoli* is sold at most vegetable stands in the markets. Check that it is fresh, clean and free of bugs. Good, ripe broccoli should be of a healthy dark green color. Avoid anything grey or yellow.

Brócoli can be cooked or eaten raw, but studies claim that steamed *brócoli* provides more nutrients and produces less flatulence. *Brócoli* is great in salads or as a side dish with garlic and sesame seeds. Try it with rice and veggies, like in a stir-fry!

CABBAGE / *KOL* (Mexico) *REPOLLO* (Central America)

HIGH IN: Vitamins C and K, and Folates.

ALSO CONTAINS: Fiber, Manganese, Vitamins B6, B5 and B1, Potassium, Calcium, Iron, and Magnesium.

Cabbage is extremely high in **vitamin K**. A serving of one cup of cooked cabbage contains almost over 90% of the daily-recommended intake. Vitamin K is essential for maintaining healthy bones. It strengthens the skeleton, reducing bone loss and therefore the risk of bone fracture. Vitamin K can also help Alzheimer's disease patients by limiting neuronal damage in the brain.

The vitamin C content of cabbage is also good. Cabbage actually contains more vitamin C than oranges. Vitamin C is a powerful **antioxidant** that boosts immunity, fights cancer-causing free radicals, promotes proper functioning of the immune system and wards off the effects of premature aging.

Red cabbage has more phytonutrients than green cabbage. The vitamin C content of red cabbage is 6-8 times higher than that of green cabbage. Red cabbage also contains anthocyanin, an antioxidant, anti-inflammatory pigment that can help lower blood sugar levels, fight cardiovascular disease, and protect the brain against and Alzheimer's.

Cabbage is a good source of **fiber**, which helps add roughage to food and alleviate constipation and the many health problems associated with it. Cabbage also has considerable amounts of sulfur, a very useful nutrient in fighting infections.

Cabbage is believed to help prevent cancer, heal ulcers, strengthen eyes, detoxify the body and treat skin disorders, gout, arthritis, varicose veins, as well as fungal disorders.

HOW TO EAT CABBAGE: Kol or *Repollo* can be found at the vegetable stands in the markets. Cabbage can be cooked or eaten raw. Many studies suggest that more nutrients are available to the body in the cooked form. It can be used in salads, sandwiches, juices, or as a topping to certain dishes. Sauerkraut, fermented cabbage, is said to contain up to ten times the vitamin C of raw cabbage. Learn how to make homemade sauerkraut on page 272.

CELERY / *APIO*

HIGH IN: Vitamins A and K, Folates, and Fiber.

ALSO CONTAINS: Manganese, Sodium, Vitamin C, Potassium, and Calcium.

Celery has long been used in the treatment of digestive disorders and gallbladder or kidney stones. It can be used as a liver stimulant or diuretic. Celery contains powerful antioxidant and anti-inflammatory properties, thus can aid in cancer prevention. It is high in **vitamin** K, which helps increase bone mass, and vitamin A, necessary for maintaining healthy mucus membranes and good vision.

Celery contains cancer-fighting compounds called coumarins that can lower blood pressure, tone the vascular system and be effective against migraines. Coumarins can also enhance the activity of certain white blood cells, therefore boosting the immune system.

The anti-inflammatory agents in celery can help people who suffer from arthritis or rheumatism by reducing swelling and pain around the joints. It can have a positive effect on asthma symptoms, as well. Celery contains a chemical that lowers the level of stress hormones in the blood, allowing blood vessels to expand, giving more room to the blood and essentially lowering blood pressure.

All parts of the celery plant can be used- from the stalk to the leaves, roots to the seeds. The essential oil obtained from the plant has been used to sooth nervousness, osteoarthritis and gouty-arthritis conditions. Celery is a good antiseptic and has been used to treat kidney disorders and urinary tract infections in women.

Celery contains a good balance of potassium and sodium. Celery-based juices serve as great electrolyte replacement drinks when taken after a workout. Potassium is important in the control of heart rate and blood pressure.

Celery is believed to aid in weight loss. A tablespoon of honey in a glass of celery juice may help to reduce appetite if taken before a meal or support sound sleep if taken before bed. It is also believed to strengthen a weak sexual system.

HOW TO EAT CELERY: Apio is found in the vegetable sections of the markets. It is sold in bunches or by the stalk (*rama*). Celery seeds (*semilla de apio*) are sold separately, usually in the seed and grain areas. Seeds can be used as a spice in cooking or raw over salads. Celery stalks can be used in salads, soups, veggie dishes, and juices or on their own with a dip of choice like hummus, fava bean dip, or peanut butter. They are crisp and refreshing.

CHAYOTE / *CHAYOTE* (Mexico) *GÜISQUIL* (Central America)

HIGH IN: Folate, Vitamin C, Manganese, and Fiber.

ALSO CONTAINS: Copper, Zinc, Potassium, Vitamins B6 and K, Magnesium, and Calcium.

Chayote, sometimes known as mirliton or vegetable pear, is a light green squash-like vegetable native to Mexico. It grows on a vine and is rather bland in taste with a texture something similar to that of a potato.

Chayote, from the Nahuatl word "*chayohtli*," is high in **folate**, necessary for DNA synthesis, and **vitamin** C, a powerful **antioxidant** and immune system booster.

The **manganese** content in chayote is good for providing energy. Its copper, along with iodine, helps to keep the thyroid gland healthy, aiding in hormone production and absorption. Vitamin B6 can improve memory function and the electrolyte mineral, magnesium, can help prevent muscle cramps.

The edible seeds of the chayote squash are rich in **amino acids**. The fruit has antioxidants that help rid the body of cancer-causing free radicals. The folate present in the flesh helps prevent the build up of homocysteine in the body, an overabundance of which is linked to coronary disease.

HOW TO EAT CHAYOTE: Chayote or *güisquil* is usually found in the vegetable sections of the markets. The vegetable is light green, fist-sized, pear-shaped and wrinkly. The inner flesh is off-white. All parts of the *chayote* are edible. It can be cooked like a potato or squash. Some forms of chayote have small thorns all over the outside of the fruit. These can be carefully peeled away after the fruit is pared. Some *chayotes* are covered in little hairs that dissolve when boiled. White, sweet chayote (*perulero*) can also be found.

Try chayote steamed or boiled in stews, soups, or in rice and veggie plates.

CHILI PEPPERS / *CHILES*

HIGH IN: Vitamins A, B6, C and K, Calcium, Potassium, Fiber, and Riboflavin.

ALSO CONTAIN: Manganese, Iron, Niacin, Magnesium, and Protein.

Chili peppers originated in the Americas and were exposed to the world through the European trade route in the early 16th century. The word "chili" most likely comes from the Nahuatl term *chilli* or *xilli*. The plants were domesticated over 6000 years ago and are still staples in contemporary Mexican cuisine.

Chili peppers are exceptionally high in **vitamins** C and A as well as potassium and calcium. Vegans would benefit by adding some chili to their diet to help boost calcium levels.

Cayenne, one of the major components of hot peppers, can help to lower cholesterol and triglyceride levels, reduce bloating and gas, ease stomach pain and aid in food digestion. Curiously, the presence of cayenne may actually be important to reduce the occurence of stomach ulcers.

Chili peppers contain another active component called capsaicin. A study published in Cancer Research states that capsaicin has the potential to cause certain cancer cells to commit suicide in lab mice. It is also used in topical creams as a treatment for ostheoarthritis and other pains due to light injury or inflammation.

Capsaicin has extremely anti-inflammatory and antibacterial properties and can also help to relieve migraine or sinus headaches as well as sinus infections and allergy related syptoms. Many weight loss supplements contain capsaicin as it increases metabolic activity and helps to burn off fat and calories. Capsaicin may also be useful in protecting the heart as it reduces cholesterol, triglycerides, and prevents the formation of blood clots. Many cultures around the world who include chili peppers in their standard diet boast lower rates of heart attack and stroke than those who don't.

HOW TO EAT CHILI PEPPERS: Chiles are usually found in the seed and spice sections of the markets. There are many different types and strengths. Some of the most common are *jalapeños*, *chiles verdes*, *chiles de árbol*, *chipotle*, *ancho*, and *guajillo*. They can be found fresh or dried, even smoked. Be adventurous! Try them all!

The milder peppers like bell (*chile morrón* or *pimiento*) and anaheim (*poblano*) are typically found in the fruit and vegetable stands.

CORN / *ELOTE (MAÍZ)*

HIGH IN: Vitamin B6, Fiber, Magnesium, Manganese, Selenium, Thiamin, Phosphorus, Protein, and Niacin.

ALSO CONTAINS: Copper, Iron, Zinc, Riboflavin, Omega 6, Potassium, and Folates.

Corn is one of the most important and versatile crops of the Americas. When grown naturally, it contains tons of **vitamins, nutrients** and **protein**. The ancient Aztecs, Mayans, and many North American tribes used corn as the main staple food in their diets. Whereas corn has now found its way into almost everything we eat it the form of sweeteners, starch, bulk fiber, or animal feed, it is still used in Mexican cuisine the way it has been used for centuries to make tortillas, *tamales*, *pozole*, *atoles*, and more.

The ancient Mexican people saw themselves as the "People of Corn." They prayed to the God of Maize, *Centeotl*, and understood that the corn, or maize, was an essential part of their diet. Legend has it the *Quetzalcoatl*, the creator God of the East, turned himself into a black ant and brought forth maize kernels from deep within the Mountain of Sustenance to strengthen the newly created and weak, developing humans.

In Mexico, corn grains are soaked and cooked in an alkaline solution like limewater, a process called nixtamalization, to increase the nutrient content, reduce toxins, make them easier to grind and easier to digest. Native Americans used a similar process, cooking with ash, to produce hominy - processed, dried, and preserved corn kernels.

Corn, a fruit by botanist definition, is high in folic acid, a B vitamin that prevents dangerous homocysteine buildup and aids in enzyme metabolism and DNA synthesis and guards against neural-tube defects at birth. It is very rich in fiber, which helps in digestion and lowers the threat of disease. Corn is full of antioxidants that are necessary for growth and good health. It even contains trace nutrients like selenium and manganese.

Unfortunately, in much of North America, the quality of corn has been compromised to produce higher yields. Take advantage whenever you can and try authentic red, blue, white, brown, or black corn. This type of corn may or may not be organic, but it is most likely GMO-free.

HOW TO EAT CORN: In Latin America, *maíz* is the whole plant or dried, processed product and *elote* is the corn-on-the-cob. In Central America you may hear the name *choclo* used. *Masa* is the ground corn flour used to make tamales or tortillas. *Masa harina* is basically polenta and *maizena* is cornstarch. Each of these products is sold separately throughout the markets. You can find *elote* or *choclo* either cooked or uncooked to suit your needs.

EGGPLANT / *BERENJENA*

HIGH IN: Fiber, Vitamin K and B6, Folates, Antioxidants, and Sodium.

ALSO CONTAINS: Manganese, Iron, Copper, Potassium, and Vitamins B1, B3 and B5.

Eggplant, also known as aubergine, isn't an overly nutritious food. More than anything else it boasts high levels of **fiber** and **antioxidants**. Of course those are two crucial components to a healthy diet. Research states that chlorogenic acid is the dominant antioxidant compound found in eggplant. It is antimutagenic, meaning it protect cells from mutating into cancer cells, antiviral, and has the capacity to fight free radicals and lower bad cholesterol.

High levels of nasunin, a phytonutrient flavonoid, are found in eggplant. Nasunin is known to help protect the fats surrounding the cell membranes of the brain. The purple skin of eggplants contains phyto-chemicals called anthocyanins. These antioxidants have potential health effects against cancer, aging, inflammation, and neurological diseases.

Eggplant has the ability to absorb cooking oil and other flavors it's cooked with almost like a sponge. The high fiber in eggplant helps maintain a healthy digestive track and lengthens the feeling of fullness after eating.

HOW TO EAT EGGPLANT: Berenjena is found in the vegetable sections of most markets. They are of a deep purple color and an oblong bulb shape, ranging from hand size to head size. The inner "meat" of the eggplant is of an off-white color and full of tiny edible seeds. The tough skin is edible, as well, and contains beneficial compounds. Check for soft spots, wormholes, or discoloration when selecting *berenjena*.

Many people like to soak their eggplants in salty water before cooking to take out some of the bitterness. You can cut the bulb into cubes or flat strips and soak them for an hour in a bowl of purified water with a tablespoon of salt. If you want your eggplant to absorb more flavor during cooking, instead of soaking them, lightly salt the cut pieces and set them between two dry paper towels with a plate or something heavy on top for an hour. The salt and paper towels will draw out the bitterness. The drier eggplant will absorb oils, spices, salsas, and marinades.

Eggplant should be cooked until it's quite tender. Alternately you can cut it into flat, wide strips and grill it. Try rubbing a little olive oil over the strips first.

MEXICAN TRUFFLE / *HUITLACOCHE*

HIGH IN: Lysine, Vitamin B6, Fiber, Magnesium, Manganese, Selenium, Thiamin, Phosphorus, Protein, and Niacin.

ALSO CONTAINS: Copper, Iron, Zinc, Riboflavin, Omega 6, Potassium, and Folates.

Hiutlacoche is essentially a plant disease caused by the pathogenic fungus Ustilago maydis, which infects otherwise healthy corn plants. This "smut," long detested by American farmers as merely a blight, feeds on the corn, decreasing the overall yield. Plant ovaries are attacked, making the kernels erupt with greyish-black pus, forming mushroom-like nodules all around the ear. These nodules are a sought-after culinary delicacy in Mexico.

The word huitlacoche (or *cuitlacoche*) comes from the ancient Nahuatl language. The best translation sums the name up to mean "sleeping excrescence," referring to the fungus's ability to stunt the corn's development, leaving it thus "sleeping," and the tumors then formed by the infection. Huitlacoche was used by the Aztecs as a staple food often found in tamales and stews. Past civilizations like the Aztec or Zuni people viewed the mushroom-like growth as a symbol of life and used the fungus medicinally, sometimes to induce labor. The parasite actually forces metabolic change inside the corn, creating new, healthier nutrients.

Huitlacoche is packed with unique **proteins**, **minerals**, and **nutrients** that didn't exist in the corn's original state. It contains a very high level of lysine, an essential amino acid needed to make strong bones and fight infection. Lysine helps to build muscle and keep skin looking young. The combination of amino acids in huitlacoche and corn, together, form a high-quality complete protein. Huitlacoche also contains more disease-fighting Beta-glucans than oatmeal. These are sugars found in the cell walls of cereals, yeast, bacteria, algae, fungi, and some plants, such as oatmeal or barley. Their soluble fibers help to reduce the risk of heart disease by lowering cholesterol in the blood. Though not technically a mushroom, corn fungus contains ergothioneine, an antioxidant amino acid found in mushrooms known to boost the immune system and protect against the formation of cancer-causing free radicals.

Many farmers regard infected *maíz* as "devil's corn," but more and more chefs are introducing huitlacoche to the American and European pallets as the "Mexican Truffle." Its slightly smoky, earthy, nutty, mushroom-like edge meets a creamy, sweet corn, almost cheesy middle that diners go crazy for. Traditionally, it makes an appearance in Mexican quesadillas, tacos, empanadas, enchiladas, or stews. People joke that huitlacoche isn't much to look at but once someone's tasted it, they'll always crave it.

Huitlacoche, as a disease, can destroy farm machinery and decimate 5 to 10 percent of a crop. As a culinary delicacy, it can be produced inexpensively but sold for over 5 times the price of ordinary corn. Some US farmers have begun to purposely infect sections of their crop in order to produce greater profit, harvesting the excrescences when they are about 2 to 3 weeks old.

HOW TO EAT MEXICAN TRUFFLES: Huitlacoche can be found in the special interest sections or around the outer circles of most Mexican markets. You may find it near someone selling nopal cactus pads or squash flowers. It looks almost like dirty grey, deformed teeth. The chunks range from thumbnail to thumb-sized. It can be cooked like any mushroom or vegetable.

OKRA / *OKRA*

HIGH IN: Vitamins C and K, Manganese, Folates, Magnesium, Fiber, and Calcium.

ALSO CONTAINS: Vitamin A, Riboflavin, Thiamin, Potassium, Protein, Copper, Phosphorus, Zinc, and Vitamin B6.

Okra, or gumbo, has been classified as a superfood for its exceptionally high **nutrient** and **vitamin** offering. One cup of okra can provide you with about 150% of the daily recommended intake of vitamin K, 130% of manganese, 90% of folates, 50% of vitamin C, 30% of fiber, and 10% of protein among many others. It is one of the green vegetables with the highest levels of **antioxidants**.

The **fiber** found in okra is of a superior quality and helps maintain the health of the gastro-intestinal tract. The fiber works hand in hand with okra's mucilage to control the absorption rate of sugar into the bloodstream and they help to trap excess cholesterol, metabolic toxins, and surplus bile, slipping it out through the stool. The mucilage assures easy passage of waste from the body, sooths irritated membranes, and creates temporary protection for the intestinal tract.

Okra is very alkaline and helps neutralize overactive acids. It can treat ulcers and keep joints limber. The calcium present in okra, as well as in many green vegetables, is easily absorbed by the body. Okra contains a good dose of **amino acids**, including L-tryptophan and sulfur amino acids.

Available in most Mesoamerican regions, okra is normally very affordable and extremely nutritious. It is used for maintaining healthy skin, relieving constipation, treating symptoms of asthma, weakness, exhaustion, lung inflammation, and sore throat. It can help prevent diabetes, cataracts, atherosclerosis, and the effects of trans fats.

Okra seeds can be roasted and ground and make a caffeine-free substitute for coffee.

HOW TO EAT OKRA: Okra, okre, or *okro,* is grown throughout Mexico and Central America. It is not always apparent in the markets, but if you ask around enough you can usually find it. The pods are green, round with ridges, about four inches long with a pointy tip. They almost resemble green chilies.

Some people are turned off by the texture of okra. You can control this to a point depending on how you cook it, but the slimy part is very good for you. Okra can be sliced raw and added to salads, breaded and pan-fried, grilled, or cooked up in a soup. It's great in a coconut curry. It can be sautéed to top off a rice plate or stuffed and baked. Experiment!

PUMPKIN / *CALABASA*

HIGH IN: Vitamins A and C, Potassium, Fiber, Copper, Manganese, Copper, and Riboflavin.

ALSO CONTAINS: Iron, Phosphorus, Magnesium, Vitamin B6 and E, Folates, Niacin, and Zinc.

"Calabasa" is a term used in Latin America to describe many forms of squash. The kind I'm talking about here is the typical big, orange, Halloween-style pumpkin.

Pumpkin flesh is extremely high in **vitamin A,** a powerful natural **antioxidant** that is required by the body to maintain the integrity of skin and mucus membranes. Vitamin A is also essential for vision and can help protect against certain cancers. A cup of mashed pumpkin provides about 245% of the recommended daily intake of vitamin A.

The antioxidant zeaxanthin is also found in pumpkin. Zeaxanthin filters ultra-violet rays inside the macula lutea in the retina of the eyes. This helps protect against eye damage and age related degeneration of the vision.

Pumpkin is also rich in antioxidant carotenoids like alpha and beta-carotene, which are known for keeping immune systems strong and healthy, reducing inflammation, breaking down the buildup of cholesterol, preventing cataract formation, and slowing the aging process.

Zinc also boosts the immune system, promotes reproductive health and adds to bone density, preventing osteoporosis. Magnesium is required for the maintenance of bones and teeth and various biological functions.

Both pumpkin flesh and seeds contain the **amino acid** L-tryptophan, which counteracts depression and creates a general sensation of wellbeing. The phytosterols present in pumpkin can replace cholesterol in the body and lower cholesterol levels in the blood. Regular consumption of pumpkin and squash (flesh and seeds) has the potential to improve health remarkably.

HOW TO EAT PUMPKIN: Calabasa applies to many forms of squash both spherical and oblong. They come in many colors and sizes with many other titles. In Guatemala, many pumpkin-like squash are called *ayote*. *Chilacayote* and *güicoy* are other names you may hear. *Caiba* and *tacaco* are smaller, similar vegetables you may want to try.

Calabasas are sold all over the markets. They are sometimes available with other vegetables and sometimes sold at stands on their own. All parts but the stem are edible, however some have tougher skin that is very difficult to chew if it isn't thoroughly cooked. If you don't enjoy the skin you can cut the flesh away from it. Certain *ayote* are very challenging to open and may require a hammer or big rock to break them into smaller pieces. Once they are cooked, they soften considerably.

Pumpkin and its extended family can be cut or broken into pieces and then boiled, steamed, baked, or roasted. It can later be mashed or puréed and served like potatoes. Try it with grilled zucchini. The seeds can be eaten raw, boiled, or toasted. They are highly nutritious and contain much protein.

SQUASH / *CALABASA* (Mexico) *AYOTE* (Central America)

HIGH IN: Vitamins A and C.

ALSO CONTAINS: Vitamins B6 and E, Manganese, Potassium, Folates, Fiber, Phosphorous, Magnesium, Niacin, and Iron.

Although there are many types of squash available in Mesoamerica, this page focuses more on the winter variety like pumpkins, butternut, or acorn. The summer varieties are covered on the zucchini page. Winter squash tends to have a tougher skin than summer squash, though it is still edible and full of **nutrients**.

Winter squash are an excellent source of carotenes, strong cancer-fighting pigments found in richly colored vegetables and fruits. The abundant **fiber** found in squash plays a major role in eliminating toxins from the body and preserving prostrate health. Squash helps maintain good vision and protects skin from damaging sun exposure and dehydration. The vegetable contains coumarins, nutrients that interact with others in the body to thin out the blood, lowering blood pressure. The manganese present in squash helps to build bones and create enzymes as well as process fats, carbohydrates and glucose.

HOW TO EAT SQUASH: There are many varieties of *calabasa* or *ayote*. Sometimes vendors don't specify or have a particular name for each. Squash is typically sold in the fruit and vegetable sections of the markets. Some kinds of squash have such a tough skin that they have to be broken with a hammer or big rock... or conversely smashed on the ground to be opened.

Ayote, probably from the Nahuatl word *ayotli*, are best steamed or baked as boiling robs the food of valuable nutrients. The peel is an integral part of the food and should not be discarded. The seeds are also edible and can be dried or toasted as desired. When steaming squash, check both the flesh and peel to make sure they are soft enough to be eaten.

ZUCCHINI / *CALABACÍN*

HIGH IN: Vitamin C, Fiber, Potassium, Manganese, Niacin, and Antioxidants.

ALSO CONTAINS: Vitamin A and K, Riboflavin, Magnesium, Phosphorus, and Copper.

Zucchini, like many green vegetables, is a good source of **antioxidants** and **vitamins**. It is similar to most vegetables featured in this book in that it is high in **nutrients** and low in calories, making it a good choice for people who wish to lose weight.

The peel of the zucchini is rich in dietary **fiber**. This fiber helps move food through the digestive system and can lower cholesterol in the body by binding itself to bile acids that the liver makes from cholesterol for digesting fat. The fiber attaches itself so well that it immediately forms a crowd and makes it more difficult for the fat to be digested, thus forcing the liver to create more bile acid from existing cholesterol in the body.

Vitamins A and C work as antioxidants and can further help this digestive process by preventing the cholesterol from oxidizing and potentially causing atherosclerosis or colon cancer.

Zucchini also has a positive effect on the cardiovascular system. It contains a good amount of the intra-cellular electrolyte, potassium, which helps regulate blood pressure, can relieve stress, and protect against heart attack, stroke, and other serious health conditions.

Zucchini contains a notable amount of manganese, which helps the body metabolize proteins and carbohydrates, aids in the production of sex hormones, and catalyzes the synthesis of fatty acids and cholesterol. Manganese is also essential for the production of proline, an amino acid that promotes the formation of collagen, thus allowing for healthy skin and proper wound healing.

Zucchini has a high water content and can help keep the body hydrated. It also has the potential to help cure asthma, lower homocysteine levels, prevent the onset of multiple sclerosis, support the arrangement of capillaries, and aid in proper prostate function.

HOW TO EAT ZUCCHINI: Calabasín is sold in the vegetable sections of the markets. In many countries of Central America, it is still called "zucchini." The skin of the fruit is edible and contains many vitamins and fiber. If you choose to eat the whole *calabasín*, make sure to wash it thoroughly.

Zucchini can be sautéed and added to salads or pastas. It's great on sandwiches. If you have access to a grill, try lightly coating strips of zucchini in olive oil (or leaving them dry) and cook them over the fire.

Cactus & Coconut

ALOE VERA / *SÁVILA*

HIGH IN: Fiber, Vitamins A, B1, B2, B6, C, and E.

ALSO CONTAINS: Protein, Magnesium, Manganese, Zinc, Copper, Chromium, Calcium, Potassium, and Iron.

Aloe vera is actually a member of the succulent family rather than the cactus family. The gel of its inner leaves is widely used as a topical ointment to treat skin disorders, burns, insect bites, wounds, rashes, and acne. The components found in aloe leaves have cleansing and anti-septic properties, which act powerfully against bacteria, viruses, fungi, and yeast. Aloe gel is known to heal scars, skin blemishes, and chronic itch. The properties of aloe let it penetrate quickly through the skin layers and even as deep as muscle tissue and bone, making it very useful in rejuvenating tissue cells, keeping skin healthy, bright, elastic and wrinkle-free.

Aloe vera can also be taken internally to treat blood pressure, internal tissue damage, arthritis, ulcers, digestive disorders, heartburn, irritable bowel syndrome, and to boost the immune system. It also aids as a laxative. 20 out of 22 **amino acids** are found in aloe gel, including 7 of the 8 essentials. Aloe is rumored to help in the absorption of the **vitamin** B12. It contains plant sterols, which may help to prevent heart disease and phytochemicals known as saponins which are may improve the immune system, cholesterol levels, and bone health.

An enzyme found in aloe vera is thought to stimulate hair growth. Using the gel as a shampoo can aid in blood circulation, lowering stress, and reversing symptoms of hair loss. Applying a mask of aloe gel to the face from time to time can help treat acne and wrinkles. The use of aloe is well known to treat sunburns. A little gel applied to the toothbrush with toothpaste can help prevent gum disease and strengthen immunity in the mouth.

HOW TO EAT ALOE VERA: Sávila can be bought at most markets, though you may need to ask several times to find it. Start in the vegetable stands and see where they lead you. *Sávila* is sold by the leaf. Look for long, flat, green, pointy leaves with small spines along each side. They look something like devils' tongues.

When you are ready to eat it, cut widthwise into the leaf. A section of about two inches could be considered a portion. Only cut one portion at a time and leave the rest intact. The leaf should be refrigerated if possible. The open end will seal itself. Now cut away the outer green part and save it for later. Toss the gooey gel into a blender and mix it up with your favorite juice. The flavor of plain aloe isn't exciting... actually a bit unpleasant, but other fruits or veggies easily mask it when blended together.

The inside layer of the leftover green skin can be used to apply to the face, body, or to treat a cut. Wipe it where you want it and let it sit about 20 minutes before washing it off.

COCONUT MEAT / *CARNE DE COCO*

HIGH IN: Saturated fat, Fiber, Manganese, Copper, Selenium, and Iron.

ALSO CONTAINS: Protein, Phosphorous, Potassium, Zinc, Magnesium, and Folates.

Coconut meat is the solid white stuff found on the inside of the coconut "canon ball." The quantity and density of the meat differs depending on the age of the nut. Whereas younger coconuts are used for drinking, older coconuts are better for their meat content. More mature or "dry" coconuts are used to make coconut milk. The milk is made by blending the coconut meat with the remaining coconut water, or by using normal drinking water when necessary. The older a coconut becomes the thicker and tougher its meat gets. Most people prefer to eat the tasty, smooth meat from a mid-aged coconut.

Like coconut water, coconut meat is a natural health booster. Its **fiber** helps relieve constipation and aids in proper bowel function. The oils found in coconut work as antibacterials and antifungals preventing ulcers, gum disease, ringworm, athlete's foot, thrush, pneumonia, and other diseases. Coconut can help protect the skin from the harmful effects of the sun and promote healthy complexion and beautiful hair.

Coconut meat is high in manganese, a trace mineral that helps metabolize **fats** and **proteins**. Manganese also supports both the immune and nervous systems and stabilizes blood sugar levels. It also aids in the assimilation of other **nutrients** like iron. One cup of coconut meat contains 14 percent of the recommended daily intake of potassium and 39 percent that of copper. Copper aids in your sense of taste and is important for the production of red blood cells.

Coconut improves the absorption of calcium and magnesium and supports the development of strong bones and teeth. Although coconut meat is high in saturated fats, these fats are made up of primarily *medium chain* fatty acids. Unlike *long chain* fatty acids, they do not contribute to high cholesterol because they can be broken down much more easily in the body. Research suggests that moderate consumption of coconut may even help to lower bad cholesterol levels.

For centuries, the coconut has been used in traditional medicine to cure or treat a number of diseases and health problems including: constipation, malnutrition, upset stomach, vomiting, weakness, flu, gingivitis, jaundice, asthma, Herpes, dysentery, typhoid, pancreatitis, intestinal worms, throat infections, gonorrhea and urinary tract infections to name a few.

HOW TO EAT COCONUT MEAT: Carne de coco is usually just scooped out the same coconut used for drinking. When the water runs out the coconut is cut in half with a machete and the meat can be scooped out with a spoon. However, if the coconut is very young it might not contain much meat. On the other hand if it's too mature the meat turns hard and is very difficult to get out. If the meat can't be removed simply with a spoon you may try to cut it into squares with a knife and pop them out one by one with a spoon. A flat screwdriver can be handy as well as the small tools sold in paint stores to open paint cans.

Near to the markets you can often find delicious, fresh *carne de coco* for sale in small plastic bags. Check the freshness and if you're in Mexico you may want to try it with hot chili sauce and lime!

COCONUT WATER / *AGUA DE COCO*

HIGH IN: Potassium, Manganese, Magnesium.

ALSO CONTAINS: Vitamin C, Riboflavin, Niacin, Thiamin, Iron, Zinc, Folates, and Calcium.

The curious thing about coconut water is that it's practically identical to human blood plasma. Coconut water (not to be confused with coconut milk) has been used in blood transfusions in tropical regions. The juice is completely sterile, stored inside the coconut's impenetrable shell, and the electrolytes it contains match the electrolyte balance of human blood. During World War II, in emergency situations surgeons saved the lives of wounded soldiers in the pacific thanks to coconut water, straight outta the nut!

Coconut water has high levels of the electrolyte potassium. Potassium reacts with sodium in the body to create the electrical impulses needed for energy and muscle contraction. These same impulses are those that drive the heartbeat and maintain nerve conduction. Low levels of potassium or sodium in the body can lead to physical fatigue.

Completely compatible with the body, coconut water is a pure and natural isotonic drink with sugars, **vitamins, minerals,** electrolytes, enzymes, **amino acids,** cytokine and phyto (plant-based) hormones all in perfect balance. It is quickly absorbed into the bloodstream and extremely beneficial to human health. The fluid is composed of many bioactive enzymes that aid in digestion and metabolism.

Cytokinins are a class of phytohormones believed to have many anti-aging and anti-carcinogenic properties. This group of hormones regulates growth, development and aging. The level of *cytokinins* in the body can determine the rate at which cells eventually undergo degenerative changes and die. When there are more of these phytohormones available the cells enjoy a longer period in their round, plump, youthful state allowing for more elasticity and better hydration throughout the skin. The effects are also noted below the surface in muscles, bones, and connective tissues. Overall, coconut water and oil are said to produce many anti-aging effects on the body.

Coconut water contains *lauric acid* which is present in the milk of breastfeeding mothers. In tropical regions coconut water is often fed to newborn babies. It is viewed as superior to processed infant formula. It has other properties that can be very helpful in breaking up and preventing the formation of kidney stones. Drinking coconut water with a teaspoon of olive oil for three days is believed to kill intestinal and stomach worms.

Coconut water also contains *monolaurin*, an anti-viral, anti-bacterial monoglyceride used to kill viruses such as HIV, Herpes, flu, and various pathogenic bacteria. Coconut water is great for treating hangovers and helps reduce vomiting. This fantastic fluid is also believed to relieve urinary ailments, detoxify the body, improve immunity, reduce high blood pressure and bad cholesterol, rehydrate the body, increase metabolism, boost energy, and control diabetes.

HOW TO DRINK COCONUT WATER: In Latin America, *agua de coco* is usually only found near to the coasts or in the big cities where there is a demand. Often times someone with a machete will be selling young, green, ready-to-drink coconuts out of the back of a pickup truck. They are not typically sold inside the markets but usually on a street corner near to the markets. Many times *agua de coco* will be offered in small plastic bags with pieces of the soft meat inside and a straw sticking out of the top. If you buy the whole coconut, don't forget to ask them to cut it in half ("*Usted puede partirlo, porfavor?*") when you finish drinking the water so you can scoop out the meat. A karate chop hand motion usually gets the message across if you don't speak Spanish.

PRICKLY PEAR CACTUS / *NOPAL*

HIGH IN: Fiber, Protein, Vitamin C, Calcium, and Antioxidants.

ALSO CONTAINS: Vitamin A, B1, B2 and B3, Magnesium, Potassium, and Iron.

The nopal cactus has roots in Mexican mythology. One legend states that the displaced *Mexica* tribe was led by a vision given to them by their god, Huitzilopochtli. They were instructed to search until they encountered an eagle with a snake in its mouth. They wandered through the desert for many centuries until they came upon an island of Lake Texcoco. There they witnessed an eagle perched on a nopal cactus gripping a snake in its beak. The people recognized this sign and settled on the island, eventually building the great Aztec capitol, Tenochtitlan. In Nahuatl, nopal is translates to *nochtli*, and Tenochtitlan means "*place of the nopal.*" The emblem on the Mexican flag represents this story.

Nopal cactus has been consumed for over 12,000 years for its legendary properties. Aztec kings and warriors believed nopal to be a supreme plant food. Both the pads and fruit can be eaten. The pads are a great source of soluble and insoluble **fibers**, high-quality **protein** and **antioxidants**. All 8 essential **amino acids** can be obtained from them, making the pads better amino acid providers than most other plants. Vegans and vegetarians need to make sure they get sufficient essential amino acids in their diet and the prickly pear cactus is a great place to start.

The fibers in nopal pads help slow the absorption of sugar into the bloodstream, maintain bowel regularity, and satiate hunger. Fiber also helps protect against certain cancers, reduce levels of bad cholesterol, absorb toxins, and clean the colon.

Prickly pear cactus contains a high amount of *mucilage*, which helps balance the pH of the stomach and sooth the mucus membranes of the stomach lining. It controls excess gastric acid production and is thought to stimulate the healing of stomach ulcers and reduce stomach inflammation. It is also believed alleviate joint pain, aiding in arthritis treatment. Many athletes use the juice of prickly pear fruit after workouts for its anti-inflammation and rehydrating properties.

The antioxidants in the pads help to lower oxidative stress and maintain healthy cells. They can help reduce the formation of plaque along blood vessel walls and slow the effects of aging. Consuming cactus before ingesting alcohol can counteract the effects of overdrinking by rehydrating the body and improving liver function, therefore relieving the rotten feeling of a hangover.

HOW TO EAT PRICKLY PEAR CACTUS: Nopal can be found in the vegetable or special interest (assorted stuff) areas of the markets. The size of the pads differs from about the size of one to two hands. They are green and flat and typically full of small spines. The spines need to be cut off before cooking or eating the plant. To do this quickly, scrape the pad horizontally with the blade of a sharp knife. Many times the cactus is sold de-spined and ready to eat. It may be offered in plastic bags, already cut into strips or squares. Once the pad has been cut, like most foods it begins to degenerate. If you have time and a good knife, I recommend buying the uncut cactus and preparing it yourself.

The nopal has a very distinct texture. Some people don't like it at first. It's chewy and gooey, not unlike asparagus crossed with okra. It bears a slight lemony taste and is best grilled or can be blended raw with other fruits and veggies to drink. Try it in tacos or quesadillas alongside grilled mushrooms or black beans.

Leaves & Greens

CHEPIL / *CHIPILÍN*

HIGH IN: Vitamin C, Iron, Calcium, Riboflavin, Thaimin, and Beta Carotene.

ALSO CONTAINS: Protein, Fiber, Niacin, and Phosphorus.

An herb fairly unknown outside of Southern Mexico and Central America, *chepil* is commonly found within that region. It is often used in tamales, soups, and quesadillas.

Little scientific study has been published about *chepil*. The Central American community regards it as a highly nutritious plant on par with moringa. The dried leaves are said to contain high levels of protein and other nutrients that could successfully battle malnutrition.

An old Mayan legend tells that *Chac*, the rain god, fell helplessly in love with *IxChel*, the moon goddess. Alas, his love was not returned and *Chac* grew angry, covering the entire sky with a veil of black clouds that obstructed the people's view of their beloved moon. The thick clouds churned and incessant rain fell for three years, flooding villages and destroying crops. When *IxChel* saw that the Mayans were destitute, on the verge of death, she succumbed to the only option she believed could save the people; to marry *Chac* and convince him with her beauty to put a stop to the endless storm. However, on their wedding night, after convincing him of this, *IxChel* escaped. She turned herself into tiny green leaves that fell from the sky like rain. These leaves were eaten by the people and saved them from certain demise. They were called "*Chepil-Ix*," which means 'leaves of the moon.'

HOW TO EAT CHEPIL: Known as *chepil* in Mexico and *chipilín* in Central America, the leaf is commonly found in the herb or vegetable sections of the markets. It is a medium-small green leaf that can be used like spinach or other leafy green. Wash it well and cut it up for a salad or cook it in a soup or with some veggies. Some say the dried leaves are more potent. They can be used to make tea.

EPAZOTE

HIGH IN: Vitamin C and Calcium.

ALSO CONTAINS: Manganese, Potassium, Iron, Copper, Zinc, Selenium, Vitamin A, and Antioxidants.

Epazote is an herb native to Mexico, Central and South America. It grows in many places like a weed but is traditionally used in Mexican cooking. The herb is said to curb the effect of flatulence caused by eating beans. Epazote, also known as *apazote*, wormseed, Jesuit's tea, or Mexican tea, adds a unique and savory taste to any dish. For these two reasons black beans are typically cooked with a few sprigs of epazote. Eggs and soups are also spiced up with this pungent leaf.

The ancient Mayans were accustomed to drinking epazote tea. Its leaves are composed of many monoterpene compounds, such as ascaridole, which are toxic to intestinal worms. Drinking epazote tea often is believed to help steer clear of worm infestation.

Epazote adds a distinct flavor in cooking. For people unfamiliar to herb it may be hard to place. The name of the plant is derived from the Náhuatl (Aztec) *epazotl*, meaning "skunk" (*epatl*) and "dirt, sweat" (*tzotl*). Many find it unappealing on its own, but the strength of the smell blends well with food and gives Mexican gastronomy that special touch.

HOW TO EAT EPAZOTE: Epazote is not easily found in markets south of Mexico. However the vegetable sections of Mexican markets will definitely carry the herb. *Epazote* can be cooked with beans, in soups, with vegetables, or made into a tea. It is a common ingredient in street foods like *sopes, huaraches, quesadillas,* etc... Use care when cooking as the taste is strong. A couple sprigs should usually do the trick. When found in Central America, the plant may be referred to as *apazote.*

*NOTE: Epazote can induce abortions in pregnant women. Use with caution.

KALE / *COL RIZADA*

HIGH IN: Vitamins A, C, and K.

ALSO CONTAINS: Manganese, Copper, Calcium, Potassium, Vitamin B6, Iron, Sulfur, and Magnesium.

Kale has been tagged a superfood due to its intensely high concentration of **vitamins** K, C, and A. One cup of kale contains more than the recommended daily intake of vitamin C, at least twice that of vitamin A, and six times the recommended intake of vitamin K.

Kale, per calorie, has more iron than beef and more calcium than milk. It's loaded with **antioxidants** and **fiber** and contains a good amount of sulfur. Kale contains many antiviral and antibacterial agents and is one of the best sources of beta-carotene. Kale also has strong anti-inflammatory properties and can help fight asthma, arthritis, and autoimmune disorders.

The ancient Greeks and Romans recognized kale for its healing and detoxifying nature. It's great for vision, skin, and cardiovascular support. Kale is a form of cabbage whose leaves don't grow into a head. It can be eaten raw or cooked. Studies show that there are benefits to both methods. However, when cooking kale, always steam or stir-fry it as boiling lets much of nutritional value escape into the water.

HOW TO EAT KALE: Col Rizada can be found in the fruits and vegetable areas of the markets. Kale leaves are tough and dark green with wild curly ridges along the sides. Wash it well and eat it raw in a salad, juice it, or steam it with some garlic and lemon (or lime) juice.

*NOTE: When you can't find kale, you can probably find chard (*acelga*). The taste, texture, and preparation options are similar. It's good to use in the place of kale.

LOROCO

HIGH IN: Protein, Fiber, Calcium, and Phosphorus.

ALSO CONTAINS: Vitamins A, B (niacin), and C.

Loroco is an edible flower native to southern Mexico and Central America. Originally known as *quilite*, meaning "edible herb," the flower bud has a long tradition is the region's gastronomy. Loroco is a natural aphrodisiac. The small, pulpous buds have an enticing buttery, nutty taste. They are often used in Salvadoran *pupusas*, sauces, or rice dishes. Loroco has spasmodic properties which help in relaxation.

Fresh loroco flowers are difficult to find outside of El Salvador or Guatemala. They have a unique taste enjoyed by many. Don't pass them up if you see them. You will be pleasantly surprised.

HOW TO EAT LOROCO: *Loroco* is sold in clusters of opened and unopened buds on a stem. The green unopened buds look like early 1900's stick grenades. The opened flowers are small and white. Normally the cluster is comprised of mostly partially opened buds. They are quite common in El Salvador but will require some effort to locate in other areas.

Loroco can be cooked or steamed and added to salads, pastas, soups, sandwiches, and just about whatever else you want. Try them on a creamy veggie pasta with crushed, roasted peanuts.

SOME OTHER EDIBLE FLOWERS OF INTEREST FOUND IN CENTRAL AMERICA:

PITO: A small red flower reminiscent of a bird's beak or tiny tongue. Make sure to buy mature red flowers because the unripe ones lack taste and texture.

FLOR DE IZOTE: This is the national flower of El Salvador. It is the medium-sized white flower that grows out of the tall, palm-like yucca plant. The flower is slightly bitter, but cooking with salt will reduce that some. Typically eaten on salads.

MORINGA OLEIFERA / *MORINGA*

HIGH IN: Protein, Fiber, Vitamins A and C, Potassium, Magnesium, Antioxidants, and Calcium.

ALSO CONTAINS: Zinc, Manganese, Phosphorus, and Copper.

Moringa, found in tropical zones around the world, has been dubbed by many cultures as the "Tree of Life" or "Mother's Best Friend." It thrives in almost impossibly dry climates with little or no human attention. Nearly every part of the tree can be utilized and is found to be beneficial to the human body.

Studies claim that moringa leaves contain seven times the **vitamin** C in oranges, four times the calcium in milk, four times the vitamin A in carrots, two times the **protein** in milk, three times the potassium in bananas and twice the amount of iron in spinach. The leaves are used in dry powder form, in teas, or added fresh to salads or cooked dishes. Dried leaves are rumored to have more **nutrients** than fresh.

Moringa seeds grow in long, skinny pods sometimes referred to as "drumsticks." Immature pods can be cooked up in soups or curries and are especially high in vitamin C. The meat of mature pods is used in soups and the seeds can be eaten like peas or roasted like peanuts. The seeds boast 18 **amino acids**, including all essential amino acids. They have anti-inflammatory and antiseptic qualities. Crushed seeds are known to purify dirty water, drawing out the impurities and rendering it drinkable.

Moringa has been used traditionally in Africa, India, and Asia for centuries in folk medicine. The bark of the moringa tree contains alkaloid compounds that support the nervous system. A juice is made from bark and leaves to treat diabetes and high blood pressure. The tree is believed to cure an estimated 300 diseases.

HOW TO EAT MORINGA: Moringa, sometimes called *morungai* or *malunggay* is rarely found in Latin American markets. Most people who consume parts of the plant have a tree in their yard or know where to find one. The trees grow wild and a little asking around will usually lead you to one. They appear sad and barren most of the year. The leaves are green and rounded, about the size of a fingernail. They grow symmetrically, evenly dispersed on both sides of the branch.

Cut a few small branches, tie them upside down, and hang them somewhere dry in the shade for about a week. When the little leaves are completely dry and crispy put them in a bag and crush them up or use a mortar and pestle if you have one on hand to grind the leaves into a powder. Of course, you can also grind dried leaves in a blender. This powder can then be sprinkled over cereals, added to shakes, tossed over salads, etc.

Fresh leaves can be eaten in salads or cooked in the place of spinach or other greens. A heaping tablespoon of dry or fresh leaves can be used to make tea. The unripe green pods can be cut up and cooked in soups or vegetable curries.

SAGE / *SALVIA*

HIGH IN: Vitamin K, Calcium, and Potassium.

ALSO CONTAINS: Vitamins A and B6, Manganese, Magnesium, and Iron.

Sage isn't so common in the markets. However, if or when you do find some it's worth picking up. Fresh leaves add a delicious touch to any meal and can be chewed fresh for good breath and oral wellbeing. Dried leaves make a fabulous tea.

Sage has a long history of use as a medicinal plant. It has both **antioxidant** and anti-inflammatory properties. It has been used to treat gingivitis, sore throat, and rheumatoid arthritis. It is known to be antimicrobial, anxiolytic (reduces anxiety), anhidrotic (prevents perspiration), and anti-hypertensive (counteracts high blood pressure).

Sage tea is a potent source of antioxidants that help defend against disease causing free radicals in the body. The tea has the ability to relieve tension and headaches and settle frayed nerves. Try some after a long, hot, turbulent chicken-bus ride.

HOW TO EAT SAGE: If you have trouble locating *salvia* in the local markets, try the naturalist shops (*tiendas naturistas*). They tend to stock a variety of herbs and medicinal items that don't make it to the general markets. Sage leaves are of a grey/green color, thin, fuzzy, and about two to three inches long. Try fresh or dried sage in your meals or as a relaxing tea in the afternoons.

SORREL / *ACEDERA*

Acedera is found in many Central American markets. It can be used in salads or soups. The leaves are long, green, and tongue shaped. They are said to be rich in Vitamins A, B9, and C and are also a good source of iron, magnesium, and calcium. Sorrel has a spicy, tangy flavor that adds a little pop to any plate. It loses a little of that when it's cooked.

HIERBA MORA (MACUY/QUILETE)

Hierba mora is of the nightshade family. In Guatemala it is known as *macuy* or *quilete*. The leaves are a little wider than *acedera* with a point at the tip. *Hierba mora* is great in soups, vegetable curry, or veggie rice dishes. Many nightshades have a reputation as being poisonous. Rest assured, if it's being sold in the market, it's safe to eat. Just use extreme caution picking wild leaves by yourself.

HOW TO EAT SORREL & HIERBA MORA: Acedera and *hierba mora* can be found at most vegetable stands in the larger Central American markets. They may be hard to distinguish at first so it doesn't hurt to ask. Use either in salads, soups, or sautéed in vegetable or rice dishes.

SPINACH / *ESPINACA*

HIGH IN: Vitamins A and K.

ALSO CONTAINS: Folate, Vitamin C, Manganese, Magnesium, Potassium, Iron, Fiber, and Calcium.

Unfortunately, many people overlook spinach when putting together a salad or adding some garnish to a plate or sandwich. Most types of lettuce are just about devoid of nutrients when compared to spinach. Although it may not have the satisfying crunch of iceberg lettuce, spinach can deliver a whole storehouse full of goodness for the body.

Spinach is extremely rich in **vitamins** A and K. Vitamin A strengthens and protects the barrier zones of the body, such as mucus membranes, respiratory, urinary, and intestinal tracts. It works to help filter what makes it into the bloodstream, thereby supporting the immune system.

Vitamin A, along with the carotenoids lutein and xanthene, is beneficial for eyesight. The three can help prevent blindness, cataracts, eye ulcers, and dry or itchy eyes.

Vitamin K is essential in maintaining strong, healthy bones. It promotes the fortification and mineralization of the skeletal system while simultaneously preventing the formation of calcium in the tissue, too much of which can lead to the hardening of arteries, causing heart attack or stroke. Vitamin K actually promotes the synthesis of *osteocalcin*, a **protein** beneficial for maintaining bone density and strength.

Spinach is said to contain more than a dozen individual flavonoid components working together to make it one of the toughest cancer-fighting foods available. The leaves contain a carotenoid that encourages prostate cancer cells to destroy themselves and prevents them from reproducing. *Kaempferol*, a powerful **antioxidant**, is also found in spinach. It prevents the formation of cancerous cells and reduces cancer cell proliferation.

It is believed that spinach can protect the brain from the effects of premature aging by preventing the harmful effects of oxidation on the brain. Some of the same antioxidants at work in the brain can help protect the body from osteoporosis, atherosclerosis, high blood pressure, and skin ailments.

HOW TO EAT SPINACH: Espinaca can be found in the fruit and vegetable sections of the markets. It is usually sold in bunches. Check for fresh, clean leaves without bruises or blemishes. The leaves should be thoroughly cleaned and disinfected.

Use *espinaca* in salads or sandwiches. It can be cooked, added to soups, or used raw in green juices. Some people say that spinach provides more antioxidants and **nutrients** when cooked. However cooking for too long or with too much heat can destroy all the good stuff. When cooking, try steaming your spinach as opposed to boiling. This allows the leaves to retain more nutrients that would otherwise be lost in the cooking water.

SQUASH FLOWER / *FLOR DE CALABAZA*

The squash flower is used often in Mexican cooking. It's easy to find in the markets or even growing on the side of the road in rural areas. It is typically used in quesadillas, soups, tamales, or sautéed veggie plates. The flower is slightly sweet and a little chewy. It adds texture, flavor, and color but is not extremely high in nutritional content. It does contain, of course, some **fiber**, **protein**, and a few **vitamins**.

HOW TO EAT SQUASH FLOWERS: Flor de calabaza is not found in any one place in the markets. They are usually sold by whoever has them available at the time. Look in the vegetable sections or the assorted booths. You will sometimes see them with the herbs or the seeds or with an *abuela* on the corner. Look for closed, delicate orange and white blossoms about the length of your finger. They appear almost like crumpled up tissue paper and will be displayed in bags or on a tray.

The squash flower can be sautéed, steamed, or cooked and eaten whole. Try it with a black bean or vegetable soup, with rice and vegetables, or cooked up in a salsa. They are delicious!

TREE SPINACH / *CHAYA*

HIGH IN: Protein, Vitamin C, Potassium, and Calcium.

ALSO CONTAINS: Fiber, Vitamin A, Iron, Phosphorus, Niacin, Thiamin, Carotene, and Riboflavin.

More commonly known as *chaya*, tree spinach is believed to have originated in Mexico's Yucatan Peninsula. It was regarded as a miracle plant by the Maya and is still widely used in Mexico and some parts of Central America for its medicinal properties. It is believed to better blood circulation and vision, aid in digestion, increase calcium content in the bones, prevent anemia, as well as treat lung problems and diabetes.

Chaya is also said to improve liver, thyroid, and cerebral functions. Some say it reduces arthritic pain, acts as a decongestant, and helps keep the colon clean. *Agua de chaya* is a popular medicinal drink in the Mesoamerican region. The plant is believed to have substantially higher levels of **nutrients** and **vitamins** than most other leafy greens.

However, like many leafy green vegetables, tree spinach contains toxins. Although the plant is often consumed in raw form, it is not recommended to do so as the low levels of *hydrocyanic glycosides* (cyanide) compounds can create potential health risks. Steaming or cooking the leaves renders these toxins harmless and the food can then be consumed without worry. With that in mind, chaya should *not* be cooked in aluminum as a chemical reaction can occur which may cause diarrhea.

HOW TO EAT CHAYA: Chaya leaves are about the size of a small hand. The have three points and smooth curves. Not commonly sold in any distinct area of the market, you will have to look closely and ask around for it. Many families have a *chaya* plant in their yard, so the demand for market supply is low. The leaves are highly beneficial, though, and a little searching is worth the effort. *Chaya* may be more commonly found in Mexican markets. The word *chaya* in some other places like Nicaragua often refers to the *chayote squash*.

Chaya is often used as spinach in cooked dishes. It can also be used in salads, sandwiches, or teas. Some forms of *chaya* have small stinging hairs on the backside of the leaf. Heat destroys these hairs.

WATERCRESS / *BERRO*

HIGH IN: Vitamin K, A, and C.

ALSO CONTAINS: Protein, Manganese, Calcium, Potassium, Vitamin E, B6, and Magnesium.

Watercress is one of the world's oldest know vegetables, cultivated since ancient times for food and medicinal values in Europe, Central Asia, and the Americas. It is a nutrient-rich aquatic plant found in abundance near springs and slow moving waterways.

This magnificent herb has been dubbed numerous times as a superfood for its high **vitamin** content. Watercress is extremely rich in vitamins K and C. Vitamin K aids in forming and strengthening healthy bones. Adequate levels of vitamin K in the diet can help limit neuronal damage in the brain and, therefore, has a potential edge supporting the treatment of patients with Alzheimer's disease. It has been stated that 100 grams of watercress contain more vitamin C than an orange. Vitamin C helps maintain connective tissue, prevents iron deficiency, and boosts immunity.

Watercress leaves contain *gluconasturtiin*, a glucosinolate compound that gives the herb a sharp, peppery taste. Studies suggest that certain elements of *gluconasturtiin* work as powerful cancer preventing inhibitors.

Watercress is also a good source of **minerals** like copper, calcium, potassium, magnesium, manganese and phosphorous. For an herb, its leaves are surprisingly high in **protein**. The herb is believed to purify the blood, relieve phlegm, stimulate the thyroid, aid in weight loss, promote healthy hair and skin, normalize blood pressure, and help in digestion. Regular inclusion of watercress in the diet is found to prevent osteoporosis, anemia, vitamin A deficiency, and believed to protect from cardiovascular diseases and colon and prostate cancers. Hippocrates, the father of modern medicine, built his first hospital near to a stream where watercress grew.

HOW TO EAT WATERCRESS: Berro is a leafy green herb that looks similar to mint with rounded leaves. It can be found in the vegetable sections of the markets. Look for fresh, clean plants. After thorough cleaning, watercress can be used in salads or on sandwiches, cooked in soups, or even added to veggie drinks. The leaves and stems are both consumed.

NOTE: Due to its growing environment, watercress is prone to infestation by parasitic eggs and worms that thrive in aquatic conditions. Before eating, it is very important to thoroughly clean the leaves and stems. Wash it under clean running water and then soak it about half an hour in salt water. You can also use a commercial disinfectant of the type often sold as drops in markets and grocery stores.

Legumes

BLACK BEANS / *FRIJOLES NEGROS*

HIGH IN: Protein, Antioxidants, Fiber, Copper, Phosphorus, Manganese, Magnesium, and Iron.

ALSO CONTAIN: Calcium, Zinc, B6, Folic Acid, Thiamin, and Riboflavin.

Black beans are one of the most common beans available. Most beans share a very similar nutritional make up. They are high in dietary **protein** and **fiber**, which help regulate the absorption of sugar into the blood stream and keep you feeling fuller for longer. White beans by far have the most iron. Kidney beans are somewhere in the middle. Beans are high in **antioxidants** that work together with the fiber to clear out the intestines and eliminate cancer-forming free radicals. Beans are said to be very successful in reducing the risk of colon cancer.

Dry beans are a great source of low fat protein. They contain about 21 to 25 percent protein by weight and the little fat that they do contain is predominately **unsaturated fatty acids** (the good guys that stabilize the cholesterol in your blood). However, as black beans have the highest **amino acid** score, they, like all dried beans, are still missing one essential amino acid. That means that their protein is not "complete." Luckily, brown rice (which is missing a *different* amino acid) does contain what the beans lack. Thus, eating black beans and brown rice together "form" a complete protein. In many parts of Latin America this is called "*casamiento*" (marriage) and the two foods have been mixed and served this way for centuries.

Beans are packed full of complex carbohydrates to be converted to energy by your body. This energy fuels your muscles and brain. Dry beans also contain phytochemicals that can help reduce the risk of many diseases.

Black beans are extremely rich in *molybdenum*, a trace mineral that helps the body break down and detoxify sulfites. Many people have a negative reaction to the sulfites naturally present or added to certain foods like wine, salads, or some processed items. These sensitivities may cause rapid heartbeat, headache, or increased asthma symptoms.

HOW TO EAT BLACK BEANS: Frijoles negros and most other *frijoles* can be found in the seed and grain sections of the markets. They are usually sold in bags be the kilo or half kilo. Be sure to try the other types of *frijoles* as well: *PINTO* (red), *BAYO* (tan), *AZUFRADO HIGUERA* (yellow), *BLANCO* (white) and many, many more.

GAS ATTACK! Unfortunately beans also carry along some complex sugars that cause digestive issues. The enzymes necessary to break down these sugars are not available in the human body, therefore microbial reactions within the intestines can cause gas and, of course, flatulence.

But don't turn back! Pre-soaking and thoroughly cooking the beans should remove these sugars. It may also be necessary to toss out, rather than consume, the cooking water. Add a couple sprigs of *epazote* herb while you're cooking the beans and this will further help to lower the gassy effect.

Dried beans should be soaked for at least 8 hours before cooking. Cover them with plenty of water, as they will probably double in size during that time. Once soaked, drain and rinse the beans. Now you're ready to cook. For a black bean cooking recipe, see page 25.

CHICKPEAS / *GARBANZOS*

HIGH IN: Protein, Fiber, Folate, Manganese, Copper, Phosphorus, Iron, and Magnesium.

ALSO CONTAIN: Zinc, Potassium, Thiamin, Vitamins B6 and K, Selenium, and Calcium.

7,500-year-old remains of cultivated garbanzo beans have been found in the Middle East, making them one of the oldest domesticated crops. They are the base ingredients for foods like falafel and hummus. Garbanzos, or chickpeas, are very high in dietary **protein** and **fiber**. They are said to contain almost twice the amount of protein compared to cereal grains. The fiber in garbanzos helps to regulate cholesterol levels in the body.

Darker beans have a higher nutritional value. The outer husk of the seed contains many **vitamins** and **nutrients**. It is not necessary to discard this husk after the garbanzo has been cooked.

Garbanzos are a great source of the trace element *molybdenum*. They have exceptionally high levels of manganese and folate and provide a good amount of iron. Garbanzos also offer a notable amount of *selenium*, a trace mineral that works as a co-factor in antioxidant enzymes that protect the body from cellular damage. Selenium is also essential for normal functioning of the immune system and thyroid gland.

HOW TO EAT CHICKPEAS: Garbanzos can be found in the seed and grain sections of the markets. They are fingernail-sized, light to dark tan, wrinkly, balloon shaped beans.
Dried *garbanzos* can be soaked and cooked like any other beans (page 24).

FAVA BEANS / *HABAS*

HIGH IN: Protein, Fiber, Folate, Manganese, Copper, and Phosphorus.

ALSO CONTAIN: Magnesium, Iron, Potassium, Thiamin, Zinc, Vitamin B6, and Calcium.

Fava beans, broad beans, and butterbeans are all similar and often confused with lima beans or kidney beans. Many times in the markets any bean of this particular size or shape is sold as "*habas*." The fava will be of a light beige color. You can find them dried or toasted and occasionally fresh. You can't go wrong with any of the "broad beans," but the favas in particular are great to make a creamy hummus-like spread (page 34).

Broad beans contain L-Dopa, a precursor of neuro-chemicals in the brain such as dopamine, epinephrine, and nor-epinephrine. Dopamine in the brain is associated with mental clarity and smooth, controlled body movements. A diet high in fava beans my help prevent Parkinson's disease and dopamine responsive dystonia disorders.

A cup of fava beans provides almost half the daily-recommended intake of folates. Folates, along with B12, are the essential components of DNA synthesis and cell division. The beans also contain many **vitamins** that function as co-enzymes in carbohydrate, **protein**, and **fat** metabolism. They offer one of the highest plant sources of potassium, an important electrolyte of cell and body fluids.

HOW TO EAT FAVA BEANS: Habas can be found at most seed and grain stands in the markets. Look for kidney-shaped off-yellow beans about the size of the end of your thumb. If you want them to cook with, buy the dried or fresh beans. If you're just looking for a quick snack you can take the roasted and salted variety.

GREEN PEAS / *CHÍCARO* (Mexico) *ARVEJAS* (Central America)

HIGH IN: Protein, Fiber, Vitamins A, C and K, Manganese, Folates, and Thiamin.

ALSO CONTAIN: Phosphorus, Vitamin B6, Magnesium, Niacin, Riboflavin, Iron, Potassium, Copper, and Zinc.

Green peas are one of the most nutritious leguminous vegetables, rich in phytonutrients, minerals, **vitamins**, and **antioxidants**. Peas have exceptionally high levels of vitamins C and K, which aid in overall immune system strength, strong bones, and minimize damage to organs and body tissue. Vitamin C, in particular, has incredible potential in preventing or drastically reducing the development of almost all types of cancer. The other phytonutrients and antioxidants in green peas help in neutralizing the free radicals in the body, thereby reducing blood vessel damage and the accumulation of plaque on the artery walls. Peas contain the phytosterol *B-sitosterol*, which is good for lowering cholesterol levels in the blood.

Green peas are a great source of high quality **protein**. They have been found to aid in energy production, nerve function, and carbohydrate metabolism. Peas contain the special plant protein, *lectin*, which plays a major role in dissolving clumps of red blood cells that could later become problematic blood clots.

Peas can be useful in lowering cholesterol and homocysteine levels, strengthening eyesight, detoxifying the body, and supporting healthy organs, bones, and tissue.

HOW TO EAT GREEN PEAS: Chícharo or *arvejas* can be found in either the seed and grain areas of the markets or with the vegetables. When dehydrated, they are easy to confuse with dried green lentils. Fresh, dried, or frozen, peas can be boiled with or without salt until tender. Cooking times will vary depending on how you buy the peas.

Green peas can be eaten by themselves, in a salad, as a soup, or with rice and veggies. Some other pea variations you may want to try are: **SNOW PEAS** (*Arbejas Chinas*), **STRING BEANS** (*Ejote*), or **PURPLE STRING BEANS** (*Ejote Morado*).

INGA BEAN

HIGH IN: Protein, Fiber, Antioxidants, Calcium, and Phosphorus.

ALSO CONTAIN: Vitamin A, B1, and C.

This is a special treat. Affectionately known as the "ice cream bean" to many English speakers, the *Inga Edulis Mart* has many names throughout Latin America. In Mexico it is often called *cuil*; in Guatemala, *cushín*; in El Salvador, *paterna*; in Panamá, *guaba*, and in some regions it is known as *pacay*.

The beans are encased in a long, green pod that is jokingly referred to sometimes as a "*machete.*" Within the pod the seeds are wrapped up in a sweet, edible, cotton-like white **fiber** that tastes similar to vanilla ice cream. After feasting on the sweet stuff you can cook the beans with some salt to complete the nutritious snack.

Eating inga beans raw won't kill you, but they do contain a toxic compounds known as trypsin inhibitors (also found in soy beans) that prevent the production of the enzyme trypsin in the pancreas. Trypsin is needed in digestion as it converts **protein** into **amino acids**. Cooking the beans destroys this toxic compound.

HOW TO EAT INGA BEANS: Inga beans are found sporadically throughout Central America. They tend to be sold by individuals on the outer edges of the markets. The pods are brownish and almost the length of your forearm. The pod can be peeled apart and the "cotton" can be eaten raw. The beans should be boiled before eaten.

SIMILAR PODS: The "ice cream bean" is very unique, but some other pods are shaped the same. In Costa Rica you may want to try the **CARAO**, a long round, brown pod full of dark, sticky, chewy seeds. These slightly bitter seeds are said to be very high in iron and used to cure anemia.

Also in Costa Rica you can find the shorter orange/brown **GUAPINOL** pods, full of a chalky, powdery substance. This powder can be eaten raw (have a toothbrush ready… it's sticky!) or made into a drink. A basic drink recipe would be 2½ cups milk of choice, 2½ TBS *guapinol* powder, 2 TBS crushed cacao or cocoa powder, 1 TSP honey, and 1 TSP vanilla. Mix it all in a blender. But be prepared… you will probably need a hammer to break into the *guapinol* pod!

LENTILS / *LENTEJAS*

HIGH IN: Protein, Fiber, Folates, Manganese, Iron, Phosphorus, Copper, Thiamin, and Potassium.

ALSO CONTAIN: Magnesium, Vitamin B6, Zinc, Riboflavin, Niacin, Selenium, and Calcium.

Lentils are said to be one of the highest sources of plant-based **protein**. They can be cooked more quickly than most other legumes and can be prepared in many ways. Lentils were one of the first domesticated crops in the Near East and have become a staple food in many cultures. They can now be found all over the world.

Like most plant-based proteins, dry lentils are incomplete in that they are deficient in a couple essential **amino acids**. However, sprouting the lentils creates these amino acids therefore rendering the protein complete (see sprouting section). Of course, they can also be combined with brown rice or other grains in order to balance the amino acid factor.

Lentils are a great source of iron, an element that binds to certain proteins responsible for oxygen transport in the body. Iron absorption can be increased by the presence of **vitamin** C in the body, but decreased by excess calcium, magnesium, or zinc.

A half a cup of cooked lentils provides you with about a third of the daily requirement of **fiber**, but they also include some anti-nutritional properties that can block digestive enzymes or reduce the bioavailability of dietary minerals. Soaking the lentils in warm water overnight before cooking can reduce these effects.

Lentils are also packed with folate, an important B vitamin that protects against coronary artery disease, birth defects, and certain cancers.

HOW TO EAT LENTILS: Lentejas can be found in the seed and grain sections of the markets. You will find them available in myriad colors from brown to green, red, yellow, black, or pink. The brown pulses cook more quickly but tend to become mushy while the green lentils take more time to prepare, but hold their shape and are a great addition to salads.

It is not necessary to soak *lentejas* before cooking, but soaking will activate more of the positive properties of the lentils. Soaked or not the lentils will need to be boiled until tender. They are delicious by themselves or great with rice or soups.

PIGEON PEA / *GUANDÚ*

HIGH IN: Protein, Fiber, Folates, Manganese, Copper, and Phosphorus.

ALSO CONTAIN: Magnesium, Potassium, Iron, Zinc, Calcium, Niacin, and Selenium.

Pigeon peas are widely consumed on the Indian subcontinent, much of Africa, and parts of Asia. They are grown on most of the Caribbean Islands and commonly found in Costa Rica or Panama.

Pigeon peas are a well-balanced human food. The small green and black peas are highly nutritious and believed to cure cough, poisoning effect, stomach pain, gas troubles, swelling of internal organs, or acidity. The leaves of the plant are also used to treat jaundice, inflammation, urinary infections, and skin problems.

HOW TO EAT PIGEON PEAS: Guandules can be found at most markets in Costa Rica and Panama. They are small and of a mottled green and black color. The peas can be boiled alone or in a soup. They are great in a coconut curry. *Guandules* are frequently sold in cans premixed with coconut milk.

TEXTURED VEGETABLE PROTEIN / *CARNE DE SOYA*

HIGH IN: Protein.

ALSO CONTAINS: Iron, Phosphorus, Copper, Manganese, Zinc, Fiber, Calcium, and Potassium.

Textured Vegetable Protein, often referred to as "TVP," or "soy meat," is a highly processed meat imitation made from soybeans. TVP is derived from defatted soy flour. The end product are small, dried chunks that, when rehydrated, resemble ground beef. TVP, like tofu, absorbs whatever flavor the chef decides to give it. Therefore, it is often used as a meat substitute for vegetarians or even as a meat extender in non-veggie dishes. It has become widely used in impoverished communities an economic and nutritious alternative to meat.

TVP's main attraction is its **protein** content. A half-cup serving provides about 25 grams of protein. However, wide debates continue as to whether or not the protein provided is complete or not. Another benefit is that it is cholesterol free. TVP also contains a decent amount of **fiber**, iron, and other nutrients. Some manufacturers add vitamin B12 to their product. During the production process, raffinose, the hard-to-digest sugar in legumes that causes intestinal gas, is eliminated.

On the downside, TVP is often produced using hexane, a dangerous by-product of gasoline refining, to separate the fat from the protein. Traces of hexane may be found in the TVP. According to the EPA, hexane is both an air pollutant and neurotoxin. Soy also contains high levels of plant estrogens which, when over-consumed, may have negative effects on human health.

HOW TO EAT TEXTURED VEGETABLE PROTEIN: Carne de soya or *soya seca* can usually be found in the nuts and seeds sections of the markets. It may take a little hunting to track it down. They are small beige-colored crumbles sold by weight in plastic bags.

Soya seca acts like a sponge. If you want it to absorb flavor, it's best to leave it dry until you have the broth or marinade ready to go. By rehydrating with plain water before you cook it, the flavors have a harder time getting into the "meat." Rather, add the dry crumbles to the broth or soup directly. TVP can be used in place of ground beef for tacos, cooked with rice, added to chili or pasta sauce, used as a base in veggie burgers and much more. It is a highly versatile and easy to prepare product.

Seeds, Grains, & Nuts

ALMONDS / *ALMENDRAS*

HIGH IN: Protein, Fiber, Vitamin E, Manganese, Magnesium, Omega 6, and Riboflavin.

ALSO CONTAIN: Copper, Phosphorus, Potassium, Zinc, Calcium, and Iron.

Almonds, usually expensive, are worth what you pay for. The nuts are full of vital **proteins, vitamins,** and **minerals.** Almonds are eaten raw, toasted, or candied and can be used to make flour, milk, toppings, or breading.

Like most nuts, almonds are rich in unsaturated **fats,** which can help the body bring down bad cholesterol levels while feeding the muscles and organs the essential dietary fats they need to function properly. Almonds are an excellent source of the **antioxidant** vitamin E; 50 grams contain about 85% of the recommended daily intake. Almond skins contain a group of plant nutrients thought to protect the body from aging.

Almonds are high in fiber, helping you feel fuller faster. That coupled with their good cholesterol profile and ability to fight bad cholesterol makes them helpful in maintaining a healthy weight. Almonds are said to increase the blood flow to the vital organs and have, at times, been used as aphrodisiacs. The oil obtained from the nuts is very beneficial to the skin and often used as massage or hair oil. Because almonds are free of gluten, almond flour is gaining popularity as a gluten-free baking alternative.

Almonds contain a small amount of selenium which, combined with sufficient other sources, can help you meet your daily needs. Selenium, along with vitamin C, vitamin E, and beta carotene, works to block chemical reactions that create free radicals is the body. It helps stop damaged DNA molecules from reproducing, therefore it can help prevent tumors from developing.

HOW TO EAT ALMONDS: Almendras are found with the other nuts in the seed and grain sections of the markets. They are thin, wrinkly, light brown, bean-shaped nuts with a point a one end. Eat them raw, add them to your trail mix or salads, crush them and toss them over a dessert, or use them to make homemade milk (page 21).

AMARANTH / *AMARANTO*

HIGH IN: Protein, Folate, Fiber, Iron, Manganese, Magnesium, and Phosphorus.

ALSO CONTAINS: Selenium, Copper, Zinc, Calcium, and Vitamin B6.

Amaranth is one of the world's oldest grains. It was viewed as a sacred food source to Mexico's ancient Aztecs and also used by the Mayans and even the Incas as far south as Peru. During the conquest of Mexico, the Spanish became aware of the religious importance and nutritional value that amaranth held for the Aztecs and they destroyed all the plants they could find. It is now making a comeback.

In 1985 NASA sent amaranth into space to feed the astronauts who were then able to germinate plants in orbit. Amaranth grows in extremely adverse conditions, has a high nutritional value, and short growing season. During space flight in the shuttle the plant flowered and was able to remove carbon dioxide from the atmosphere and provide food, water, and oxygen for the astronauts.

Amaranth is extremely rich in high-quality, easily digestible **protein**. Some researchers believe that the protein found in amaranth is one of the most nutritious plant based proteins and could be considered on par with animal based proteins. A cup of the cooked grain is a great source of magnesium, necessary for normal heart rhythm, proper muscle contraction, and strong bones.

Amaranth grain also contains *squalene*, a strong **antioxidant** once found only in shark or whale liver oil. Squalene is able to treat or remove harmful pollution built up in the body by toxic substances in the environment, including car exhaust fumes and industrial waste. It is said that amaranth oil contains up to 8 times that of shark or whale oil. Squalene may eradicate or inhibit the growth of tumors and help reduce the effects of allergies, diabetes, arthritis, asthma, and to improve memory function.

The leaves of the amaranth plant, although harder to find, are exceptionally nutritious as well. They can be cooked and used in salads, soups, or sandwiches and are recognized to make a medicinal tea.

Although amaranth has a higher nutritional value than most other grains, it is still an incomplete protein. Combine it with beans, peanuts, or lentils to cover all your amino acid bases.

HOW TO EAT AMARANTH: Amaranto is not easily accessible in Central America. However, in Mexico toasted *amaranto* grain can be found at most markets. It looks like tiny popcorn. Uncooked grains look like small, tan poppy seeds but, unfortunately, are harder to find. The uncooked grains cannot be eaten raw, but can be cooked for about 20 minutes like quinoa, oats, rice, or other grains. They make a great breakfast cereal with fruit and honey or can be added to soups or pasta dishes. Amaranth does not contain gluten so ground flour made from the grain is a good alternative for people enjoying a gluten or wheat-free diet.

NOTE: You can toast your own amaranth seeds to make the little white popcorn-like balls you find in the markets. Heat a deep pot or pan over medium heat (no oil) and pour in about 2 TBS of amaranth seed. Don't put too much as they all need to be touching the hot surface. Stir the seeds around with a wooden spoon until they begin to pop. Have something ready to top the pot as the seeds are sure to go flying everywhere! Quickly remove from heat when most of the seeds have popped so they don't burn. Et voilà!

BARLEY / *CEBADA*
&
WHEAT BERRIES / *BAYA DE TRIGO*

HIGH IN: Protein, Fiber, Phosphorus, and Iron.

ALSO CONTAIN: Antioxidants, Selenium, Magnesium, Copper, and Vitamins B1 and B3.

Barley (a grain used to make beer) and wheat berries (the whole grain form of wheat flour) are commonly found in the markets. They are easily confused and sometimes sold as the same thing. Not to worry as both are nutritious and easy to prepare.

Either can be used as a rice substitute, in salads and soups, or even to make drinks (page 128). They have a crunchy, nutty flavor and are quite filling due to the high fiber content.

HOW TO EAT BARLEY OR WHEAT BERRIES: Cebada and *Baya de Trigo* would be found in the seed and grain sections of the markets. The two look almost identical as small, light brown, oblong seeds. Barley is a bit more pointed at the ends while wheat berries are more rounded.

Cooking either *cebada* or *baya de trigo* is more or less similar to cooking rice (page 23), though you may want to add more water.

BROWN RICE / *ARROZ INTERGRAL*

HIGH IN: Fiber, Manganese, Selenium, and Magnesium.

ALSO CONTAINS: Protein, Vitamin B6, Thiamin, Niacin, Calcium, Potassium, and Copper.

Unfortunately, the majority of rice eaters in the world now eat white rice. Brown and white rice are essentially the same grain, but white rice has been further processed to give it a longer shelf life, change the taste/texture, and make it easier to cook. The tough outer husk is peeled away and the grain is then polished, leaving it white. Sadly, the discarded layer contains most of the **nutrients** and **vitamins** that the rice has to offer. What's left afterwards isn't so nutritious.

Some big companies enrich their white rice, adding a few vitamins and **minerals** to the vacant grain. However, only a fraction of those vital elements are returned and many that are stripped away in processing are lost completely. The **fiber** available in brown rice is an example. Fiber helps satisfy your diet, aids in digestion, and is known to combat colon cancer. Polished white rice contains very little fiber.

White rice is converted more quickly to sugar and can cause sharp sugar spikes in the body. Studies show that eating white rice actually increases the risk of developing type 2 diabetes while a few helpings of brown rice each week can lower the risk of developing the disease.

Brown rice is very high in manganese, a trace mineral that helps derive energy from proteins and carbohydrates. Manganese is part of a compound known as superoxide dismutase, an **antioxidant** that prevents damage from free radicals created during the energy production process. It also plays a key role in the synthesis of fatty acids. The niacin present also aids in energy production. Brown rice contains selenium, which helps regulate thyroid function and has the potential to destroy cancer cells. Selenium also works together with vitamin E in protecting the body against heart disease, atherosclerosis, and stroke and is helpful in relieving the symptoms of asthma and rheumatoid arthritis.

Brown rice is believed to be beneficial in maintaining a healthy body weight. Studies suggest that the grain can help lower bad cholesterol levels and slow the progression of plaque build-up in the artery walls. Brown rice contains plant lignans, which can help protect against heart disease and certain types of cancer. Anti-inflammatory phytonutrients are found in brown rice as well as magnesium, a nutrient essential to maintaining strong bones.

HOW TO EAT BROWN RICE: Arroz intergral is not always easy to track down in the markets. Ask for it in the seed and grain sections, but it is not always available. *Arroz intergral* spoils more quickly that *arroz blanco* due to its husk and unprocessed state. You may also want to ask in the *tiendas naturistas* (health food shops).

For recommendations on cooking brown rice, please see page 23.

COCOA BEANS / *CACAO*

HIGH IN: Protein, Fiber, Magnesium, Iron, Antioxidants, and Phosphorus.

ALSO CONTAIN: Copper, Calcium, Potassium, Zinc, Sulfur and Vitamins C, E, and B-Complex.

Domesticated in Mexico almost 4000 years ago, cacao has now spread across the world, mostly in the form of chocolate. The Maya believed "*kakaw*" was a food of the gods. The beans were often used as currency in the Mayan and Aztec cultures. The word "chocolate" may have roots in the Aztec drink named "*xócoatl*," meaning bitter water. This was a bitter, frothy drink seasoned with vanilla and chili pepper said to be refreshing and invigorating.

Cacao is the base ingredient for dark chocolate. The beans are processed, ground, and sweetened to produce what is typically sold in stores. However raw cacao beans and processed chocolate are two very different food items. The information found here relates strictly to raw cacao.

Cacao beans are sometimes referred to as "Nature's Anti-Depressant." They contain three neurotransmitters associated with a healthy mood and positive state of mind: Serotonin, dopamine, and phenylethylamine. The beans, or seeds, also contain tryptophan and monoamine oxidase inhibitors, which allow the serotonin and dopamine to circulate longer in the bloodstream. Tryptophan, by producing serotonin, can lessen anxiety and reduce sensitivity to pain. These key elements are what often give people that euphoric feeling while eating chocolate.

Also present in cacao is magnesium, a **mineral** that supports the heart and cardiovascular system. Magnesium strengthens the heart and improves its ability to pump blood effectively.
Some research suggests that raw cacao provides one of the richest sources of **antioxidant** flavonols available. It is said to contain up to three times the levels found in green tea and twice that of red wine. These antioxidants can help protect your skin and organs from damages caused by cancer-inducing free radicals.

HOW TO EAT CACAO BEANS: Raw or toasted cacao beans are found throughout Mexico and Central America. They are most often discovered in the seed and grain areas of the markets but sometimes you will find them with the herbs or even vegetables. The beans are dark brown and oblong about the size of the end of your thumb. Look for raw beans (*crudos*), not toasted (*tostados*), as the heat will have killed many of the beneficial properties.

Cacao beans can be eaten raw if you enjoy the taste. They are slightly bitter. You can add them to smoothies or make delicious deserts. There are a number of good drinks that use ground cacao.

ALSO TRY PATAXTE! Pronounced "patáshte," *pataxte* are white cacao beans and the original base ingredient for white chocolate. They are much more difficult to find, so grab them when you can!

CASHEWS / *NUÉZ DE MARAÑON, NUÉZ DE LA INDIA*

HIGH IN: Protein, Copper, Vitamin E, and Manganese.

ALSO CONTAIN: Magnesium, Iron, Fiber, Phosphorus, Omega 6, and Vitamin K.

Cashews are actually seeds that grow on the underside of a curious tropical fruit called *jocote marañon*, or cashew apple. This fruit is said to have originated in South America, which leads us to believe that the other common name for cashews, the "India Nut," would have come about later. Portuguese originally delivered the *"caju"* to India where the tree flourished and India is now the world's largest producer and processor of the seed. The name *"marañon"* may have roots in the northern Brazilian state of Maranhao where the food was originally cultivated.

Cashews are well-balanced nuts rich in energy and **nutrients**. They are high in calories, but low in bad cholesterol, and in moderation have the potential to help maintain a healthy weight. Cashews contain selenium, an important micronutrient that works as a co-factor for **antioxidant** enzymes in the body and plays a role in the proper functioning and protection of the thyroid gland. The nuts also contain a small amount of *zea-xanthin*, an important flavonoid antioxidant that can help protect the inner eyes from UV damage and prevent age related eyesight problems.

The high levels of copper in cashews aid in the production of energy and melanin, a skin and hair pigment. Copper supports the development of connective tissue and bone, the cross linking of elastin and collagen, and the utilization of iron in the body. Copper is also necessary for proper brain function and used to break down the **fat** in your food.

The outer shell of cashew nuts, however, contains a toxic skin irritant called *urushiol*. Even though this caustic compound is not found in the nut itself, the oils from the shell don't allow for cashews to be eaten raw. The reaction caused by *urushiol* can be toxic or fatal. Therefore all cashew nuts are either roasted or sundried inside the shell to kill the toxins or roasted or fried after being shelled. The heat destroys the toxic compounds, rendering the seed fit to eat.

Want to prepare your own cashew nuts from some fresh fruit you bought? See page 27.

HOW TO EAT CASHEW NUTS: *Nuéz de marañon* (or *de la India*) can be found ready to eat in many places. If you don't find them in the markets, check in the super markets. The tan, moon-shaped nuts are never cheap. However, they cost less when you prepare them yourself. Of course each fruit only has one nut, so you would have to eat a big bag of *jocote marañon* in order to get just a handful of cashew nuts. And the curing process takes time.

Cashews can be added to breakfast cereals, trail mixes, or tossed into salads. They are delicious when used in cooking. Try them over rice and vegetables or in a curry dish. Cashews can also be ground and filtered to make milk or cream.

CHIA SEEDS / *SEMILLA DE CHÍA*

HIGH IN: Protein, Fiber, Calcium, Phosphorus, Manganese, and Omega 3.

ALSO CONTAINS: Copper, Zinc, and Omega 6.

The word "chia" comes from the ancient Mayan language and means strength. The plant was domesticated by pre-Colombian Mexican cultures about 4500 years ago. The tiny seeds have been experiencing a surge in popularity in recent years due to their phenomenal health benefits.

Chia seeds are a balanced blend of **protein, carbohydrates, fats,** and **fiber**. They are one of the only plant-based sources of complete protein. The seeds are exceptionally high in tryptophan, an **essential amino acid** that produces niacin and serotonin in the body. Tryptophan is known to aid in good sleep, relaxation, weight reduction, and mood stabilization.

The essential fatty acid omega 3 is plentiful in chia seeds. Essential fatty acids cannot be synthesized by the body, but must be obtained through diet. They are known to make cell membranes more flexible and to make nutrients more readily available. Omega 3 is highly important for brain and memory performance. It can also help to reduce pain or inflammation and protect against certain diseases and depression. Deficiencies in essential fatty acids can be detrimental to the immune, cardiovascular, nervous, and reproductive systems. Conversely, a diet rich in these beneficial fats can help lubricate joints, boost metabolism, and promote lean muscle mass.

Chia is an excellent source of **antioxidants**, said to contain even more antioxidants than blueberries. The levels of antioxidants present in the seeds help the oils from going rancid, aiding to a much longer shelf life. They also contain strontium, which helps to assimilate protein and produce high energy. The seeds are said to have almost five times more calcium than cow's milk.

HOW TO EAT CHIA: Chía is known as *"chan"* in Guatemala and El Salvador. Usually sold in small plastic bags in the seed and grain sections of the markets, they are tiny black and grey pellets, not unlike poppy seeds in appearance.

Chía can be eaten raw. The seeds do not need to be ground to ensure absorption, like flaxseed. Grinding them before eating, however, does allow the body to take advantage of more of their benefits. Ground or whole they can be tossed into a juice or smoothie, or over a salad or pasta.

A typical drink consumed in Mexico and Central America is *"chía fresca,"* fresh fruit juice or limeade with a few tablespoons of *chía* seed. Submerged in liquid for at least twenty minutes, the seeds transform into a gelatinous substance believed to benefit stomach and digestion. *Chía* seed can also be ground into flour and used in baking or added whole to breads or puddings.

FLAXSEED / *LINAZA*

HIGH IN: Protein, Fiber, Omega 3, Antioxidants, Manganese, Magnesium, Phosphorus, Copper, Selenium, Iron, Calcium, Potassium, and Zinc.

ALSO CONTAINS: Omega 6, Thiamin, Folate, Vitamin B6, and Niacin.

Flaxseed, or linseed, is extraordinarily high in nutritional value. It boasts exceeding **antioxidant** and anti-inflammatory properties. The seeds are extremely rich as a complete **protein** and have a high level of **essential fatty acids.** Flaxseeds are a great course of **vitamin** E, a powerful antioxidant and cell membrane protector. The **fiber** load is enormous.

Tiny flaxseeds contain a high volume of lignans, a class of phytoestrogens believed to be very effective against cancer. These same lignans, believed to slow the aging process, are said to contain powerful antioxidant and anti-inflammatory properties associated with lowering the risk of artery-clogging plaques and diabetes.

Flax contains the Omega 3 fatty acid ALA (alpha-linolenic acid), an essential fatty acid not produced by the body. Some fatty fish contain the non-essential fatty acids EPA or DHA, but the body can make these from ALA. Fish can also contain dangerous levels of mercury. Like many plant-based foods, flax contains trace amounts of cadmium and cyanide which can be dangerous at extremely high doses. Heat will destroy these compounds.

It is recommended to consume at least two tablespoons of flaxseed per day to enjoy its many benefits.

HOW TO EAT FLAXSEEDS: Linaza should be found in the seed and grain sections of the markets. They are tiny, oblong brown or golden seeds that almost resemble rice. The hull is tough and protects the seed for up to a year. The body can better absorb the seed once it has been ground, but the shelf life diminishes greatly once the hull is cracked. Try to buy whole flax seeds and grind them yourself little by little as you use them (see seed grinding pg.).

Ground *linaza* can be added to smoothies, salads, or baked goods. *Linaza* can be used as a very effective egg replacer in baking.

JICARO SEED / *SEMILLA DE JÍCARO, SEMILLA DE MORRO*

HIGH IN: Protein, Fiber, Iron, Calcium, and Potassium.

ALSO CONTAIN: Vitamin C, and Antioxidants.

According to Mayan legend, the jicaro tree grew out of the liberation of the people. The fruit appears in the *Popol Vuh*, the sacred Mayan book of creation and history. The Hero Twins, *1 Hunajpu* and *7 Hunajpu*, fail in a ball game and, as punishment, the demonic *Xibalbans* kill them and hang their skulls from the jicaro tree. Some say this is a mythical representation of the skull-like appearance of the fruit and the carrion smell of the tree in flowering season. The story states that one of the skulls later splits in the hands of the *Xibalban* princess *Ixquic*, thus impregnating her and begetting the second, successful generation of Maya Hero Twins.

Scientific research of the nutritional value of the jicaro seed is still in its infancy. Also known as crescentia or Mexican Calabash, the seeds are often used in Central America to combat anemia. A type of *horchata* drink is mixed from ground rice, jicaro seed(or *morro*), water, and spices. The seed can also be used in baking.

In recent years much attention has been given to the jicaro tree - a tough, drought-resistant plant that has potential to generate food and economic wellbeing to the impoverished inhabitants of Central America's wastelands. The tree can grow and survive in extremely adverse climates with very little water. Its thick, long roots penetrate dry, infertile soil and layers of clay to reach the nutrients far below.

Jicaro is an evergreen tree that bears hard, nutritious fruit year-round that can be hollowed out and used as gourds. The pulp can be fed to livestock. The fruit is not typically consumed by humans but can be used to promote bowel movement, vomiting, moisten the skin, treat chest and respiratory disorders, and stop diarrhea. A decoction made from the pulp can be applied to the skin to stop bleeding and to treat dermatitis, hemorrhoids, or bruises.

A decoction of leaves, flowers, and stem is used as a vaginal wash and for pain of hearing. A mixture of fruit and leaves can stop pain, sanitize, improve appetite, stimulate menses, and promote cough to remove phlegm from the chest. An easily digestible, high-quality vegetable oil can be pressed from the seeds. The bark and wood are good for use in cooking fires.

All these fine qualities make the jicaro tree a potential cash crop for impoverished communities living on low-quality lands.

HOW TO EAT JICARO SEED: Semilla de morro or *jícaro* is most commonly found in Honduras, El Salvador, and Nicaragua. The small, dark seeds appear as lentils and are sold whole or ground. They are very high in protein and iron and can be added to a milk or drink of choice for a quick shot of essential vitamins and minerals. For a common *horchata de jícaro* recipe, see page 123.

OATMEAL / *AVENA*

HIGH IN: Protein, Fiber, Manganese, Selenium, and Phosphorus.

ALSO CONTAINS: Manganese, Thiamin, Zinc, Iron, Copper, and Omega 6.

Oatmeal could be named as a staple in a vegetarian traveler's diet. It is cheap, easy to prepare, and packed full of **protein, fiber, vitamins**, and **minerals**. Mix it with some fruit and nuts and, nutritionally, it becomes a tough dish to beat.

Oatmeal is made up of soluble and insoluble fibers. The insoluble fibers and resistant starches in oatmeal are more difficult for your body to digest. These fibers have a slowing effect on the absorption speed of sugar from your food, essentially normalizing blood sugar levels and creating a steadier stream of energy. Oatmeal contains a fiber known as beta-glucan, thought to make your immune system respond more rigorously to infections. Beta-glucan has been shown to significantly reduce cholesterol levels, lowering the risk of weight-related illnesses such as stroke, diabetes or heart attack.

Oatmeal has one of the best amino acid profiles of any grain and a higher concentration of well-balanced protein than most other cereals. Oats contain phyto-chemicals, which have been associated with protection from chronic diseases such as cancer.

The mostly monounsaturated and polyunsaturated fats found in oatmeal work as natural lubricants for your skin. Oatmeal can be ground into a fine powder and used as a cleansing face mask. Cooked (and cooled) oatmeal can be applied to the skin for ten minutes to treat acne. It can also be used as a revitalizing shampoo.

The high fiber content, especially if you are eating raw oatmeal, can be difficult for your system to get used to. It is not uncommon to experience excess intestinal gas and bloating for the first week of continual oatmeal consumption. Your body should normalize after that and you will notice a new stability in energy levels. If bloating continues you may have an allergic reaction to the avenin or possible gluten contained in the oats.

HOW TO EAT OATMEAL: Avena ("*mosh*" in Guatemala) can be found in the seed and grain sections of most markets. It is widely consumed in Latin America. Try to buy whole oats and not the instant stuff as they retain more nutritional value. Oatmeal will usually be sold in bags or out of big bins. Look for larger, cut or rolled pieces about the size of your pinky nail, but the ground oats are still good for you.

PEANUTS / *CACAHUATE* (Mexico) MANÍ (Central America)

HIGH IN: Protein, Fiber, Folate, Niacin, Thiamin, Vitamin E, Copper, Manganese, Phosphorus, and Iron.

ALSO CONTAIN: Antioxidants, Magnesium, Potassium, Zinc, and Selenium.

Peanuts are one of the most commonly found nuts. They are a great source of dietary **protein** and unsaturated **fats**. Easy to get, typically affordable, and simple to eat, peanuts are a perfect pocket food for traveling vegetarians. Carry them around by themselves or make your own trail mix (page 275). Toast them a little and add them to your salads or shakes.

Resveratrol, a polyphenol **antioxidant**, is plentiful in peanuts. This compound is believed to slow the effects of aging and protect against cancer. Studies show that resveratrol reduces the rick of stroke, heart disease, Alzheimer's, degenerative nerve diseases and viral/fungal infections. Resveratrol is also found in the skin of red grapes.

Peanuts contain high-quality **amino acids** and are an excellent source of vitamin E, necessary for healthy cells, skin, and mucus. Peanuts are packed with B-Complex vitamins and are especially high in niacin which helps improve blood flow to the brain and therefore better brain function.

Many markets in Latin America sell ready-shelled peanuts with the dark reddish brown skins intact. Peeling away this skin is not necessary before eating the seed. The skin, although it adds a slightly bitter taste, actually contains very high levels of vitamins and antioxidants. Some studies suggest that boiling the peanuts whole can increase the overall antioxidant count greatly.

HOW TO EAT A PEANUT: It would be difficult to find a person in the world who has never come in contact with a peanut. Like most other items in this section of the book, you would likely find peanuts in the seed and grain section of the market but peanuts are commonly found for sale on street corners as well. And there are always options: raw (*crudo*), toasted (*tostado*), salted (*con sal*), roasted with salt, garlic, and lime (*preparado*), candied (*con dulce*), etc... Try them all.

PUMPKIN SEEDS / *PEPITORIA, PEPITAS*

HIGH IN: Protein, Fiber, Zinc, Magnesium, Copper, Vitamin E, Antioxidants, and Omega 6.

ALSO CONTAIN: B-Complex Vitamins, Potassium, and Iron.

Pumpkin seeds are a great source of high-quality **protein**. They are high in calories but the **fat** content is made up primarily of mono-unsaturated fats that help lower bad cholesterol in the bloodstream.

Tryptophan and glutamate are two **amino acids** found in pumpkin seeds. These two are converted into serotonin and GABA (Gamma-Aminobutyric Acid), respectively, both of which are guilty of helping people get good sleep and reducing anxiety, stress, and nervous irritability. Pumpkin seeds are also a great source of the **antioxidant** vitamin E, known to protect skin and mucus membranes from damage.

In short, it is believed that pumpkin seeds can help reduce the risk of prostate and ovarian cancer, improve bladder functions, fight depression, lower bad cholesterol levels, and remove intestinal parasites.

HOW TO EAT PUMPKIN SEEDS: Pepitoria, pepitas, or *semilla de calbasa* will usually be found in the seed and grain areas of the markets. Typically the seeds are sold hulled and toasted. They are of a light green color about the size of a fingernail. Raw seeds are slightly more nutritious as the heat used to toast them can destroy some of the vitamins and minerals, but you'll still be doing yourself a favor by eating the toasted seeds.

SESAME SEEDS / *AJONJOLÍ*

HIGH IN: Protein, Fiber, Iron, Selenium, Manganese, Magnesium, Copper, Phosphorus, Zinc, Folate, Omega 6, and Vitamin B6.

ALSO CONTAINS: Calcium, Vitamin E, Thiamin, Niacin, and Potassium.

Sesame is believed to be the oldest domesticated oilseed crop. The seeds are highly nutritious, rich in quality vitamins and minerals. Sesame seeds have a high amount of mono-unsaturated fats, especially oleic acid, which helps bring down LDL (bad cholesterol) and raise HDL (good cholesterol).

The seeds are abundant in **antioxidants** like sesamol and sesaminol that aid in ushering unwanted disease-causing free radical cells out of the body.

Fine quality dietary **protein** and **amino acids** are found in sesame seeds as well as a very high concentration of folates, manganese, magnesium, iron, and calcium. B-Complex vitamins are also readily available. All of these elements are essential to maintain health, replenish bones, and produce red blood cells, enzymes and hormones, as well as regulate cardiac and skeletal well-being.

HOW TO EAT SESAME SEEDS: Ajonolí are better absorbed if ground, like in tahini, but can be eaten raw or toasted just as well. They are tiny off-white seeds with a crunchy, nutty flavor likely found in small plastic bags or big barrels in the seed and grain sections of the markets. Sesame seeds can be thrown over a salad or cooked vegetable dish, used whole or ground to bread (cover) a food item, or used in drinks and salsas. The oil can be used for cooking at low temperatures or as a salad dressing.

WALNUTS / *NUÉZ*

HIGH IN: Protein, Fiber, Omega 3 & 6, Manganese, Copper, Magnesium, and Phosphorus.

ALSO CONTAIN: Vitamin B6, Folate, Thiamin, Zinc, Potassium, Iron, and Calcium.

Many nuts claim their superiority as the "King of Nuts." Walnuts are yet another contender. One thing that seems to be accepted commonly, however, is that walnuts contain a higher **antioxidant** value than many others nuts. Some say that certain antioxidants present in walnuts are two to fifteen times as potent as vitamin E. Eating just a handful of walnuts per day could greatly affect a person's general well-being.

Walnuts contain plenty of high-quality **protein** and **fiber**. They are rich in the phyto-chemicals melatonin, ellagic acid, vitamin E, and carotenoids, all of which have potential health benefits against cancer, aging, inflammation, and neurological diseases. Six or seven walnuts have enough antioxidants with high oxidant radical absorbance capacity (ORAC) to help scavenge disease-causing free radicals from the body.

It is not uncommon to hear of walnuts regarded as a "brain food," not only for their cerebral shape but also because of the high levels of **essential fatty acids** they contain. Walnuts are higher in ALA omega 3 fats and contain the perfect ratio of omega 6 to omega 3 fatty acids; 4:1. The human brain is made up of around sixty percent fat so these essential fatty acids are necessary for proper brain function. Walnuts contain the amino acid l-arginine, which improves the elasticity of blood vessels and may help reduce the risk of Alzheimer's disease by blocking the formation of dangerous plaques in the brain.

Walnuts are also believed to be effective in preventing gallstones in women, get rid of intestinal parasites, ensure proper functioning of the thyroid gland, and prevent heartburn, high blood pressure, and various skin disorders.

Walnuts contain melatonin, a powerful antioxidant that also induces good sleep. Quinone juglone, a nutrient found in walnuts that is not readily available in many other foods, is said to help prevent metabolic syndrome, type 2 diabetes, and cardiovascular problems.

HOW TO EAT WALNUTS: Nueces can be slightly more evasive than peanuts or almonds but you should look for them in the seed and grain areas of the markets. Wrinkly brown chunks (look like little brains) about the size of the end of your thumb, they will sometimes be sold in specialty stores or supermarkets. Walnuts can be eaten raw, added to your trail mix, or tossed in with your salads. They can also be crushed and sprinkled over desserts.

Plants vs. Pills

Introduction to Natural Remedies

Natural remedies to common illness have been used since the dawn of humankind. Sadly though, with the rise of industrialized nations, much of this knowledge has been lost or pushed aside. Unlike much of mass-produced medicine, these ancient cures can help to alleviate many ailments and have little to no negative side effects on the human body.

First and foremost, the way you eat and treat yourself on a daily basis can protect you from sickness and help you recover more quickly if you do become ill. Your body and its supply of vitamins and nutrients are on the front lines when a disease or virus attacks. By keeping those defense systems strong and well tuned you can save yourself a lot of time and trouble.

You won't always be able to cure yourself with natural remedies, but when you feel something creeping in, fight back from the get-go and you'll have a better chance of beating it on your own!

I remember a time while traveling in Ecuador that I incurred such a nasty intestinal infection that, after a couple days, I really began to fear for my life. This occurred some years ago and I knew much less about food and nutrition than I do now. I assumed I had contracted the illness due to some bad tap water I drank in Cuenca City a few days before. Now I found myself in a teeny tiny town without a doctor.

My guts felt twisted and compressed, as if someone had beaten them with a sledgehammer. I was constipated and dizzy. A mild fever lay over me like a warm, moist blanket. Curled up in a ball, I passed the nights wide-awake, writhing in pain on the small, lumpy bed of the closet-sized room I had rented. Three days passed without food or sleep, not a moment of peace. I tried everything I could think of to expel the demons from my guts and relieve my bowels. Nothing worked. Finally, I forced myself to crawl down from the hotel and hobble, hunched-over, into town and over to the mini-pharmacy across the street from the plaza.

I nearly collapsed on the counter as I tried to explain my symptoms to the young attendants. Their brows arched in concern as they listened attentively. My Spanish was poor and my voice was feeble but in the end they assured me that they understood and sold me about 12 different pills of god-knows-what. Some, they said, were to take immediately, some for later, some to help sleep, some for the pain, and a few to repeat again the next day. I quickly popped one in my mouth as I stumbled out the door.

Safely back in my room I popped a couple more pills and tried to stretch out on the bed, but the intense abdominal pain immediately wrenched me back into a fetal position. After rolling back and forth on the mattress for about half an hour the pain receded some. The pills' magic infiltrated my bloodstream, slowly pulling me down into a deep slumber that lasted all through the night. I woke the next day feeling much better and within two days I was back to normal.

Ironically, the valley in which that small town sits is famous for its natural, plant-based medicines and the incredible health and longevity of its inhabitants. I didn't find this out until a few years later and felt a little embarrassed to have wasted those days in agony, eventually submitting to pharmaceutical pills to cure my woes. Perhaps I could've discovered an herb growing right next door to my room like *sangre de drago* or *hierba buena* that would've done the same trick!

Plants and herbs have powerful effects and can provide just about everything the human body needs. Unfortunately most of us know as much about them as we do about nuclear physics. Like I said before: I'm no doctor. This section of the book mentions some traditional cures for minor ailments that may work for most people. If you find yourself seriously sick, don't hesitate to talk to a doctor and, if needed, take the prescribed medicines.

Natural Remedies

Not feeling so hot? Spending an extended or even short period of time on the road can exhaust your body. You are exposed to stress, germs, lack of sleep, lots of parties, uncomfortable travel conditions, unfamiliar climates, and, of course, new and different alimentation. It's inevitable that you'll get sick in some way at some point during your trip. It happens to the best of us. But don't get down...get better.

Here are some tips to help fix yourself up, naturally. Mother nature has a great big pharmacy that grows all over the earth. Give her special medicine a try.

COMMON COLD:

*Teas (page 249): Cinnamon, chamomile, garlic, ginger, green, honey, lime, neem, or peppermint.

*Drink at least 8 to 10 glasses of water per day. Avoid coffee, cola, and caffeinated drinks.

*Gargle with salt water. Gargle with a mix of salt water and cayenne. Gargle with a mix of honey and apple cider vinegar.

*Use nasal spray or saline rinse. Make your own by mixing ¼ tsp sea salt with ¼ tsp baking soda in 8 ounces of warm, sterile water. Use a plastic or bulb syringe (found at pharmacies) to push the mixture into your sinuses.

*Get extra doses of vitamin C through vitamin pills or raw fruits and veggies.

*Mix raw garlic, raw ginger, and chili peppers into your meals.

*Blow your nose often. Expel mucus.

*Apply hot or cold packs around congested sinuses.

*Inhale steam. Create humidity with a humidifier or take a steamy shower or sponge bath.

*Stay warm and rested.

CONSTIPATION:

*Teas (page 249): Chamomile, fennel, or senna.

*Drink plenty of liquids, especially water. Also try apple juice or drink warm water with lime juice 3 times a day.

*Soak raisins or prunes in water overnight and drink the water in the morning.

*Coffee and bitter foods help to stimulate the digestive tract.

*Eat a lot of fiber. Try foods like grains, cereals, corn, sweet potatoes, cactus, beans, apples, apricots, bananas, figs, dates, or even guava fruit with seeds.

*Eat fennel seed, flaxseed, and sesame seed.

*Eat magnesium-rich foods like kale, broccoli, and spinach.

*Eat foods that contain probiotics like sauerkraut, kombucha tea, or tempeh.

*Rhubarb is a natural laxative. Steam it, make it into a pie, or make a purée with apples and honey.

*Limit intake of processed or refined foods like chips, salty snacks, pastries, white bread, and basic "junk food."

*Increase oil intake. Pour some olive oil over your salads or make a dip from olive oil and herbs.

*Exercise and movement help to keep you regular. Walk, stretch, run, or work out.

DIARRHEA:

*Teas (page 249): Chamomile, ginger, or blackberry.

*Drink plenty of fluids, including coconut water.

*Eat lightly salted crackers and toast. Even burnt toast. The charcoal helps stop diarrhea.

*Avoid caffeine, alcohol, acidic fruits, dairy products, sugar, fatty foods, and spicy foods.

*Although most high-fiber foods should be avoided, you may benefit from eating certain bland and easy-to-digest foods such as: noodles, carrots, potatoes, bananas, blueberries, and apples or applesauce.

*Avoid cold drinks. Drink warm, soothing teas and water or juice at room temperature. Avoid carbonated drinks.

*Get your hands on probiotics found in fermented foods like sauerkraut, tempeh, or miso. Also try probiotic drops or capsules if you can find them.

FEVER:

*Teas (page 249): Basil, garlic, ginger, lemongrass, linden, mint, or oregano.

*Drink plenty of cool water and juice.

*Make apple or raisin water by boiling 3 parts chopped apples with 4 parts water, or 1 part chopped raisins with 7 parts water. Simmer for a few minutes, strain, let cool, and drink.

*Take a cold bath or shower.

*Eat fresh pineapple.

*Don't eat heavy foods. Actually, don't eat much at all. The saying, "starve a fever," means don't give it extra ammunition, *aka* nutrition.

*Avoid spicy foods, stressful situations, and exercise.

*Place an ice pack on your forehead to help lower temperature.

*Make yourself comfortable and get good rest.

HANGOVER:

*Teas (page 249): Ginger, green, honey with lime, oregano, or peppermint.

*Drink lots of water, including coconut water or *horchata*.

*Drink orange juice and other fruit juices. Even pickle juice.

*Hair of the dog: Have a *michelada*, *tequila*, or *mezcal*!

*Eat easy to digest food like bananas, toast, soup, *chilaquiles*, or rice.

*Eat *nopal* cactus before drinking alcohol to lower the effects of hangover. Eat prickly pear fruit before *and* after.

*Get all the sleep and rest that you need.

*Use an ice pack or cold towel on your forehead or neck to relieve pain.

HEADACHE:

*Teas (page 249): Chamomile, lemon, or lime.

*Drink lots of water.

*Apply used lime peels to sides of your temples.

*Eat foods that contain calcium and magnesium. Cayenne or hot chili peppers can also be helpful.

*Apply ice pack to your forehead, temples, or the back of your neck.

*Take a warm bath or shower, a nap, or maybe a walk.

*Sit or rest in a quiet, low-lit place.

HEARTBREAK:

*Drink plenty of tequila, mezcal, and rum.

*Go out. Be amongst people. Dance, laugh, and party.

*Get plenty of exercise. Swimming is recommended as it both raises heart rate and metaphorically "washes off the past." Running also provides a great cardio workout and helps to sweat out the bad spirits.

*Practice yoga and meditation.

INTESTINAL PARASITES:

Intestinal parasite infection is less common, but it could happen at any time due to tainted water or food. Typical symptoms can include fatigue, abdominal pain, diarrhea, vomiting, lack of appetite, and persistent gas or bloating. Try these suggestions if you think you've picked up some unwelcomed bugs. However, if symptoms persist or worsen, please see a doctor.

*Teas (page 249): Garlic, golden seal (*sello de oro/sello dorado*), neem, oregano, *epazote*, or wormwood (*ajenjo*).

*Add raw garlic, raw onion, and raw cloves to each meal.

*Eat raw papaya seeds mixed with honey three times a day.

*Eat plenty of fresh pineapple.

*Eat large amounts of raw pumpkin seeds. Use in conjunction with a laxative like senna tea.

*Drink 1 TBS of apple cider vinegar in a cup of water every day until symptoms lessen.

*Drink juice made from the ground hulls of unripe black walnuts (*cáscara molida de nuéz negra*, sometimes found in *tiendas naturistas*).

*Adopt a high-fiber diet, including foods rich in vitamins A and C.

*Avoid coffee, refined sugars, refined foods, and alcohol.

NAUSEA:

*Teas (page 249): Aniseed, cinnamon, cloves, cumin, fennel, ginger, or mint.

*Drink cranberry juice or lemon/lime juice mixed with honey.

*Drink 1 tsp of blended onion juice mixed with 1 tsp grated ginger and honey.

*Mix the juice of 1 lime with ½ tsp sugar in a cup of warm water. Add ¼ tsp baking soda, mix again, and drink.

*Avoid fatty or hard to digest foods. Eat light foods like salted crackers.

*Heat up a cup of your almond, cashew, or coconut milk and crumble a piece of toast into it. Eat slowly.

*Hold a whole clove in your mouth for 5 to 10 minutes.

SUNBURN:

*Drink plenty of water.

*Apply fresh aloe vera gel, directly from the leaf, or use moisturizing lotion with aloe.

*Apply moisturizer to the skin immediately after you bathe.

*Take a cool oat bath by adding 1 cup of oatmeal to your bath water. Air dry afterward. Don't use a towel.

*Mix instant oatmeal with water in a bowl (or blend whole oats with water in a blender). Apply the oatmeal to burned skin. Place a wet washcloth over the oatmeal and leave it for 15 minutes. Remove cloth and oatmeal. You can wash your skin without soap or leave the oatmeal residue for extended healing and soothing effects.

*Try the above procedure with potato pulp (potato and water mixed in a blender), chamomile tea, or honey.

*Soak a cloth in cold water to make a cool compress. Apply to burned areas. Also try mixing baking soda into the water.

*Eat foods high in vitamins C and E.

Medicinal Teas

This little part of the book provides information and instructions on how to prepare a handful of useful and tasty teas that you may want to try during your trip. When used medicinally to treat something such as a cold, the tea should be taken three times a day every day until the symptoms are gone... and then a few extra days to prevent them from returning.

Most of these teas are safe to drink on a daily basis, unless otherwise noted. But keep in mind that pregnant women and people with delicate health conditions or allergies should always check with their doctor first.

ARANTO TEA / *TÉ DE ARANTO*

Good for treating cancer, calming the body, and relieving anxiety.

Aranto leaves are somewhat difficult to encounter. They will most likely be found in the health and herbal medicine shops known as "*tiendas naturistas*".

Aranto has a reputation among Central American tribes for its perceived ability to cure cancer. It is also used to treat schizophrenia, panic attacks, and certain phobias. The tea has an overall calming effect on the body and is also rumored to help repair damaged organs. It is believed to help in cases of diabetes, lung and respiratory disorders, as well as digestive, circulatory, and reproductive problems.

A paste made from moist aranto leaves can also be applied to help treat wounds that won't close or heal.

To make 1 cup of tea:

-Pour a cup of boiling water over about 3 or 4 aranto leaves.

-Let stand, covered, 10 minutes.

-Uncover, strain if necessary, and drink.

Aranto tea is best NOT mixed with other teas.

AMARANTH TEA / *TÉ DE AMARANTO*

Good for treating diarrhea, bleeding from the bowels, sore throat, or excessive menstruation.

Amaranth leaves are often more difficult to find than the raw grain. If you don't see them in the markets, ask. Fresh or dried leaves can be used to make tea, but if you encounter a large chunk of fresh leaves you may want to dry them out to preserve them.

Amaranth tea, taken internally, can help clear up stomach or intestinal issues. The tea can also be gargled to treat mouth lesions or sore throat. It can be used externally to treat skin rashes. Amaranth tea is said to slow aging, improve the skin, lower bad cholesterol in the body, and strengthen artery walls.

To make 1 cup of tea:

-Pour a cup of boiling water over 4 or 5 amaranth leaves.

-Let stand, covered, 10 minutes.

-Uncover, strain if necessary, and drink.

Amaranth tea is best NOT mixed with other teas.

BOUGAINVILLEA TEA / *TÉ DE BUGAMBILIA*

Good for cough, respiratory problems, and sore throat.

Bougainvillea plants can be found all over Mexico and Central America. They are the big bushes with rose-like stems and bright, delicate flowers that almost look like colored tissue paper. The most common bougainvillea flowers are white, red, purple, and orange but there are many shades and mixtures among them.

Bougainvillea tea is made from the flowers. More precisely the dark red or purple flowers. Traditionally, this tea is used to cure persistent cough and lung or respiratory problems. Mixed with honey it is also helpful in cases of sore throat.

To make 1 cup of tea:

-Bring 1½ cups of water to a boil.

-Add 7-10 washed purple or red bougainvillea flowers.

-Let flowers simmer over low heat for about 5 minutes.

-Remove from heat, strain, and add 1 tablespoon of honey.

-Let cool down enough to drink.

OPTION: Add a cinnamon stick while boiling the leaves and/or lemon juice as the water cools.

CHAMOMILE TEA / *TÉ DE MANZANILLA*

Good for sleep, stomachaches, intestinal cramps, and colds.

Chamomile tea is most famous for its relaxing and soothing properties and is often taken before bed to promote restful sleep. It has recorded medical usage as far back as Greek and Egyptian times.

Chamomile is great to boost the immune system and fight colds. It also aids in digestion and can help in a variety of stomach problems as well as irritable bowel syndrome. It has even been shown to relieve cramping during menstruation.

A paste made of moist chamomile leaves can be applied to wounds to promote speedy recovery.

To make 1 cup of tea:

-Boil 1½ cups of water in an open pot.

-Remove from heat and add a handful of chamomile flowers.

-Let sit for 3 minutes and then strain water into a cup to drink.

OPTION: Mix your chamomile with peppermint for the digestive effects.

CINNAMON TEA / *TÉ DE CANELA*

Good for fighting colds, reducing intestinal gas, inflammation, and promoting fresh breath.

The volatile oils found in cinnamon help break up mucus and defend the body from the microbial attack. Cinnamon is said to help regulate blood sugar levels and soothing upset stomachs. It is also believed to aid in weight loss.

To make 1 cup of tea:

-Bring 1½ cups of water to boil with 1 cinnamon stick.

-Turn down flame and let simmer 5 minutes.

-Remove from heat, strain, and let cool down enough to drink.

EPAZOTE TEA / *TÉ DE EPAZOTE*

Good for improving digestion, removing parasites, and preventing flatulence.

Epazote is a Mexican cooking herb also known as Jesuit tea, wormseed, pigweed, and Mexican tea. It is very helpful taken after meals as a digestive aid can help reduce intestinal bloating and flatulence. Epazote tea is known for its power to expel intestinal parasites. It is also used to treat people with nervous disorders.

A paste made from moist epazote leaves can be used to sooth arthritic joints, athlete's foot, or insect bites.

To make 1 cup of tea:

-Boil 2 cups of water with a medium-sized stem and leaves of the epazote plant.

-Once boiling, reduce heat and let simmer for 3 minutes.

-Remove from heat, strain if necessary, and let cool down enough to drink.

Pregnant women should *NOT* drink epazote tea as it is known to induce miscarriage.

GARLIC, LEMON, and HONEY TEA /
TÉ DE AJO CON LIMA Y MIEL

Good for fighting colds and respiratory problems.

Garlic has oils that inhibit cough and cold microbes and are effective decongestants. Honey is believed to have antimicrobial qualities that help the immune system fight off infection. Lemon has the ability to reduce mucus and alter the body's pH balance, making it less hospitable to viruses and bacteria.

To make 1 cup of tea:

-Chop up 2 to 3 cloves of garlic.

-Bring 1½ cups of water to boil.

-Lower heat, add garlic to water, and let simmer for 1 minute.

-Remove water from heat and add about 2 tablespoons of honey and 2 tablespoons of lemon (or lime) juice.

-Stir together and let cool down enough to drink.

Drink this mix twice a day until symptoms are relieved and then for a couple days after to keep sickness from returning.

NOTE: Limes may be easier to find in Mexico and Central America. You can substitute the lemon for lime.

GINGER TEA / *TÉ DE GENJIBRE*

Good for digestion, preventing nausea and vomiting, fighting colds and flu, limiting flatulence, and reducing inflammation.

Ginger tea has a long history of use as a digestive aid and stomach soother. It is said to help reduce intestinal gas, promote the secretion of digestive juices, neutralize stomach acids, and prevent indigestion.

The tea is also said to freshen breath and cure sore throats. Ginger is responsible for good blood circulation and can help relieve feelings of nausea. It can be used to treat diarrhea.

To make 1 cup of tea:

-Chop up about 1½ TBS of ginger root.

-Add the ginger to 1½ cups of water and bring to a boil.

-Once boiling, reduce flame and let simmer 10-15 minutes.

-Remove from heat, strain, and let cool enough to drink.

OPTION: Add a little lime (or lemon) juice and/or honey.

LEMONGRASS TEA / *TÉ DE LIMÓN*

Good for digestion, cancer treatment, sleep, detoxifying, and nervous system support.

Lemongrass tea has been used traditionally to aid in digestion, fight off infection, and alleviate symptoms of the common cold. It acts as a detoxifying agent that can help cleanse various internal organs and eliminate toxins like uric acid and cholesterol from the body.

The aromatic active ingredient, citral, found in lemongrass helps in digestion and has also been found to have a devastating effect on cancer cells. In test tubes studies, citral caused cancer cells to destroy themselves, known as "programmed cell death" or "cell suicide," while leaving the healthy cells unharmed.

Lemongrass tea is highly beneficial to the nervous system. It makes the nerves stronger and keeps them active and healthy. The tea can be used to treat disorders such as vertigo, shaky limbs, lack of reflexes, and Alzheimer's or Parkinson's diseases.

Lemongrass has a calming effect on the body and can help in cases of insomnia. It possesses astringent and antimicrobial qualities, which keep skin and eyes clean and shining. It can also bring down fever and high blood pressure. Used externally, lemongrass tea can be used as an anti-fungal treatment and help heal cuts, bruises, or arthritic pain.

To make 1 cup of tea:

-Bring 1½ cups of water to boil.

-Add about 2 heaping tablespoons of fresh or dried lemon grass leaf.

-Lower heat and let simmer for 5 minutes.

-Remove from heat, strain if necessary, and let cool down enough to drink.

**OPTION*: Add a tablespoon of honey to the finished tea. You can also boil ginger with the lemongrass.

LINDEN TEA / *TÉ DE TILO*

Good for sleep, fighting colds, fever, and upset stomach.

Linden tea, also known as lime, *tilia* or *tila*, is widely used to treat upset stomach or diarrhea. It can help reduce stress, anxiety, or irritability. Linden flowers contain essentials oils that lower inflammations of the respiratory system.

Linden tea can slightly raise the body's temperature, helping it fight against infections. The elevated body temperature simultaneously induces sweating, which doesn't allow the system to overheat. By promoting perspiration, linden can actually help fight fevers.

Linden flowers contain farnesol, believed to have sedative properties that aid in sound sleep. Taken before bed, it can help individuals who suffer from insomnia.

The aromatic herb also helps to relieve a stuffy nose and clear nasal passages as well as break up mucus from the throat. It is said to be successful at easing digestion, treating stomach pains, and alleviating gas pressure.

To make 1 cup of tea:

-Pour boiling water over 1½ TBS of linden flowers and leaves.

-Cover and let sit 5 minutes.

-Uncover, strain if necessary, and drink.

MINT TEA / *TÉ DE MENTA*

Good for sleep, digestion, headaches, and respiratory problems.

Mint tea makes a great before or after dinner digestive aid. It helps break down fats and provides relief from intestinal bloating and gas. Mint is also helpful in opening up blocked nasal passages and alleviating some symptoms of the common cold.

Mint tea is said to sooth headaches and relieve stress. It has a calming effect on the body and aids in sound sleep. The freshness of mint tea can help cure bad breath. Mint also contains some vitamin C and antioxidants.

When mint is not available, peppermint (*hierba buena*) is equally delicious and effective.

To make 1 cup of tea:

(If using fresh mint leaves cut or rip them up a little)

-Pour boiling water over about 2 TBS of fresh or dried mint leaves.

-Let stand, covered, 10 minutes.

-Uncover, strain if necessary, and drink.

OPTION: Add a tablespoon of honey or lime juice to the finished tea. You can also add a chunk of ginger to the water as you boil it.

MORINGA TEA / *TÉ DE MORINGA*

Good for digestion, nausea, diarrhea, skin beautification, energy, and metabolism.

The moringa tree sprouts small round leaves that are full of vitamins and antioxidants. A tea can be made from moringa leaves that will help normalize sugar levels in the body and promote energy. The energy provided by moringa is not sugar-based, doesn't cause sugar spikes, and lasts longer.

Moringa tea is helpful in fighting indigestion, boosting the immune system and metabolic rate, aiding vision, sharpening the brain, and improving liver, kidney, and circulatory system functions.

Moringa helps in building collagen fibers within the skin, thereby reducing wrinkles and other signs of aging. It is said to reduce the risk of esophageal cancer. The anti-inflammatory properties of moringa can provide relief from rheumatoid arthritis. The tea is said to promote the feeling of general wellbeing.

The moringa tree grows wild in Mexico and Central America. It may or may not be sold in natural medicine stores (*tiendas naturistas*). Most likely, if a store can't provide you with moringa they can tell you where to locate a tree and you can cut your own.

To make 1 cup of tea:

-Pour boiling water over 2 TBS of fresh or dried moringa leaves.

-Cover and let steep 5 minutes.

-Uncover, strain if necessary, and drink.

NEEM TEA / *TÉ DE NEEM*

Good for cough, colds, nausea, vomiting, stomach pains, oral and skin astringent, cancer treatment, and killing parasites.

The neem tree is native to India and has some 4000 years or recorded medical use there. The tree is affectionately referred to as "Sacred Tree," "Heal All," "Nature's Drugstore" or "Village Pharmacy."

Neem, when taken as a tea, has the power to reduce nausea, vomiting, and abdominal pain associated with infection. It is used to eliminate intestinal parasites. The tea is also prescribed to treat respiratory ailments like cough, cold, asthma and allergies. It may help purify the blood and treat symptoms of pneumonia, malaria, dengue, and AIDS.

Neem leaves can be used to prepare insect repellant. The concoction has a pungent odor that keeps mosquitos, fleas, and lice at bay. The same mixture in stronger doses can be used as an agricultural insecticide. It doesn't actually kill the insects, but rather deters the insects from feeding or laying eggs and even suppresses the hatching of pre-existing eggs. The problematic insects starve to death within a couple days. Curiously, neem, as an insecticide, only affects pests without harming the beneficial bugs.

People in India use the chewed end of neem twigs as a toothbrush. It is common to chew a neem leaf before or after a meal. The plant is full of antimicrobial, antiviral and antibacterial properties. It is very effective in preventing bad breath, gum disease, plaque, and cavities.

Neem can be used externally to treat skin problems such as fungal infections, rashes or wounds. Recovery time is minimized by taking the tea internally as well during treatment. The tea works as an anti-inflammatory and can be applied externally to joints to ease arthritic pain.

The tree is recognized as a functional contraceptive. The oils kill sperm on contact and, while consuming the herb, reversibly lower fertility in both men and women without affecting hormones or libido. It has a reputation for protecting against sexually transmitted diseases, including HIV.

Some studies state that neem tea can destroy cancer cells on contact. It protects against chemically induced carcinogens by boosting antioxidant levels.

To make 1 cup of tea:

-Boil 3 neem leaves in 1½ cups of water for 3 minutes.

-Strain, if necessary, and let cool down enough to drink.

-Add 1 or 2 TBS of honey as neem has a very bitter taste.

Other uses:

-Boil 6 neem leaves in 2 cups of water for three minutes to make a mouthwash. When cool, use it to gargle and rinse the mouth daily. It can also be used for sore throats or as an eyewash in case of infections.

-Boil 6 neem leaves in 2 cups of water for three minutes to make an insect repellant. When cool, apply to skin to repel mosquitos and such. Lasts for a couple of hours.

-A paste made from crushed neem leaves can be used to heal skin infections or cuts. It can also provide relief from insect bites.

NOTE: Neem may be hard to find in the markets. It grows wild in hot, dry areas of Mexico and Central America. Once you know how to spot it, you can gather your own leaves, twigs, and seeds. Neem tea is a medicinal tea. The taste alone might discourage you from drinking it for pleasure, but keep in mind that it shouldn't be overused.

RUE TEA / *TÉ DE RUDA*

Good for stomach pains, nervous disorders, headache, cough, and chest congestion.

Rue has been used for centuries as a medicinal herb. Shakespeare refers to it a few times in his plays. Rue tea has been used to calm hysterics, to induce abortions, or even as an aphrodisiac. Rue has anti-inflammatory, antispasmodic, antifertility, and antihistamine properties. It contains rutin, an antioxidant that helps prevent damage to DNA caused by free radicals. It is also believed to support and strengthen blood vessels and lower blood pressure.

Rue can be used topically to reduce inflammation and ease pain associated with arthritis, sprains, dislocations, or injuries to the bones. Crushed rue leaves can be placed on the temples or in the ear canals to alleviate headaches. Either the tea or crushed leaves can be used as insect repellant.

The tea is helpful in treating symptoms of the common cold such as congestion, dizziness, weakness, muscle tightness, earaches, and fever.

To make 1 cup of tea:

-Pour boiling water over 1 TBS of dried rue leaves.

-Cover and let sit 5 minutes.

-Uncover, strain if necessary, and drink.

NOTE: Rue is a medicinal herb. Use it with extreme caution as too much can be poisonous. More than a gram a day should not be consumed. Obviously, pregnant women should never take rue as it can induce miscarriage.

SENNA TEA / *TÉ DE HOJA DE SEN*

Good for relieving constipation.

Senna contains *anthraquinones* and *sennosides*, which are powerful laxatives and bowel irritants, respectively. Tea made from dried senna leaves is helpful in overcoming constipation or clearing out the system before a fast or cleanse.

Senna should be used as a medicine and not for the long term. Prolonged senna use may lead to liver damage. Senna tea may cause side effects such as muscle cramps or skin rash in sensitive individuals.

To make 1 cup of tea:

-Pour boiling water over about 2 TBS of senna leaves.

-Let stand, covered, 10 minutes.

-Uncover, strain if necessary, and drink.

Senna tea is best NOT mixed with other teas.

Sprouting

The process of bringing a dried seed, grain, or legume to life is called *sprouting*. In this process the complex compounds stored within the seed are broken down into more simple forms, creating food and fuel for the plant to begin growing. These biochemical changes help to greatly increase the nutritive value of the food. Sprouts often contain more available proteins, amino acids, vitamins and minerals than cooked grains or legumes. They become, essentially, a predigested food more readily absorbed by the body.

By soaking and sprouting the seeds, many anti-nutrients are destroyed or diminished. Anti-nutrients, like phytate, bind to enzymes or other nutrients and won't allow for their absorption into the body. Sufficient soak time (12 to 24 hours) causes a significant decrease in the anti-nutrients as they are leached into the soak water. As the seed germinates, anti-nutrient levels are further reduced to negligible or nothing.

Cooking is another effective way to cure legumes or grains, but some vitamins may be destroyed or damaged by the heat.

HOW TO SPROUT: Although some seeds are easier to sprout than others, almost all can be done. I recommend lentils to start out with because they are very common, highly nutritious, and easy to sprout. I will also include directions for sprouting chia seeds, as they become sticky and the jar method is ineffective.

To sprout, your seeds will need air, warmth, and minimum indirect sunlight. They need to be kept clean and moist. Not all seeds sprout the same. Some will take longer or call for different methods. Patience is key while learning to sprout new seeds.

LENTILS:

You will need:
¼ cup lentils -- about a liter-sized jar or glass
A paper towel or two
A rubber band
Clean water
A strainer, cheesecloth, or bandana is helpful

Directions:
Rinse the lentils thoroughly and place them in the jar or glass, cover with water and let soak for at least 12 hours.

Drain water and rinse lentils again. Let excess water dry from lentils (preferably in a strainer) and place moist lentils back in the jar. Cover the mouth of the jar with the paper towel, securing it with the rubber band. Place jar in a warm place out of direct sunlight and let sit for 24 hours.

Uncover jar and rinse the lentils again (either inside the jar or in the strainer). Let excess water drain from the jar, making sure there is no water at the bottom or the lentils will spoil. Replace the paper towel and let the jar sit another 24 hours.

Repeat for about three days, rinsing lentils daily, until sprouts have grown to two or three inches. Ready to eat!

NOTE: The lentil seed left on the end of the sprout is edible. It contains nutrients but has a slightly bitter taste and can be removed if desired. Your sprouts can be used in salads, sandwiches, juices, stir-frys, or just eaten in small handfuls throughout the day.

CHIA:

These directions are suitable to sprout chia seeds. Generally smaller seeds can be sprouted this way. However, unlike the chia seeds we're working with here, most other seeds will need to be rinsed and soaked first (see Lentils).

You will need:
¼ cup (or less) chia seeds
A plate or tray
A couple paper towels (or any other clean, porous medium that holds water)
Clean water

Directions:

Thoroughly moisten the paper towels and lay them out, doubled up, on the plate or tray. Sprinkle the dry chia seeds onto the paper towels, trying to allow them each a little space of their own.

Place tray in a warm, low light environment. It is not necessary to cover the seeds, but if there are any insects present it may be a good idea. Get creative. They will need to breath, so use something like another paper towel, strainer, bag with holes in it, etc.

Keep the paper towels moist, but not soggy. The best way to do this is with a spray bottle if one is available. Tip the tray or plate after watering to allow any excess liquid to drain. Check the paper towel for moisture a couple times a day.

When the plants begin to grow you can move them into more light. Make sure to keep the paper towels moist.

After a few days the plants should have a couple small green leaves. They are ready to eat. Cut the just above the paper towel and enjoy.

Other things to sprout:

Garbanzos
Black beans
Pinto beans
Amaranth (use chia method)
Sesame seeds (use chia method)
Brown rice
Pumpkin seeds
Sunflower seeds

NOTE: Kidney bean and soybean sprouts are <u>toxic</u>. *Do not eat them raw.* If you choose to sprout these legumes, the resulting sprouts *must be cooked* before they can be consumed. The heat destroys the toxins.

Fermentation

SAUERKRAUT

Sauerkraut is shredded cabbage in a fermented state. It's highly nutritious and tastes best when homemade! However, the fermentation process takes 3 to 4 weeks so plan ahead!

Ingredients:
½ head of green or red cabbage (or mixed)
Salt

Directions:
You will need two open-mouthed containers of about half a liter capacity. The easiest to recycle in Mexico/Central America would be a plastic yogurt or margarine container. The base of one container must be able to fit into the mouth of the second container.

Remove one of the large outer leaves of cabbage. Slice the remaining cabbage into thin strips. Pack some cabbage strips about three fingers high into one container and sprinkle some salt over the top. Add another three fingers of cabbage strips and sprinkle some more salt over the top. Repeat this process until the container is full, sprinkling a little salt over the top.

Place the intact cabbage leaf (cut to size) over the top of the shredded cabbage and press down. Try and cover all the cabbage strips. Now fill the second container with water and close it with the original top, if available. Place the water-filled container on/in the cabbage container directly over the cabbage leaf. This water acts as weight to continually push down on the cabbage. Of course, any object of similar weight and diameter will work. The idea is to squeeze the water out of the cabbage.

Leave the containers in a cool, clean environment overnight.

Check the container the next morning to see if water has been expelled from the cabbage. There should be enough to cover all the cabbage and top leaf. If not, add enough drinking water to completely submerge the cabbage. What's under the water will begin to ferment. Any cabbage sticking out of the water will rot.

Leave the cabbage in a cool, dark spot, periodically cleaning of any foam or scum that begins to develop on the surface of the water. After 3 or 4 weeks you can check the sauerkraut to see if it's done. It should have a strong odor and tart, tangy taste.

Use your sauerkraut in sandwiches, soups, or salads. Store it in water and keep it refrigerated. Sauerkraut can keep for a month or more.

NONI JUICE

Noni fruit is used to make a highly nutritious juice used medicinally to treat many diseases as well as clean and fortify an already healthy body. You can read more about noni fruit on page 166.

Directions:
If you have access to a noni tree, pick the fruit when it is ripe (soft and yellowish green) but before it turns white. You'll need about 6 to 8 pieces. Wash them thoroughly and lay them outside to dry in the sun. Within a few hours the fruit should begin to turn translucent. The skin will become softer and a foul smell will permeate from the noni. This is good and normal.

Now pack the noni into a clean and sterile mason jar or any old glass container with a lid. There should be some extra space in the jar. A good ratio would be at least 3:1 noni and extra space. Put the lid on the jar tightly but don't worry about making it airtight. The enclosed nonies will now need to sit in a warm place for about 6 to 8 weeks to fully ferment.

A juice will be secreted naturally during this period. The longer the juice sits, the darker it will become. This means it's becoming more potent. At the end of the fermentation process there will remain just a mushy mess inside the jar. Use a tight mesh strainer, cheesecloth, or bandana to separate the juice from the mush. Save the juice, toss the mush. Transfer the juice to a smaller glass container.

Your noni juice can be stored in or out of the fridge. It should last at least 2 years. Use it often, but it moderation and in small quantities as the high levels of potassium could become damaging to the kidneys if overused.

REJUVELAC

Rejuvelac is a high protein, fermented liquid believed to aid in digestion and energy production. It can be added to your veggie juices or taken on its own if you enjoy the pungent taste. Rejuvelac is made from grains, typically wheat, rye, oats, barley, or quinoa. For this recipe we will use wheat berries to make 1 gallon of liquid.

Ingredients:
¾ cup wheat berries
Water

Directions:
Thoroughly rinse grains. In a pot or jar cover grains with sufficient water and let them soak for 8 to 12 hours. They should expand in size.

Drain and discard the water. Transfer the grains to a strainer and rinse well. Allow excess water to drain and then move the grains back to the jar. Cover the jar with a paper towel or light bandana and secure it with a rubber band. Leave the jar in a warm place out of direct sunlight. The grains should begin to sprout by the next morning.

Let the grain sprouts continue to grow for 24 to 36 hours. Rinse and drain them again, changing the paper towel, two or three times during sprouting. You can rinse them in the same jar, allowing for excess water to drain thoroughly afterwards, or gently move them back to the strainer to wash and drain.

Once well-sprouted, add 1 cup of the sprouted grain to a blender along with 2 cups of drinking water and blend for a few seconds. Pour contents into a one-gallon container. Add enough drinking water to fill the container. Cover the mouth of the container with a paper towel, screen, or bandana to keep bugs and dust out. Let the liquid stand at room temperature at least 24 hours. Longer fermentation makes stronger rejuvelac. Too much time will spoil it.

When ready, strain the liquid into another clean container or jar (or into a medium-sized pot while you wash the jar, later returning the rejuvelac to the original jar). It should have a fermented aroma and taste slightly sour. If it tastes too bland or obviously spoiled, something went wrong. Rejuvelac can be stored up to four days in a refrigerator. Cover it loosely with a cloth or paper towel, but don't put a tight lid on it.

*NOTE: Since rejuvelac needs some warmth to ferment, it's best made in hot or controlled climates. The fermentation process won't work in the cold. However, direct sun should also be avoided. Rejuvelac can also be used to add taste and extra nutrition to vegan cheeses (page 32).

Quick Snacks for the Road

As a vegetarian or health-conscious eater it's always a good idea to plan ahead before you make a journey. There's no guarantee that you'll come across something that suits your diet during the trip. Much of the what's sold at rest stops and by the vendors who board the buses is deep fried, non-veggie, or unsatisfying. Sometimes you'll get lucky, but just in case you may want to eat a fulfilling meal beforehand and carry some snacks along with you in you bag.

*Oranges, apples, or mangoes. Some great fruits to help keep vitamins and sugars flowing through your bloodstream. Bananas are also good to keep energy levels up, but notorious for getting squashed and making a mess in your bag. Eat those before you go!

*Trail Mix. This one is easy to throw together with a trip to the market. Pick up whatever you can find; peanuts, raisins, walnuts, almonds, dried fruit. . . take about a ¼ kilo of each and toss it all together into a bigger bag. Shake it up well and -- bang! Trail mix.

*Palanquetas. Nut and seeds bars fused together with melted cane sugar. These can be found in rectangular bar form or as discs, usually in the markets or street corners in Mexico. They usually include peanuts, pumpkin seeds, raisins, sesame seeds, and/or puffed amaranth.

*Make a quick sandwich. Slice bread is usually sold in complete loaves. If you don't want to carry so much, pick up a couple buns from the bread shop (*panadería*) slice them up and build your own sandwiches. Avocado, carrots, raw garlic, spinach, *chaya*, mushrooms, grilled *nopal* cactus, zucchini, hummus, etc. Get creative. Bag it up and stash it for later.

*Carrots and celery. They're full of vitamins and can handle a bumpy road. Make the meal more complete with some peanut butter or your own homemade hummus.

*Dried fruits. Always a treasure when you come across a good batch of dried fruit in the market. It won't go bad and it will keep you feeling good.

*Baked sweet potatoes. If you have access to an oven, bake a couple of these for an hour or so and bring them along with you. Sometimes they can be found pre-baked or boiled outside the markets. The sugars and carbs provide energy and they taste great by themselves.

*Fritos de harina (page 71). While not the healthiest option, these little guys are easy to make and withstand tough travel. They'll fill you up and you can add toppings to them at your discretion.

*Tamales. In the south of Mexico or select areas of Central America tamales are sold on street corners or in the markets (see also: Street Food Guide, next). Pop a couple in your daypack before departing on a new adventure!

How I Fell in Love with Street Food
Prelude to the Street Food Guide

I went traveling to India when I was 26. Before I left, everyone I knew had to put their two cents in about where, when, how, and why I should or shouldn't do this or that. One constant recommendation was, "Don't drink the water and watch what you eat." More precisely, "You *will* get sick. So be ready for it!"

Of course, by then I already knew the affinity many people have for exaggerating the possible negative aspects of travel. I had been around the block a few times but this was my first sojourn into the nitty-gritty of a largely developing country. The anticipation and wonder were deeply felt. It still makes me laugh when folks offer advice about a place they've never been to themselves, but I have to admit that after being hit with so many warnings regarding the food and sanitation that I, myself, had become a little skeptical.

When I touched down in the republic, I became immediately leery about what I put in my mouth. I ate at a couple of restaurants and even ventured to try some deep-fried veggie *samosas* sold from a cart on a well-kept corner near to a tourist zone of New Delhi. Everything was delicious and nothing made me feel in the least bit out of sorts.

It wasn't until about a week later in the city of Agra where I had befriended a young motor-rickshaw taxi driver that I had my first encounter with the real deal Indian street food. The young driver's name was Ali, a mostly devout Muslim who confessed to enjoying a little too much alcohol from time to time. He drove me to some of the best sights in Agra during my short stay and took me to eat one night at what he confided to be the best spot in the city... one that most people didn't even know about.

Ali drove us into a part of Agra that I hadn't yet been to. The street lamps were dismal, few, and far between. Dust shone in the headlights of the wanton traffic that buzzed all around us. His rickety rickshaw sputtered ahead, weaving through the mass, and finally off of the avenue and onto a backstreet that opened into a small, low-lit alleyway. Towards the end of the alleyway I could make out a gathering of tarps and carts, lit from above by a string of bare light bulbs burning in the dry desert night. It looked like a small carnival and we headed straight for it.

Arriving at the congregation I saw people sitting around the carts eating, drinking, and laughing. Behind and around them were more people talking, eating, pushing, or squeezing to get ahead of each other and as we neared them Ali honked a few times and slowly cut through the crowd. Some of the men yelled things at him and pointed to me. "They never saw some people like you here," he said. "But don't worry. They are my friends. My big mouth friends, haha!" he laughed. "Come." Ali parked the three-wheeled rickshaw next to a couple other rickshaws and taxi sedans. We got out and he led me back into the nucleus of the food extravaganza.

Enveloped in an avalanche of aromas we stepped around people, between carts, and over hungry dogs until Ali stopped and gave a great cheer and hug to a middle-aged man working over an assembly of hot pots. He motioned for me to take a seat on an over-abused plastic stool while he haggled for the right to another stool from a pair of the man's customers who had just finished eating. Having won, Ali sat beside me and said with a beaming smile, "Yes! Good vegetarian food for you, my friend. Cheap and best!" He ordered from the man at the pots and we were instantly presented with multi-partitioned metal trays loaded with scrumptious-smelling vegetables, lentils, sauces, and warm *naan* bread.

From the first sight of the food stalls I was struck with apprehension and a list of excuses began to rattle through my brain that I hoped I could use to dissuade Ali from stopping here to eat. I was sure that this experience would serve as my grand introduction to the sickness I had been warned so much about. Simultaneously, a small voice hovering somewhere inside my left ear reminded me that if the locals were eating it, it must be okay. This place sure was full of locals. It was also full of dogs and trash and car exhaust. As we parked the rickshaw and entered into the mix, these two opposing forces grappled within my mind and left me speechless, unable to make any objection. By the time we made it to the hot-pot man and sat down I judged that it would be extremely rude for me to ask to be excused and eat somewhere else. And now that the food had been ordered and we sat face-to-face with shiny trays of extremely aromatic edibles, my stomach growled, my mouth began to water, and I saw no other option but to dig in and deal with the consequences later. I thanked Ali and we ate.

The food was incredible. Thick, complex, and wholly satisfying. The flavors blended together immaculately and it was cooked to perfection. Meandering into a mellow meditation, my mind was wiped blank as I devoured the meal. I sat in dizzy ecstasy afterward until Ali shook me from my coma and said that it was time to move on and make room for the next customers. I floated on a cloud back to the rickshaw and as we made our way towards my hotel I thought about everything I had eaten in India up until that point. Each meal had been tasty and thoughtfully presented, but what we ate that night had something else to it. Heart, maybe. Love. Food cooked by the people for the people. Ancient recipes passed down for generations, prepared by friends and family. I felt as if I'd been cheated so far. As if the food I'd been served in sterile, brightly lit restaurants lacked the history and honesty present in the meal I'd consumed that night. It seemed that the street food we enjoyed was created so naturally and communally that it just had to be right. Rather than eating Indian food, it felt like we were eating India. Everything else seemed like a show.

Maybe it was the atmosphere. Maybe it could be blamed on my initial doubt, but it would be a massive understatement to simply say that I was impressed. I couldn't thank Ali enough and from that moment on I made it a point to seek out dark alleyways and out-of-the-way food cart hang-outs in order to procure the best of any country's culinary catalog.

And I never did get sick. Never from food, at any rate, and I do believe that my adherence to a vegan diet definitely helped that. By avoiding meat and dairy products I've sidestepped the greater risk zone of foodborne illness and kept my body full of vitamins and minerals to fight off any bad bacteria that I might encounter. So, *Don't Fear the Street Food*, I say! That's where it's at! Just be smart about it. Do use your instincts, but don't let them intimidate you. Eat wise and be happy.

Street Food Guide

Eating out as a vegetarian on the road can be difficult. The smells, tastes, and appearance of the food is foreign, as well as the language. When I get stuck trying to order a meal at a place that doesn't ordinarily serve vegetarian fare I've found it much more effective to tell a vendor what I *do* want rather than what I *don't*. For a cook who's not accustomed to preparing vegetarian food it can seem very alien and daunting to create such an abnormal meal. Help them along by specifying what you do eat. Rather than asking for vegetarian food, try asking simply for vegetables. Instead of asking what they can *make* you, tell them what you *want*.

In bigger cities or tourist towns you can probably track down a vegetarian restaurant or two. However, if you're on a budget and want to experiment with local cuisine and eat amongst the people, try the street food.

Eating on the street is cheap, quick, and easy. Cooked vegetarian food offers little threat to your health, though if you have a sensitive stomach you may want to be cautious of raw veggies kept in water or leafy greens, like lettuce. However, most water used in and around food carts is purified water.

Common veg-friendly street food ingredients:

Beans (*frijoles*)
Rice (*arroz*)
Mushrooms (*champiñones/hongos*)
Potatoes (*papas*)
Avocado (*aguacate*)
Guacamole
Cactus (*nopales*)
Cabbage (*kol, repollo*)
Corn fungus (*huitlacoche*)
Squash flower (*flor de calabasa*)
Lettuce (*lechuga*)
Pico de gallo (mix of onion, lime, cilantro, tomato)
Salsas (red and green)

MEXICO

In Latin America, Mexico by far has the most diverse menu for vegetarian street food. A common doubt for vegetarians when eating out is whether or not the beans were cooked with lard. Rest assured most of the beans sold on the streets were cooked with just water. It's cheaper and means they can be eaten by anyone. Better for business. However, lard may be used on the grill to prepare the food. Often there is an alternative. Ask to substitute lard (*grasa/asiento*) for oil (*aciete*). Some tortillas are made with lard. If you are concerned, just ask.

Many street food vendors carry the same items and won't mind if you prefer to mix and match to create your own version of these traditional favorites. Of course, they'll probably look at you funny and call their friends over to get a kick out of what you're eating.

When ordering vegetarian plates, be sure to specify exactly which ingredients you would like and ask that they add nothing else (*solo eso y nada más*).

Quesadillas:
A folded corn tortilla with or without melted cheese inside. Usually comes with your choice of black beans, potatoes, mushrooms, *huitlacoche*, and/or squash flowers.

Huaraches:
Typically thick, long, blue corn tortilla with or without cheese and your choice of black beans, mushrooms, cactus, potatoes, and green or red salsa.

Sopes:
Thick, lightly fried corn tortilla topped with your choice of black beans, cheese, lettuce, onions, and/or tomato.

Tortas:
Mexican tortas are similar to sub sandwiches. Some typical ingredients are black beans, lettuce, onion, tomato, cheese, avocado, and mayonnaise.

Elote:
Corn on the cob. Served plain or with lime and chili powder. Some vendors offer mayonnaise.

Esquite:
Corn off the cob. Served with lime juice in a small cup.

Tostadas:
Fried corn tortilla with beans, lettuce or cabbage, tomato, guacamole, and cheese if you wish.

Tamales:
Corn dough (*masa*) with a filling. The most widely encountered vegetarian tamales are made with black beans or *chepil* leaves. Also keep and eye out for pineapple with raisin or black beans with squash.

Tlayudas:
The "Mexican Pizza!" *Tlayudas* are native to the state of Oaxaca. They are large toasted corn tortillas loaded with toppings. Veggie options usually include black beans, cabbage, mushrooms, cactus, tomatoes, avocado, squash flower, *huitlacoche*, and lettuce. *Tlayudas* are most definitely filling.

Chilaquiles:
Fried corn tortillas, green or red salsa, cheese if you wish, and an egg on top. Usually comes with beans on the side. Vegans, ask for no cheese and avocado instead of egg. Extremely satisfying for breakfast after a long night of fiesta.

Churros:
A trip to Mexico wouldn't be complete with trying a *churro*. Long, tube shaped, deep-fried flour treats topped with cinnamon and sugar.

GUATEMALA

Guatemala and most of Central America don't offer the quantity or variety of street food found in Mexico, at least not vegetarian friendly. But there are still some options.

Arroz con Frijoles:
This is a staple for vegetarian travelers in Latin America: a nice, clean helping of rice and beans. In Guatemala, typically black beans (refried or liquefied), and white rice.

Rellenitos:
Deep-fried mashed plantain balls full of blended black beans.

Plátano Frito:
This one is common all throughout the region. Fried plantain. With or without sweet cream.

Tamalitos de Chipilin:
The Guatemalan version of *tamales de chepil.*

Tostadas:
Fried corn tortilla with beans, lettuce or cabbage, and cheese if you wish.

Atole:
Atoles are hot, thick, rich drinks typically made from corn (*elote*), plantain (*plátano*) or other fruits. They are quite fulfilling on a cold day. Sometimes they contain milk (*leche*). If it concerns you, just ask.

Arroz con Leche:
This one obviously isn't for the vegans. White rice and milk made into a chunky rice pudding.

EL SALVADOR

Pupusas:
These savory little treats are one of El Salvador's culinary claims to fame. They are similar to sopes (*gorditas*) or *arepas*. Thick corn tortillas filled with beans, squash, cabbage, *loroco* or other on-hand ingredients. I recommend squash or *loroco*. Don't miss out!

NICARAGUA

Gallo Pinto:
Again, this is the classic rice and beans plate, however in Nicaragua whole red beans typically take the place of black beans and it is often served with fried plantain, sometimes called "*maduro*" as in ripe plantains.

COSTA RICA

Sopa Negra:
Spicy black bean soup. Usually served with an egg. It is sometimes possible to substitute the egg for some avocado.

Casamiento:
More rice and beans. *Casamiento* means marriage. The combination of beans and rice provide you with all the essential amino acids, creating a complete protein. Therefore, they're served together. In some areas the plate is called "*casado*."

BEVERAGES

Good liquids to try while you're out cruising the streets.

Agua de Coco (straight outta the coconut)
Jugo de Caña (sugar cane juice)
Horchata (sweet rice milk – sometimes contains dairy milk)
Vampiro (juice made from beets, carrots, celery, and citrus fruit)
Clorofila (alfalfa and mixed greens juice)
Champurrado (hot, sweet, cinnamon chocolate drink)
Atole (thick, sweet drink usually made from corn, sesame, or plantain)
Tejate (a cold, invigorating drink found in the south of Mexico
        made from cacao, corn, and ground mamey seed)
Tepache (a cold, refreshing drink found in the south of Mexico
        made from fermented pineapple rinds)

Farewell

And now, dear friends, we've about reached the end of the book. I want to thank you for joining me on this journey and entrusting me as your guide. I wish you the best as you continue to grow, learn, live, and love. Take care of yourself. Take care of your body. It's the only life and the only body you'll get - at least this time around. Make it count. I look forward to sharing more food, thoughts, and adventures with you in the future. Until then...

In the meantime I'll leave you with an appendix made up of vital nutritional data that could prove extremely beneficial to your daily dietary routine. Enjoy!

Pieces of the Puzzle

NUTRIENTS:

A nutrient is described as any substance that nourishes an organism. Nutrients come in the form of vitamins, minerals, proteins, fats, carbohydrates, water, oxygen, and even sunlight. The following information briefly outlines how a variety of nutrients are needed, working together, to sustain the human body.

ANTIOXIDANTS:

Oxygen is essential to almost all life forms on earth. Without it, the body's cells would die. But like most other things in life, to achieve a state of wellbeing involves balance. Too much oxygen can also destroy the cells. Oxygen is a highly reactive, corrosive chemical. When you look at metal or materials that have been left outside for a while, you see the effects of oxygen. The iron gates of a fortress can be brought down by oxygen, crumbling and corroding it one atom at a time. This process is called oxidation and it is happening right now in every living human body.

Oxidation happens when certain molecules interact with oxygen. The oxygen can strip them of an electron, leaving them as an unbalanced, positively charged ion. These molecules, called free radicals, naturally want to rebalance themselves and will try to rob an electron from their neighbor. The chain reaction that is thereby initiated is called oxidative stress and can be the precursor to many forms of illness. If proteins and amino acids are the building blocks of muscle and body tissue, free radicals are the building blocks of disease.

Antioxidants help fight oxidation. Antioxidants have the power to bind with free radicals, stabilizing them and putting a stop to the damaging domino effect they produce. If free radicals are left unchecked, these mutating cells begin to grow and proliferate, constantly disrupting and degrading the healthy functioning cells around them until disease takes hold. Antioxidants neutralize the corrupted cells and many times prevent them from dividing or growing. In this way, antioxidants also help slow the aging process.

Free radicals are found not only in the body but also in much of the environment. They are present in the air, in food, pollution, pesticides, plastic, and sunlight. The body produces free radicals in times of high physical or mental stress. Actually, free radicals are such a constant part of our existence that the body also produces its own antioxidants. However, as many of us live with stress and pollution, getting extra antioxidants is a must.

Dietary antioxidants are primarily found in plant foods. Vitamins C and E are antioxidants as well as selenium, manganese, beta carotene, and lycopene. Fresh fruits and vegetables are great sources of antioxidants. It's a good idea to get as many servings as possible including all the colors of the rainbow on a daily basis. Typically, the richer the color, the more and stronger the antioxidants!

A deficiency in antioxidants can leave the body open to attack, greatly elevating the risk of cancer, heart disease, arthritis, vision problems, accelerated aging, Alzheimer's disease, Parkinson's disease, high cholesterol, and diabetes-related damage.

Some good sources of dietary antioxidants are sweet potatoes, mangoes, carrots, apricots, broccoli, blueberries, eggplant, tomatoes, spinach, cantaloupe, collard greens, guava, papaya, pink grapefruit, cranberries, blackberries, artichoke, red beans, nuts, watermelon, and prunes. Each type of food offers its own antioxidants. The body needs a good mix to help it maintain balance. No one antioxidant can provide the protection offered by the many antioxidants working together.

FATS:
The good, the bad... the wide world of fats. The human brain is about 60% fat. Many of the vital organs like the kidneys, heart, and intestines are cushioned in a layer of fat that helps to hold them in place and protect them from injury. Fats are in integral source of energy. So why does fat get treated like a four-letter word?

Well, not all fats are the same. Humans tend to run into problems when consuming saturated fats, trans fatty acids (trans fats), and partially hydrogenated fats. These are the bad guys guilty of clogging arteries, raising cholesterol levels, and increasing the risk of heart disease. These fats are known to elevate the levels of a type of cholesterol commonly referred to as LDL (low density lipoproteins). LDL sticks to the walls of veins and arteries making it increasingly difficult for the body to pump blood through them. As this plaque gradually builds up, dangerous blockage of the blood vessel can lead to heart attack or stroke.

These potentially negative types of fats are typically found in meat and dairy products, margarine, some highly processed cooking oils, packaged snack foods or baked goods, and fried foods.
On the other hand, essential fatty acids are vital to a healthy life. Polyunsaturated and monounsaturated fats counteract saturated fats, actually replacing them and lowering the risk of serious health problems such as heart disease. These good fats provide HDL (high density

lipoproteins) cholesterol, one of whose major functions is to get a hold of LDL and escort them, by way of the liver, out the back door. Bon voyage!

The essential fatty acids Omega 3 and Omega 6 are required by the human metabolic system. They are termed "essential" because we, as mammals, lack the ability to produce them in the body and must obtain them through diet. A proper balance between the two is ideal for optimum health, but most of the Western World is far too heavy on Omega 6. Other non-essential fatty acids are also extremely important, but the body can synthesize them from unsaturated fats - like those found in olive oil or in most seeds.

Essential fatty acids are used to repair and maintain cell membranes, allowing cells to absorb nutrition and expel waste. They are needed for the production of prostaglandins, hormone-like fat compounds, which regulate various operations like blood clotting, blood pressure, heart rate, fertility, and conception. The presence of essential fatty acids helps control inflammation and encourages the immune system to fight off infection. Proper neural development, especially in children, is dependent on these nutrients.

Fats play a big part in the overall texture and shine of the skin and hair. They make cell walls supple and flexible, improving circulation and oxygen delivery. Fat soluble vitamins, like A, D, E, and K, obviously need fats to be absorbed into. Fats lend a hand in the production of sex hormones, help move messages along the nerve wires of the body tissue, and are probably the most efficient energetic fuel source.

Fatty acid deficiency has been linked to heart disease, heart attacks, stroke, cancer, depression, accelerated aging, obesity, diabetes, arthritis, Alzheimer's Disease, ADHD, decreased memory and cognitive abilities, blood clots, poor vision, fatigue, diminished immune function, high blood pressure, tingling sensation in the nerves, and growth retardation in children and infants.

Saturated, hydrogenated, and trans fats should be avoided like dirty diapers. Good sources of unsaturated fats include nuts, seeds, pure unprocessed oils, avocados, and nut butters. Some exceptionally good sources of essential fatty acids are flaxseed oil, flax seeds, chia seeds, hempseed oil, hemp seeds, and olive oil. These particular seeds also happen to be complete proteins.

So don't hate on fats! Just learn how to choose the right ones.

FIBER:
Dietary fiber is comprised of all the plant parts that the body can't absorb. There are two types of fiber, or roughage: 1) Soluble Fiber, which can be dissolved in water and turns into a gel-like substance good for lowering cholesterol and glucose levels. And, 2) Insoluble Fiber, which is all the material that adds bulk to the stool and helps move food through the intestines at the proper rate.

Fiber helps to normalize bowel movements, protect the intestines from damage and disease, control blood sugar levels, lower bad cholesterol, and maintain a healthy weight. Fiber slows digestion and prevents the body from absorbing too much starch or sugar. It can absorb water and help the feeling of being full last longer.

A diet high in fiber can greatly reduce the risk of heart disease. Fiber binds with LDL (bad cholesterol) as they pass through the intestines, ushering them out of the body. By lowering the amount of cholesterol absorbed by the body, fiber helps to lower the amount of cholesterol that can build up in the arteries.

A diet low in fiber can result in heart disease, high blood pressure, obesity, colon cancer, irritable bowel syndrome, diabetes, or constipation.

Some high fiber foods include oatmeal, whole grains, nuts, apples, blueberries, grapes, celery, nopal cactus, carrots, beans, peas, lentils, cauliflower, broccoli, sweet potatoes, seeds, passion fruit, prickly pear, kale, Swiss chard, squash, prunes, guava, and avocado.

PROTEIN:

Proteins are essential nutrients known as the building blocks of the body tissue. They can be found in all cells of the body and are used to build, repair, and maintain muscles, organs, hair, and skin. Protein is also needed to create blood cells.

Protein is comprised of amino acids. Digestive enzymes in the stomach must first break down the amino acid chains that form the protein molecules before they can be absorbed by the body. Amino acids are identified as essential, non-essential, and conditional. Essential amino acids must be supplied by foods as they cannot be created by the body. Non-essential amino acids are made from essential amino acids or created during breakdown of food. Conditional amino acids are not usually essential except in times of high stress or sickness.

A complete protein is the term used for a food that contains all nine essential amino acids. Most plant-based foods do not qualify as complete proteins, however all essential amino acids can be derived by eating a variety of plant-based foods. These include beans (legumes/pulses), grains, seeds, nuts, algae, seaweed, fruits, and vegetables. Combining proteins, like beans and rice, provides all essential amino acids at once. Some plant-based foods that do qualify as complete proteins are spirulina, sprouts, prickly pear cactus, as well as chia, hemp, and flax seeds.

Proteins do provide some energy, but usually only when carbohydrates and lipids (fats) start to run out. When the body's supply of complex sugars (carbs) and fats gets low, it begins to pull on proteins from the muscles to keep going.

High heat can damage protein molecules. Cooking over 115° Fahrenheit destroys hydrogen bonds that hold the amino acid chains together, causing them to form enzyme-resistant bonds, changing the structure of the protein and making it basically useless to the body. The digestive system no longer recognizes these molecules as food.

CALCIUM:

Calcium is a silvery metal essential for the survival of all living organisms. It is one of the main materials that make up bones and teeth. It also plays a major role in blood clotting, the central nervous system, muscle function, and heartbeat.

When the body needs to heal an opened blood vessel, it sends more calcium in the blood platelets to that area. The higher concentration of calcium allows a protein called fibrinogen to bind together and stop the flow of blood.

Nerve impulses are triggered by calcium ions in the brain. Converting electrical impulses to chemical signals, calcium helps to release messages to be carried from the brain to all ends of the body.

The presence of calcium in neuromuscular cells helps nerve impulses to be further relayed through the muscle fibers, allowing muscles to work and move. This same process supports the muscle contractions that produce your heartbeat.

Calcium needs to be ingested and absorbed on a daily basis. Calcium deficiency can lead to osteoporosis, weak bones, brittle nails, muscle cramps, low pulse, insomnia, or heart palpitations.

Good sources of calcium include: Dark green leafy vegetables like spinach or kale, broccoli, beans, sesame seeds, almonds, oranges, and dried fruits.

COPPER:

Copper, stored primarily in the liver but present in all body tissue, is an important trace mineral that allows many critical enzymes to function properly. There is actually less copper in your body than in a penny - but it does a lot of work. Copper helps the body utilize iron. It preserves the outer lining that protects nerves. It assists in the elimination of free radicals, development of bone and connective tissue, production of the skin and hair pigment called melanin, and keeps the thyroid gland functioning properly. Copper is necessary for collagen production, red blood cell production, generation of hormones released by the adrenal gland, production of certain neuroactive chemicals, and helps regulate many hormone levels.

Copper and zinc work together to support antioxidants like vitamin C, but actually compete for absorption space. A high level of zinc may block proper absorption of copper. The dependency of vitamin C on copper also means that high doses of this vitamin may lead to copper depletion. Because of its role in iron absorption, low copper stores may lead to iron anemia.

Copper deficiency is rare, but symptoms may include weakness, fatigue, loss of hair or skin color, elevated LDL (bad cholesterol) levels, decreased immune function, skin sores, joint problems, poor thyroid function, anemia, ruptured blood vessels, or osteoporosis.

Some foods rich in copper are sesame and other seeds, cashews, cacao, turnip greens, sundried tomatoes, asparagus, crimini and shiitake mushrooms, peanuts, walnuts, dark green leafy vegetables, blackstrap molasses, garlic, beets, fennel, olives, sweet potatoes, quinoa, lentils, beans, tempeh, ginger, pineapple, and raspberries, as well as dried herbs like basil, marjoram, oregano, thyme, and parsley.

IRON:

Iron may be most famous for the role it plays in the cardiovascular system. The majority of the body's supply of iron is contained in the blood, used in the hemoglobin of red blood cells to transport oxygen from the lungs throughout all extremities of the body and bring carbon dioxide back into the lungs. Oxygen is needed for the production and maintenance of all human cells. Therefore, without iron, the body does not receive adequate oxygen and ceases to function properly.

Anemia is one of the most common signs of iron deficiency. Symptoms include weakness, fatigue, short attention span, irritability, decreased immune function, delayed cognitive development, and difficulty maintaining body temperature.

Consumption of vitamin C together with iron-rich foods increases the iron absorption rate. Excess iron is stored in the body. Vitamin A helps to release iron when needed from storage. Human bodies tightly regulate iron absorption and recycling so, although the body has no regulatory method for excreting excess iron, illness due to iron toxicity is rare.

More dietary iron is needed during times of growth, blood loss, or excessive heavy exercise. Athletes, vegetarians, children, pregnant and menstruating women are more at risk of iron deficiency.

Iron found in animal flesh (heme) is generally better absorbed by the human body than iron found in plant-based foods (non-heme). However, plant-based foods tend to contain more iron per calorie than meat and many of those foods also contain vitamin C, essential to the absorption of non-heme iron. A diet including many iron-rich vegetables and legumes combined with plenty of vitamin C should eliminate the risk of iron deficiency. Coffee, tea, and calcium can obstruct the absorption of iron and should be consumed several hours before an iron-rich meal.

Iron can be found in a variety of foods. Some good sources are: Beans (legumes/pulses), dark green leafy vegetables, dried fruits, nuts, pumpkin seeds, cacao, and whole grains.

MAGNESIUM:

Magnesium is another metal that is essential to good health. It is integral in building and maintaining strong bones. 50% of the body's total magnesium is found in the skeleton. Magnesium and calcium, both important for optimum health, have a sort of yin yang relationship. Whereas calcium helps muscles contract, magnesium helps them to relax. Calcium assists in blood clotting while magnesium thins the blood and promotes proper blood flow. The presence of magnesium is necessary for the absorption of calcium into the bones.

Magnesium is needed for over 300 biochemical reactions in the body. It's interplay with calcium helps keep heart rates steady. Magnesium helps to regulate blood sugar levels, maintain normal blood pressure, protects blood vessels, alleviate constipation, promote relaxation, and maintain normal muscle and nerve function. It even plays a part in energy metabolism and protein synthesis. Magnesium is being studied for its potential role in the prevention of diabetes.

Deficiency in this essential mineral can lead to muscle cramps or spasms, weakness, fatigue, dizziness, loss of appetite, nausea, vomiting, anxiety, insomnia, constipation, irritability, or heart palpitations.

Some good sources of dietary magnesium are: Green vegetables, beans, peas, nuts, seeds, whole grains, and cacao.

MANGANESE:

Manganese is a metallic trace element used by the body as an enzyme activator. Most of the body's store of manganese is located in the bones with the remainder found in the kidney, liver, pancreas, pituitary glands, and adrenal glands. Manganese is responsible for activating the enzymes needed to make possible the absorption of certain nutrients like vitamins B1, B7, C, and choline (a nutrient of utmost importance in cell structure and nervous system communication).

Manganese also aids in the production of sex hormones, fatty acids, and cholesterol. It facilitates protein and carbohydrate metabolism. The presence of manganese keeps bones healthy and strong, promotes optimal function of the thyroid gland, regulates blood sugar levels, maintains nerve health, and protects from free radical damage.

Symptoms of manganese deficiency can include hearing loss, infertility, weak ligaments or tendons, fatigue, brittle nails and hair, seizures, or nausea. Extreme cases may result in skeletal abnormalities or osteoporosis.

Manganese can be found in spinach, kale, chard, mustard greens, summer squash, eggplant, pineapple, strawberries, grapes, raspberries, collard greens, turnip greens, brown rice, cinnamon, cloves, thyme, black pepper, turmeric, black strap molasses, maple syrup, cucumber, peppermint, peanuts, figs, bananas, carrots, cashews, kiwifruit, bell peppers, and onions.

PHOSPHORUS:

Phosphorus is the second most abundant mineral found in the human body. It, too, works closely with calcium to provide strong bones and teeth. About 85% of the body's phosphorus can be found there. Consumption levels of phosphorus need to be balanced to ensure skeletal health.

Phosphorus also promotes proper growth, maintenance, and repair of all tissues and cells. It is needed for the production of DNA and to balance and utilize other vitamins and minerals such as vitamin D, iodine, magnesium, and zinc. The body needs phosphorus in order to take in B complex vitamins. Synthesis of proteins, fats, and carbohydrates is assisted by phosphorus, creating energy for the body to burn. Many athletes use phosphorus supplements or eat phosphorus rich foods after workouts to relieve muscle pain and fatigue.

Weak bones, bone pain, fatigue, anxiety, stiff joints, and impaired immune system can be signs of phosphorus deficiency.

Good sources of phosphorus include legumes, nuts, seeds, whole grains, potatoes, dried fruit, and garlic cloves.

POTASSIUM:

Potassium is a highly reactive metal. Along with sodium, calcium, chloride, magnesium, and phosphorus, it is a type of electrolyte that conducts electricity throughout the body. Potassium plays a role in maintaining bone health, transmitting nerve impulses, regulating fluid and electrolyte balances, keeping the body hydrated, and maintaining normal blood pressure. It also regulates muscle contractions, including heart rate.

The body needs potassium to maintain normal growth, build proteins and muscle, breakdown and use carbohydrates, and control pH balance. pH stands for "power of Hydrogen." The pH scale measures the acidity or alkalinity of a substance. The human body uses potassium to maintain the acid/base balance needed for the system to thrive. By controlling the amount of fluid in the body's cells, potassium helps to keep that balance where it should be.

Low levels of potassium can cause fatigue, weakness, muscle cramps, insomnia, depression, poor reflexes, and irregular heartbeat. Heavy exercise, excessive alcohol consumption, high stress, prolonged diarrhea or vomiting, and overconsumption of sodium and processed foods can all lead to potassium deficiency.

Some good sources of dietary potassium include sweet potatoes, winter squash, beans, peas, broccoli, bananas, prunes, dried apricots, cantaloupe, coconut water, nuts, oranges, spinach, mushrooms, and avocados.

SELENIUM:

Selenium is a micronutrient we don't hear about as often as some others, but it is extremely important and a small amount needs to be consumed on a daily basis. Selenium works with other nutrients and antioxidants such as vitamins C and E, niacin, and glutathione to relieve oxidative stress in the cells. This group prevents oxygen molecules from becoming too reactive and causing damage to healthy cells.

Selenium has been shown to inhibit the proliferation of cancer cells and induce a self-destruct sequence that pushes damaged or worn-out cells to commit suicide and be flushed from the system. Selenium also helps to repair and synthesize DNA in damaged cells worth saving. Found within certain antioxidant proteins, selenium is essential in the process of detoxifying the body and preventing the growth or spread of cancerous cells.

Along with iodine, the thyroid gland also depends on selenium to function right. Selenium is essential in the production of the thyroid's most active hormone, T3, and also regulates the amount of that hormone that is produced.

Low intake of selenium has been linked to the oxidative stress that causes blood vessel damage leading to heart disease and rheumatoid arthritis. Symptoms of deficiency also include overall weakness, muscle pain, discoloration of skin or hair, and a whitening of the fingernail beds. Iron or copper deficiency may increase the risk of selenium deficiency. Selenium plays a role in the retention of the body's supply of vitamins C and E and glutathione.

Some say that eating one Brazil nut per day can supply all the needed selenium. Some other good food sources include crimini and shiitake mushrooms, mustard seeds, barley, and sunflower seeds, as well as wheat, rice, and oat brans.

SODIUM:

With so much focus put on lowering sodium in diets, it's easy to forget that sodium is actually an essential nutrient required by all life forms to exist. Sodium absorbs water and is needed to maintain fluid levels in the body. It regulates the water balance within the cells and is needed to carry nerve impulses and allow for proper muscle function. However, overconsumption of salt can result in water retention, high blood pressure, and edema, a condition causing swelling in certain parts of the body.

Overconsumption of sodium, found in salt, is much more common than deficiency. Some athletes or heavy laborers may be concerned about the sodium lost through excessive perspiration, but as sodium is found in almost all foods, it's easy to recuperate. Problems related to a high-sodium diet can usually be managed by drastically reducing the amount of sodium (salt) ingested, regular exercise, avoiding processed and preserved foods and drinks, eating more fresh and raw foods, drinking more water, and substituting other spices and herbs for salt when cooking.

ZINC:

Zinc is a trace mineral, or micromineral, needed by the body in small doses every day. Zinc helps to balance blood sugar, stabilize metabolic rate, support the immune system, and insure optimal sense of smell and taste. Vitamin A cannot be properly transported throughout the body without the presence of zinc. Many genetic activities are regulated by zinc. It is essential for reading genetic instructions, a process called gene transcription. This is important because gene codes are basically the blueprints to our bodies. In other words, zinc plays a part in the creation of DNA.

In order for our sense of taste to function correctly, zinc must be bound to a protein called gustin. The presence of zinc and the interrelation of taste and smell means that zinc is therefore also important to our sense of smell. An impaired sense of taste or smell can be due to a zinc deficiency while a metallic taste in the mouth could be a sign of zinc toxicity.

The processing or cooking of foods can damage the zinc content. Protein deficiency as well as excessive liquid loss through sweating or sickness can contribute to zinc deficiency. When the body runs low on zinc, symptoms such as depression, weaken immune system, lack of appetite, impaired overall growth, impotence, hair loss, or diarrhea may occur.

Good sources of dietary zinc include spinach, crimini and shiitake mushrooms, asparagus, chard, green peas, oats, pumpkin seeds, sesame seeds, miso, maple syrup, toasted wheat germ, dried watermelon seeds, cacao, and peanuts.

VITAMINS:

A vitamin is described as an organic compound required by an organism as an essential nutrient in small amounts. This vital compound usually cannot be synthesized in sufficient quantities by the organism and must be obtained from diet.

Vitamins can either be dissolved into water and absorbed immediately into the bloodstream or dissolved into fat and stored in the body tissue. Water-soluble vitamins are not stored and must be used or excreted in the moment. These vitamins are important to consume on a daily basis to insure that your body gets the amount that it needs to maintain normal function. When the body takes in fat-soluble vitamins, it uses what it needs and the excess that it stored typically remains semi-permanently. On rare occasions, this can cause a problem if the person consumes too much of a certain vitamin. Conversely, a person with low fat intake may have trouble storing certain fat-soluble vitamins, which can result in vitamin deficiency.

Water-soluble vitamins are C and all the B complex vitamins. Fat-soluble vitamins are A, D, E, and K.

VITAMIN A:

Vitamin A is extremely important for good eyesight, with deficiency resulting in night blindness. When touched by light, retinol, a form of vitamin A, is converted to retinal and ignites the instant process that shoots nerve impulses to the brain, determining what it is that we see. Low levels of retinol, or vitamin A, don't allow the vision sequence to work properly.

Vitamin A is needed for the production and activation of white blood cells, supporting the immune system. It is also used in the formation of red blood cells and aids in their iron absorption process. The retinoic form of vitamin A is also important in regulating the speed of gene transcription, determining how quickly the body can assign proteins to where they are needed.

Healthy skin also depends on vitamin A. The vitamin's properties as an antioxidant help protect skin and hair from premature aging as well as lower the risk of certain cancers. Vitamin A is also needed to support healthy bones and teeth.

Deficiency in vitamin A can result in impaired immune system, night blindness, full blindness, slow bone development, respiratory infections, dry skin, and diarrhea.

Some foods that contain an adequate amount of vitamin A include kale, carrots, sweet potatoes, spinach, squash, oranges, broccoli, cantaloupe, mangoes, hot red peppers, and apricots.

VITAMIN B1 (Thiamin):

Thiamin, along with all B complex vitamins, helps the body convert food into fuel, burned to produce energy. B1 also helps the body metabolize fats and proteins and is part of an enzyme system that enables the conversion of sugar into energy.

B vitamins are needed for proper functioning of the nervous system and to maintain healthy hair, skin, eyes, and liver. Thiamin is important in the production of a neurotransmitter that allows muscles and nerves to work right. B complex vitamins are sometimes referred to as "anti-stress" vitamins for their ability to defend the immune system and help the body withstand stressful conditions.

Absorption of thiamin into the system requires adequate amounts of vitamins B6, B9, and B12.

Common symptoms of deficiencies include weight loss, weakness, panic attacks, depressed immune system, and impairment of reflex or motor skills.

Most foods contain some thiamin. Good sources include whole grain products, legumes, bran, brewer's yeast, asparagus, crimini mushrooms, spinach, sesame seeds, sunflower seeds, flax seeds, nuts, peas, and Brussels sprouts.

VITAMIN B2 (Riboflavin):

Like other B vitamins, riboflavin is needed to produce energy for the body. It also works as an antioxidant, protecting cells from oxidative damage that can lead to cancer, premature aging, and other serious health complications. Riboflavin is needed by the body to convert vitamin B6 and B9 into usable forms and is important for enzyme function and amino acid synthesis.

The name riboflavin comes from the Latin word "flavus," which means yellow. The bright yellow urine produced after taking multivitamin supplements can be attributed to high levels of riboflavin in the system.

Riboflavin is destroyed by ultraviolet light. It can also be lost in the water of foods that are boiled or soaked. Riboflavin deficiency symptoms may include migraines, fatigue, red or itchy eyes, night blindness, cataracts, anemia, numbness, inflammation of the tongue, or cracks and sores at the edges of the mouth.

Adequate amounts of riboflavin can be found in asparagus, bananas, okra, chard, green beans, leafy green vegetables, legumes, tomatoes, yeast, mushrooms, almonds, broccoli, whole grains, sesame seeds, and Brussels sprouts.

VITAMIN B3 (Niacin):

Niacin has been used clinically since the 1950's to help lower LDL (bad cholesterol), but uncomfortable to extreme side effects from high doses of the vitamin make the practice questionable. Niacin is essential in the chemical processing of fats in the body. Fat-based hormones and fat-containing structures in the body, like cell membranes, require the presence of niacin to be created. Likewise, DNA cells rely on vitamin B3 for their production and deficiency has been linked to genetic damage and a higher risk of developing cancer.

Niacin, like all B vitamins, plays a critical role in energy production. It helps to convert proteins, fats, and carbohydrates into usable energy. The vitamin is also credited with blood sugar regulation, synthesis of sex and stress-related hormones, maintenance of the circulatory and nervous systems, lowering the risk of developing Alzheimer's disease or cataracts, keeping skin healthy, and aiding in proper digestion.

Niacin deficiency can lead to fatigue, vomiting, indigestion, canker sores, depression, headache, apathy, memory loss, skin lesions, red swollen tongue, disorientation, diarrhea, and paranoia.

Good sources of dietary niacin include beets, brewer's yeast, sunflower seeds, peanuts, mushrooms, asparagus, whole grains, paprika, and sundried tomatoes.

VITAMIN B5 (Pantothenic Acid):

Pantothenic acid is critical to the production of red blood cells. It helps maintain a healthy digestive tract, allows the body to process B2 and other vitamins, and is integral in the conversion of proteins, fats, carbohydrates, and sugar into energy.

Some studies suggest that adequate doses of pantothenic acid, combined with vitamin C, may help to speed up the healing of wounds. It is also necessary for the manufacture of sex and stress-related hormones in the adrenal gland, making the body more capable to respond to high-stress situations.

Both fatty acids and cholesterol depend on pantothenic acid for their synthesis. The presence of B5 supports and transports the proteins that build and maintain cells. B5 is also important in the releasing of energy stored as fat and removing waste from the mitochondrial energy production sites.

Deficiency in vitamin B5 may be related to a burning sensation in the hands or feet, poor coordination, a tingly feeling in the muscles, muscle cramps, numbness, fatigue, irritability, apathy, sleep disturbances, restlessness, diarrhea, vomiting, water retention, acne, skin blemishes, or unwarranted stress.

Pantothenic acid takes its name from the Greek word "pantos", meaning *all*. Vitamin B5 is found in most foods. Some of the best sources are whole grains, sunflower seeds, tomatoes, avocados, corn, kale, cauliflower, broccoli, split peas, legumes, lentils, peanuts, sweet potatoes, brewer's yeast, crimini and shiitake mushrooms, asparagus, and bell peppers.

VITAMIN B6 (Pyridoxine):

Pyridoxine is necessary for normal brain development and function. It helps the body create certain neurotransmitters that carry signals throughout the nervous system from one part of the body to another. B6 is essential in the production of serotonin and norepinephrine, hormones that regulate mood, as well as melatonin, the hormone in charge of the body clock. Many amino acids require adequate supplies of pyridoxine for their synthesis, including the nucleic acids used to form DNA. Vitamin B6 is basically needed for the creation of all new cells in the body.

Pyridoxine helps to eliminate certain toxins from the body. Along with B9 and B12, it helps control the levels of homocysteine, a potentially damaging amino acid created during metabolism, in the blood. When left unchecked, homocysteine can build up in the system and lead to cardiovascular disease.

Like other B vitamins, pyridoxine is necessary for conversion of energy from carbohydrates, fats, sugars, and proteins. B6 is needed to absorb B12 and in the formation of red blood cells as well as immune system cells.

Low levels of pyridoxine can result in fatigue, depression, skin disorders, anemia, convulsions or seizures, high levels of homocysteine, decreased brain function, confusion, irritability, and mouth or tongue sores.

Good dietary sources of pyridoxine include lentils, beans, spinach, carrots, avocado, bananas, whole grains, sunflower seeds, summer squash, turnip greens, shiitake mushrooms, bell peppers, pistachios, garlic, molasses, chili peppers, paprika, and dried herbs such as spearmint, tarragon, sage, oregano, rosemary, turmeric, dill, marjoram, and bay leaves.

VITAMIN B7 (Biotin):
Biotin, also termed vitamin H, is involved in the metabolism of both sugar and fat, making them available to the body as fuel. The metabolizing of amino acids by biotin activates particular proteins needed for the strengthening of hair and nails.

Biotin is an important nutrient for proper embryonic growth, making its presence critical during pregnancy. Biotin is also required by certain enzymes that assemble the building blocks responsible for fat production in the body. This has a direct effect on skin quality as skin cells must be regenerated so rapidly and all of the body's cell membranes contain fat. Biotin, as it is used to create energy, directly supports the entire nervous system.

Biotin deficiency can cause seizures, lack of muscle coordination or muscle tone, dermatitis, cradle cap in infants, muscle cramps, hair loss, dry eyes, cracking at the corners of the mouth, swollen tongue, fatigue, insomnia, or loss of appetite.

Vitamin B7 can be found in brewer's yeast, nuts and nut butters, legumes, cauliflower, bananas, mushrooms, Swiss chard, tomatoes, carrots, and sweet potatoes. But be aware that food-processing procedures may destroy biotin.

VITAMIN B8 (Inositol):
Inositol is essential for the development of healthy cell membranes and the communication of chemicals throughout the body. However, the human body is capable of producing small amounts of inositol on its own so its classification as a water-soluble member of the B family of vitamins is under constant criticism. Generally, a vitamin must be obtained from a source outside the body.

Inositol is a type of glucose that keeps muscles and nerves functioning optimally and helps the liver process fat. As an integral part of every cell membrane, the "vitamin" positively influences cellular performance. As with choline, it is a precursor of phospholipids, essential fats that support the transportation of nutrients and electrical currents across the interior of all cells, specifically aiding brain function by ensuring proper signaling from all major neurotransmitters.

Increasing the effectiveness of vitamin E, vitamin B8 is shown to relieve nerve damage, treat skin conditions, and promote healthy hair growth. It has anti-anxiety and antidepressant-like qualities and helps prevent the build-up of damaging fats in the heart and liver. Inositol and choline, combined, produce lecithin, which assists in the absorption of vitamin B1 (thiamin), therefor supporting the conversion of nutrients into energy.

Inositol triggers the production of serotonin, helping to control moods and treat psychosomatic and psychological disorders. It has been used to treat depression. When taken as a supplement, high-level doses have been found very tolerable if the dosages are increased slowly. Any excess of the vitamin is expelled via urination.

Possible symptoms of inositol deficiency can include impaired memory, hair loss, depression, anxiety, impotence, lung disease, obsessive-compulsive disorder, panic disorder, psoriasis, eczema, polycystic ovary syndrome (PCOS), increased cholesterol, or eyesight-related issues.

Foods rich in inositol include brown rice, cereals, citrus fruits, nuts and seeds, bananas, beans, legumes, sprouts, cantaloupe, whole grains, green leafy vegetables, molasses, soy, wheat germ, and lecithin granules.

VITAMIN B9 (Folate):

Folate is extremely important for proper brain function and healthy development of DNA, especially when tissues are growing rapidly as in times of infancy, adolescence, and pregnancy. Deficiencies in folate can cause neural tube damage shortly after conception and pregnant women who don't get enough folate are more likely to have children with birth defects. It is believed that the presence of folate also keeps DNA cells healthy and free of cancer-causing mutations.

Folate works closely with vitamin B12 to produce red blood cells, therefore aiding in the distribution of iron and oxygen throughout the body. It partners up again with B12 and B6 to lower homocysteine levels in the blood. The buildup of homocysteine, a naturally occurring amino acid, can lead to heart complications and cardiovascular disease. High levels of homocysteine may also contribute to the deterioration of dopamine-producing brain cells, elevating the risk of depression or Parkinson's disease.

Like other B vitamins, folate plays a key role in the maintenance of healthy skin and the metabolizing of food for energy.

Deficiencies in vitamin B9 can lead to physical and mental fatigue, depression, irritability, confusion, insomnia, certain cancers, bone fractures, gingivitis, headache, difficulty concentrating, sore tongue, pale skin, or anemia.

Some folate-rich foods include asparagus, spinach, turnip greens, collard greens, parsley, cauliflower, broccoli, beets, lentils, beans, seeds, yeast, peanuts, Brussels sprouts, root vegetables, whole grains, avocado, and dried herbs such as rosemary, basil, coriander, thyme, bay leaf, and marjoram.

VITAMIN B12 (Cobalamin):

Although it has many functions, B12 is may be most widely talked about for the role it plays in the nervous system. B12 is needed to manufacture myelin, an insulating material that surrounds and protects many of the body's nerve cells and helps speed neural transmission. The presence of the vitamin, therefore, has a direct effect on brain function and its ability to relay and receive messages from throughout the body.

Vitamin B12 is important for the production of red blood cells. As red blood cells mature, they require information provided by DNA molecules. B12 is essential for healthy development of new cells and without it DNA synthesis becomes defective and the coding system fails. To produce new and healthy blood, nerve cells, skin cells, brain cells, etc... B12 must be present.

Vitamin B12 is needed to cycle protein through the body. Lack of the vitamin can leave many amino acids unavailable for use. Proteins are needed to create muscles and body tissue. B12 plays a pivotal role in the assembly of these molecules and the growth and development of the body.

Like other B vitamins, B12 is needed to metabolize fats and carbohydrates, making them available to the body as energy.

Most plants and animals are incapable of producing B12. Only microorganisms like yeast, molds, bacteria, and algae have been shown to be able to do so. The presence of a unique protein called intrinsic factor, made in the stomach, is necessary to transport B12 throughout the body.

Medications that affect the stomach, like aspirin or antacids, can harm the production of intrinsic factor, leaving B12 stranded and eventually flushed from the system instead of absorbed.

Vitamin B12 deficiencies can result in tingling or numbness in feet, sore or red tongue, depression, memory problems, nervousness, heart palpitations, anemia, high levels of homocysteine in the blood, weight loss, mood swings, easy bruising or bleeding, disorientation, or shortness of breath.

Vegan and vegetarians needs to be especially careful to consume adequate amounts of B12. Many may wish to take a vitamin B12 supplement in addition to food sources, just to be sure. A few foods that do contain some B12, due to bacteria or environment, are non-dairy yogurts, tempeh, seaweed (nori sushi paper), spirulina (blue green algae), and fortified nutritional yeast.

VITAMIN C (Ascorbic Acid):

Vitamin C is needed for the growth, development, and repair of all body tissues. It is used to heal wounds and build scar tissue, make skin, ligaments, tendons, and blood vessels, and repair and maintain cartilage, bones, and teeth.

As one of many antioxidants, vitamin C helps defend the body from the damaging effects of free radicals that can lead to major complications and serious disease. The presence of vitamin C in the body can lower the risk of cancer, cardiovascular disease, and joint problems. Vitamin C can help in times of common cold or flu because it protects the immune system cells from free radicals that are formed during the immune cells fight with invading microorganisms, helping the immune cells stay strong and do their job.

Vitamin C improves iron absorption and helps to recycle vitamin E supplies. It is essential to most living beings. Many mammals can create their own vitamin C within their bodies, but humans, chimps, gorillas, bats, guinea pigs, and birds are some of the few animals that must rely on outside dietary intake.

Like B complex vitamins, vitamin C is water soluble, meaning that it is not stored in the body and must be consumed daily to maintain supplies in the system. Early sailors on long sea voyages fell victim to diseases like scurvy because, on a limited diet, their vitamin C stores became so depleted. When limes were finally discovered to thwart the effects of scurvy, large amounts of limes were carried aboard ships and British sailors became known as "limeys."

Vitamin C deficiency can lead to bruising, bleeding gums, fatigue, depression, gingivitis, slow healing of wounds, chronic joint pain, anemia, dry skin or hair, and, of course, scurvy.

Many foods contain vitamin C, most of them fruits and vegetables. Some good example are oranges, cantaloupe, mangoes, kiwi, broccoli, Brussels sprouts, spinach, papaya, pineapple, squash, strawberries, sweet potatoes, hot chili peppers, turnip greens, guava, bell peppers, kale, cauliflower, parsley, blueberries, cranberries, lemons, limes, and even watermelon.

Don't forget... Every time you go pee, say goodbye to some vitamin C!

VITAMIN D:

Vitamin D is a very important vitamin found in very few foods. Most people meet their vitamin D requirements through exposure to sunlight. When UV rays strike the skin, a cholesterol is activated that is then converted into forms of vitamin D. These inert forms of vitamin D later travel through the liver and kidneys before they become completely active.

Vitamin D promotes calcium and phosphorus absorption, making it critical for proper bone growth and maintenance. Working together with calcium, vitamin D helps lower the risk of osteoporosis and skeletal disorders.

Vitamin D also works as a hormone, regulating insulin levels and blood sugar balance, calcium and phosphorus balance, blood pressure, and muscle function. The presence of vitamin D helps trigger the immune system's response to infections, allowing it to release antibacterial proteins.

Some research shows that vitamin D can also aid in the prevention of certain cancers.
Because vitamin D is stored in fat, exposure to sunlight for 15-20 minutes a day during the spring, summer, and fall months probably gives a person living in the northern latitudes a sufficient quantity to last through the winter. However, the UVB rays that induce vitamin D production do not penetrate glass or sunscreen.

Vitamin D deficiency can cause high blood pressure, stunted growth, bone pain and fractures, fatigue, depression, impaired cognitive function, muscle aches and weakness, asthma, flu, weak immune system, or cancer.

Some of the only vegetarian food sources of vitamin D are shiitake or button mushrooms and fortified tofu, cereal, or other foods. Go to the beach.

VITAMIN E:
Vitamin E is actually a group of fat-soluble vitamins that have strong antioxidant properties. By binding with reactive oxygen molecules, it can help to stabilize free radicals and lower the effects of oxidative stress, thereby protecting the body from disease and slowing down the aging process. This potential can be seen in vitamin E's ability to maintain healthy and hydrated skin, prevent cataracts and poor eyesight in elders, and protect skin from damages done by UV rays. Vitamin E works hand in hand with vitamins B3 and C, selenium, and glutathione to make this happen.

Not only can vitamin E help on the surface, but it also gets down into the tissues, increasing energy and improving muscle strength. It widens blood vessels, preventing blockage, and prevents the hardening of arteries, therefore lowering the risk of heart attack, high blood pressure, or pains due to irregular blood flow.

Vitamin E is important in the production of red blood cells and supports the immune system. Its presence is necessary to allow the transfer of information from one cell to another. Clinically, vitamin E is used to treat diabetes, prevent cancer, and protect against Alzheimer's disease. It can also have a positive effect against asthma, respiratory infections, infertility, impotence, ulcers, and allergies. It has been used to prevent complications late in pregnancy, treat brain and nervous system disorders, and epilepsy. Vitamin E is vital for the body's use of vitamin K.

Deficiency in vitamin E can result in some of the above mentioned disorders as well as fatigue, mild anemia, muscular weakness, cramps, hair loss, decreased sex drive, poor balance, sight problems, and skin disease.

Good food sources of vitamin E include almonds and other nuts, sunflower and other seeds, green leafy vegetables, avocados, asparagus, vegetable oils, cayenne pepper, bell peppers, papaya, dried apricots, olives, taro root, and dried herbs such as basil, oregano, sage, thyme, parsley, and cumin.

VITAMIN K:

If you're wondering how it is that we've just jumped from vitamin E to vitamin K, don't worry. You're not missing 5 vitamins from your diet! Although other nutrients have been categorized under those lacking letters from time to time, in this case the "K" actually comes from its German name, *koagulationsvitamin*, owing to the vitamin's ability to help blood clot, or coagulate, properly.

More accurately, without vitamin K blood would not clot at all. Working together with calcium, different forms of vitamin K are activated in a series of reactions called the "clotting cascade" that allows the body to cut off blood flow to an injured area. This process is highly regulated and kept in check by existing anticoagulants to make sure that blood clotting only takes place in emergencies and that no blockage builds up in healthy veins and arteries.

Vitamin K is also critical in maintaining strong bones, preventing fracture and excess bone demineralization. The body actually relies on vitamin K in order to use calcium to build bone. More available vitamin K may equal greater bone density.

As the relationship between vitamin K and calcium is integral in bone health, vitamin K also plays an important role in preventing the buildup of calcium, or calcification, of tissue and blood vessels- the unwanted hardening of what should be soft. Calcification of arteries and heart valves can lead to serious cardiovascular disease.

Freezing may destroy vitamin K, but heat doesn't seem to harm it. Aside from dietary sources, vitamin K is also produced in the intestines, but the use of antibiotics can kill the vital bacteria that breed it.

Chlorophyll is the substance that gives certain foods their green color. It's a storehouse of vitamin K. Foods that contain a good amount of vitamin K include dark green leafy vegetables, Brussels sprouts, broccoli, cauliflower, cabbage, asparagus, green tea, green beans, sea vegetables, spirulina, celery, cucumber, leeks, blueberries, tomatoes, chili peppers, scallions, prunes, and dried or fresh herbs such as basil, sage, thyme, and parsley.

Did you enjoy *The Bodyguard*?
Help spread the word!
Share your experience!

#bodyguardcookbook

Facebook: Paco Garden Enterprises
Instagram: @paco_garden
Twitter: @DPAC3000

GUANABANA

ICE CREAM BEAN

MAMEY